MODEL
DOUBLE TAXATION
CONVENTION
ON INCOME AND ON CAPITAL

**Report
of the OECD Committee
on Fiscal Affairs**

1977

**ORGANISATION FOR ECONOMIC CO-OPERATION AND DEVELOPMENT
PARIS**

The Organisation for Economic Co-operation and Development (OECD) was set up under a Convention signed in Paris on 14th December, 1960, which provides that the OECD shall promote policies designed:

— to achieve the highest sustainable economic growth and employment and a rising standard of living in Member countries, while maintaining financial stability, and thus to contribute to the development of the world economy;

— to contribute to sound economic expansion in Member as well as non-member countries in the process of economic development;

— to contribute to the expansion of world trade on a multilateral, non-discriminatory basis in accordance with international obligations.

The Members of OECD are Australia, Austria, Belgium, Canada, Denmark, Finland, France, the Federal Republic of Germany, Greece, Iceland, Ireland, Italy, Japan, Luxembourg, the Netherlands, New Zealand, Norway, Portugal, Spain, Sweden, Switzerland, Turkey, the United Kingdom and the United States.

* *
*

CONTENTS

*
* *

ANNEXES

*
* *

APPENDICES

I

INTRODUCTION

1.   The Council of the Organisation for Economic Co-operation and Development adopted on 30th July, 1963, a Recommendation concerning the avoidance of double taxation and called upon the Governments of Member countries, when concluding or revising bilateral conventions between them, to conform to the Draft Convention drawn up by the Fiscal Committee of the OECD.[1] Since then, the Draft Convention has been widely followed in negotiations for the conclusion of double taxation conventions.

2.   Due to the fact that certain questions had not been entirely solved, the Fiscal Committee had planned to revise it in the light of the experience that would be gained. This work was started by the Fiscal Committee and was continued by its successor, the Committee on Fiscal Affairs. The present report, which contains a new Model Convention accompanied by a recast of the commentaries, is the result of thorough and far-reaching discussions and research. The conclusions of the report contain concrete recommendations which the Committee on Fiscal Affairs suggests the Council of the OECD should make to the Governments of Member countries in order that the implementation of the Model Convention may result in further progress in the harmonization of bilateral conventions and the elimination of double taxation.

---

1. *Draft Double Taxation Convention on Income and Capital,* OECD, Paris, 1963.

II

INTERNATIONAL EFFORTS TOWARDS THE ELIMINATION OF DOUBLE TAXATION

A. HISTORICAL BACKGROUND

3.   The phenomenon of international juridical double taxation, which can be generally defined as the imposition of comparable taxes in two (or more) States on the same taxpayer in respect of the same subject matter and for identical periods, and its harmful effects on the exchange of goods and services and movements of capital and persons, are so well known that it is superfluous to stress the importance of removing the obstacles that double taxation presents to the development of economic relations between OECD Member countries. It is, in particular, most desirable to clarify, standardize and guarantee the fiscal situation of taxpayers in each Member country who are engaged in commercial, industrial or financial activities in other Member countries through the application by all Member countries of common solutions to identical cases of double taxation.

4.   Progress had already been made towards elimination of double taxation through bilateral conventions or unilateral measures when the Council of the Organisation for European Economic Co-operation (OEEC) adopted its first Recommendation concerning double taxation on 25th February, 1955. At that time, 70 bilateral general conventions had been signed between countries now Members of the OECD. This was to a large extent due to the work commenced in 1921 by the League of Nations. This work led to the drawing up in 1928 of the first model bilateral conventions and, finally, in the Model Conventions of Mexico (1943) and London (1946), the principles of which were followed with certain variants in many of the bilateral conventions concluded or revised during the following decade. Neither of these Model Conventions, however, was fully and unanimously accepted. Moreover, in respect of several essential questions, they presented considerable dissimilarities and certain gaps.

5.   The increasing economic interdependence of the Member countries of the OEEC in the post-war period and the economic co-operation established among them showed increasingly clearly the importance of measures for preventing international double taxation. The need was recognised for extending the network of bilateral double taxation conventions to all Member countries of the OEEC, and subsequently of the OECD, several of which had so far concluded only very few conventions and some none at all. At the same time, harmonization of these conventions in accordance with uniform principles, definitions, rules and methods, and agreement on a common interpretation, became increasingly desirable.

6.   It was against this new background of economic co-operation and along these new lines of thinking that the Fiscal Committee set to work in 1956 with the aim of establishing a Draft Convention which would effectively resolve the double taxation problems existing between OECD Member countries and which would be acceptable to all Member countries.   From 1958 to 1961, the Fiscal Committee prepared four interim Reports, before submitting in 1963 its final Report entitled "Draft Double Taxation Convention on Income and Capital".

B.   IMPLEMENTATION OF THE 1963 DRAFT CONVENTION

7.   The Draft Convention for the Avoidance of Double Taxation with respect to Taxes on Income and Capital, which was contained in the 1963 Report of the Fiscal Committee, has had wide repercussions.   OECD Member countries have largely conformed to it when concluding or revising bilateral conventions.

8.   The progress made towards ending double taxation between Member countries can be measured by the steeply increasing number of conventions concluded or revised over the last 20 years in accordance with the Recommendations of the Council of the OECD: 23 conventions had been concluded and 8 revised between July 1958, when the first Report of the Fiscal Committee was issued, and July 1963.   The extension and harmonization of the bilateral conventions between Member countries have accelerated since the appearance of the Draft Convention of 1963, as since then 69 conventions between Member countries have been concluded, and 49 have been revised.   These figures take into account the accession to the OECD of four new countries, Australia, Finland, Japan and New Zealand.   As of 1st January, 1977, 179 bilateral conventions for the avoidance of double taxation with respect to taxes on income and on capital had been concluded between OECD Member countries (see Table).

9.   The importance of the work of the Fiscal Committee should be measured not only by the number of conventions concluded between Member countries but also by the fact that, in accordance with the Recommendation of the Council of the OECD, these conventions follow the pattern and, in most cases, the main provisions of the Draft Convention.   The existence of the Draft Convention has made it possible to facilitate bilateral negotiations between OECD Member countries and to reach a desirable harmonization between their bilateral conventions for the benefit of both taxpayers and national administrations.   Moreover, the existence of the Commentaries has facilitated the interpretation and the enforcement of bilateral conventions along common lines.   Lastly, the impact of the Draft Convention of 1963 has extended outside the OECD area; it has been used as a basic document of reference in negotiations between Member and non-Member countries and even between non-Member countries as well as in the work of other worldwide or regional international organisations in the field of double taxation and related problems.

10.   The Fiscal Committee of the OECD had envisaged, when presenting its Report in 1963, that the Draft Convention might be elaborated upon at a later stage following further study.   Such a revision was also necessary to take account of experience gained by Member countries in negotiating new conventions or in their practical working.   To this must be added the changes in systems of taxation and the increase in international fiscal relations on the one hand and, on the other, the development of new sectors of business activity and the increasingly complex forms of organisation adopted by enterprises for their international activities.   This situation has complicated the tax problems to be solved.   For all these reasons, the Fiscal Committee and, since 1971, the Committee on Fiscal Affairs and, in particular, its Working Party N° 1, have undertaken the revision

8

NETWORK OF BILATERAL CONVENTIONS FOR THE AVOIDANCE OF DOUBLE TAXATION WITH RESPECT TO TAXES ON INCOME AND ON CAPITAL BETWEEN OECD MEMBER COUNTRIES AS AT 1st JANUARY, 1977

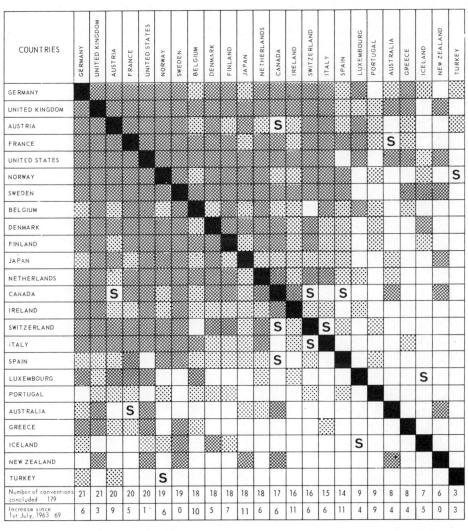

COUNTRIES	GERMANY	UNITED KINGDOM	AUSTRIA	FRANCE	UNITED STATES	NORWAY	SWEDEN	BELGIUM	DENMARK	FINLAND	JAPAN	NETHERLANDS	CANADA	IRELAND	SWITZERLAND	ITALY	SPAIN	LUXEMBOURG	PORTUGAL	AUSTRALIA	GREECE	ICELAND	NEW ZEALAND	TURKEY
Number of conventions concluded 179	21	21	20	20	20	19	19	18	18	18	18	18	17	16	16	15	14	9	9	8	8	7	6	3
Increase since 1st July, 1963 69	6	3	9	5	1	6	0	10	5	7	11	6	6	11	6	6	11	4	9	4	4	5	0	3

Convention in force before 1st July, 1963 or replacing a convention in force before 1st July, 1963.

New convention in force after 1st July, 1963

S New convention signed but not yet in force as at 1st January, 1977

of the 1963 Draft Convention and of Commentaries thereon. This work has resulted in a new text of the Convention, entitled "1977 Model Convention" as well as in new Commentaries.

III

PRESENTATION OF THE 1977 MODEL CONVENTION

11.   The 1977 Model Convention, the broad lines of which are set out in paragraphs 14 and following, provides a means of settling on a uniform basis the most common problems which arise in the field of international double taxation. In essence, the new text does not differ appreciably from the previous one, as the object of the revision of the 1963 Draft Convention was not to question its principles and general structure.

12.   During the revision, the Committee on Fiscal Affairs examined in detail many questions of a legal, theoretical or practical character which had been brought to light by the operation of the existing conventions.   On a number of points, a wide measure of agreement has made it possible to introduce amplifications to or changes in the texts of certain Articles.[1]   The essential part of the Committee's work is, however, reflected in the Commentaries on the Articles which, in some cases, have been the subject of additions, clarifications or updatings.[2]   In other cases, the Committee considered that no purpose would be served by elaborating on the diversity of situations and opinions.   Accordingly, the importance of the discussions and the work of the Committee on Fiscal Affairs is to be gauged not merely by the number and nature of the amendments made to the 1963 texts, but also by the numerous exchanges of views and experience in which Government experts engaged and which bear witness to constant international co-operation.

13.   On certain points, unanimous agreement was not possible and, like the 1963 Draft Convention, the 1977 Model Convention is accompanied by reservations.   Because of differences in taxation laws and in the economic situations and interests involved, either special rules had to be accepted, or some States lodged reservations on certain provisions of the Model Convention or expressed observations on the Commentaries (cf. General Remarks in paragraphs 24 and following).

A.   BROAD LINES OF THE MODEL CONVENTION

General

14.   The Model Convention first describes its scope (Chapter I) and defines some terms (Chapter II).   The main part is made up of Chapters III to V, which

---

1. Cf. for example, paragraphs 3 and 4 of Article 5, paragraph 2 of Article 9, paragraph 2 of Article 17, Article 19, paragraph 2 of Article 21, paragraph 5 of Article 24 and paragraphs 1 and 2 of Article 25.
2. Cf. for example, the Commentaries on Articles 5, 10, 19, 24, 25 and 26.

settle to what extent each of the two Contracting States may tax income and capital and how double taxation is to be eliminated. Then follow the Special Provisions (Chapter VI) and the Final Provisions (entry into force and termination, Chapter VII).

Scope and definitions

15.　　The Convention applies to all persons who are residents of one or both of the Contracting States (Article 1). It deals with taxes on income and on capital, which are described in a general way in Article 2. In Chapter II, some terms used in many Articles of the Convention are defined. Other terms such as "dividends", "interest", "royalties", "immovable property" and "professional services" are defined in the Articles which deal with these matters.

Taxation of income and capital

16.　　For the purpose of eliminating double taxation, the Convention establishes two categories of rules. Firstly, Articles 6 to 21 determine, with regard to different classes of income, the respective rights to tax of the State of source or situs and of the State of residence, and Article 22 does the same with regard to capital. In the case of a number of items of income and capital, an exclusive right to tax is conferred on one of the Contracting States. In this way, the other Contracting State is prevented from taxing and double taxation is thus absolutely avoided. As a rule, this exclusive right to tax is conferred on the State of residence. In the case of other items of income and capital, the right to tax is not an exclusive one. As regards two classes of income (dividends and interest), the right to tax of the State of source is limited. Secondly, insofar as these provisions confer on the State of source or situs a full or limited right to tax, the State of residence must allow relief so as to avoid double taxation; this is the purpose of Articles 23 A and 23 B. The Convention leaves it to the Contracting States to choose between two methods of relief, i.e. the exemption method and the credit method.

17.　　Income and capital may be classified into three classes, depending on the treatment applicable to each class in the State of source or situs:

—　income and capital which may be taxed without any limitation in the State of source or situs,

—　income which may be subjected to limited taxation in the State of source, and

—　income and capital which may not be taxed in the State of source or situs.

18.　　The following are the classes of income and capital which may be taxed without any limitation in the State of source or situs:

—　income from immovable property situated in that State (including income from agriculture or forestry), gains from the alienation of such property and capital represented by it (Article 6 and paragraph 1 of Articles 13 and 22);

—　profits of a permanent establishment situated in that State, gains from the alienation of such a permanent establishment and capital represented by movable property forming part of the business property of such a permanent establishment (Article 7 and paragraph 2 of Articles 13 and 22); exception: if the permanent establishment is maintained for the purposes of international shipping, inland waterways transport and international air transport (cf. paragraph 20 below);

—　income from the activities of artistes and athletes exercised in that State, irrespective of whether such income accrues to the artiste or athlete himself or to another person (Article 17);

— income from independent personal services being income attributable to a fixed base situated in that State, gains from the alienation of such a fixed base and capital represented by movable property pertaining to it (Article 14 and paragraph 2 of Articles 13 and 22);

— directors' fees paid by a company which is a resident of that State (Article 16);

— remuneration in respect of an employment in the private sector, exercised in that State, unless the employee is present therein for a period not exceeding 183 days in a year and certain conditions are met; and remuneration in respect of an employment exercised aboard a ship or aircraft operated internationally or aboard a boat, if the place of effective management of the enterprise is situated in that State (Article 15);

— subject to certain conditions, remuneration and pensions paid in respect of government service (Article 19).

19.   The following are the classes of income which may be subjected to limited taxation in the State of source:

— dividends: provided the holding in respect of which the dividends are paid is not effectively connected with a permanent establishment or fixed base situated in the State of source, that State must limit its tax to 5 per cent of the gross amount of the dividends, where the beneficial owner is a company which holds directly at least 25 per cent of the capital of the company paying the dividends, and to 15 per cent of their gross amount in other cases (Article 10);

— interest: subject to the same proviso as in the case of dividends, the State of source must limit its tax to 10 per cent of the gross amount of the interest, being interest not exceeding a normal amount (Article 11).

20.   Other items of income or capital may not be taxed in the State of source or situs; as a rule they are taxable only in the State of residence of the taxpayer. This applies, for example, to royalties not being income from immovable property (Article 12), gains from the alienation of shares or securities (paragraph 4 of Article 13), private sector pensions (Article 18), payments received by a student for the purposes of his education or training (Article 20), capital represented by shares or securities (paragraph 4 of Article 22).   Profits from the operation of ships or aircraft in international traffic or of boats, gains from the alienation of such ships, boats or aircraft, and capital represented by them, are taxable only in the State in which the place of effective management of the enterprise is situated (Article 8 and paragraph 3 of Articles 13 and 22).

21.   Where a taxpayer who is a resident of a Contracting State receives income from sources in the other Contracting State, or owns capital situated therein, which in accordance with the Convention shall be taxable only in the State of residence, no problem of double taxation arises, since the State of source or situs must grant exemption.

22.   Where, on the contrary, income or capital may, in accordance with the Convention, be taxed with or without limitation in that other State, the State of residence has the choice between the following two methods of eliminating double taxation:

— exemption method: income or capital which is taxable in the State of source or situs is then exempted in the State of residence, but it may be taken into account in determining the rate of tax applicable to the taxpayer's remaining income or capital;

13

— credit method: income or capital taxable in the State of source or situs is then taxed in the State of residence, but the tax levied in the State of source or situs is credited against the tax levied by the State of residence on such income or capital.

Special provisions

23.   These provisions concern:
— non-discrimination (Article 24);
— mutual agreement procedure (Article 25);
— exchange of information (Article 26);
— diplomatic agents and consular officers (Article 27);
— territorial extension of the Convention (Article 28).

B.   GENERAL REMARKS ON THE MODEL CONVENTION

24.   The Committee on Fiscal Affairs has endeavoured, wherever possible, to lay down in each case one single rule.   On certain points, however, it was thought necessary to leave in the Convention a certain degree of flexibility compatible with efficient implementation.   Member countries therefore enjoy a certain latitude with regard to fixing the rate of tax at the source on dividends and interest, the choice of method for eliminating double taxation and, subject to certain conditions, the allocation of profits to a permanent establishment by apportionment of the total profits of the enterprise.   Moreover, for some cases, alternative or additional provisions are mentioned in the Commentaries.

Commentaries on the Articles

25.   For each of the Articles in the Convention, there is a detailed Commentary which is designed to illustrate or interpret the provisions.   When it revised and updated the texts in the 1963 Draft Convention, the Committee on Fiscal Affairs adopted new explanations as to why new provisions had been inserted in the Article concerned or to clarify the meaning and scope of the provisions of the Article.

26.   As these Commentaries have been drafted and agreed upon by the experts appointed to the Committee on Fiscal Affairs by the Governments of Member countries, they are of special importance in the development of international fiscal law.   Although the Commentaries are not designed to be annexed in any manner to the conventions to be signed by Member countries, which alone constitute legally binding international instruments, they can nevertheless be of great assistance in the application of the conventions and, in particular, in the settlement of any disputes.

27.   Observations on the Commentaries have sometimes been inserted at the request of some Member countries who were unable to concur in the interpretation given in the Commentary on the Article concerned.   These observations thus do not express any disagreement with the text of the Convention, but furnish a useful indication of the way in which those countries will apply the provisions of the Article in question.

Reservations of certain Member countries on some provisions of the Convention

28.   All the Member countries which have participated in establishing the Model Convention are in agreement with its aims and its main provisions.

Nevertheless, a certain number of Member countries have entered, on some provisions of the Convention, reservations which are recorded in the Commentaries on the Articles concerned.[1]

29.   The Committee on Fiscal Affairs considers that these reservations must be viewed against the background of the global results which have been obtained. It is understood that insofar as certain Member countries have entered reservations the other Member countries, in negotiating bilateral conventions with the former, will retain their freedom of action in accordance with the principle of reciprocity.

Relation between the 1963 Draft Convention and the 1977 Model Convention

30.   The Committee on Fiscal Affairs has examined the problem of conflicts of interpretation which could arise as a result of changes in the text of the Articles or of the Commentaries. The Committee considers that existing conventions should, as far as possible, be interpreted in the spirit of the new Commentaries, even though the provisions of existing conventions do not yet contain the more precise wording of the 1977 Model Convention. Member countries wishing to clarify their positions in this respect can do so by means of an exchange of letters between competent authorities in accordance with the mutual agreement procedure. Even in the absence of such an exchange of letters, these authorities could use mutual agreement procedures to secure this interpretation for particular cases.

Tax avoidance and evasion; improper use of conventions

31.   The Committee on Fiscal Affairs has examined the question of the improper use of double taxation conventions but, in view of the complexity of the problem, it has limited itself, for the time being, to discussing the problem briefly in the Commentary on Article 1 and to settling a certain number of special cases (paragraph 2 of Article 17 and Commentaries on Articles 10, 11 and 12). Besides, Article 26, as clarified in the Commentary, enables States to exchange information to combat improper use of conventions, tax avoidance and evasion. The Committee intends to make an in-depth study of such problems and of other ways of dealing with them.

Multilateral convention

32.   The Committee on Fiscal Affairs has considered whether the elaboration and conclusion of a multilateral double taxation convention would be feasible. As in 1963, the Committee has come to the conclusion that, in the present situation, this would meet with great difficulties. It might, however, be possible for certain groups of Member countries to study the possibility of concluding such a convention among themselves on the basis of the Model Convention, subject to certain adaptations they may consider necessary to suit their particular purposes.

---

1. In view of the importance of the tax reform presently underway in Portugal, the Portuguese authorities have entered a general reservation on the Articles of the Model Convention, so as to be able to review their existing reservations or, as the case may be, to enter new reservations, to take account of the new legislation.

IV

CONCLUSIONS

33.   The Committee on Fiscal Affairs suggests that the Council of the OECD may wish to:

1. recommend Member countries to pursue their efforts to conclude bilateral conventions for the avoidance of double taxation with respect to taxes on income and on capital with those Member countries with which they have not yet entered into such conventions and to revise those of the existing conventions between them which may no longer be in keeping with present-day needs;
2. recommend Member countries, when concluding new bilateral conventions or revising existing bilateral conventions between them, to conform to the Model Convention, as interpreted by the Commentaries thereto and having regard to the reservations and derogations to the Model Convention, which are contained in the present report;
3. recommend that Member countries, which consider it appropriate, examine the feasibility of concluding among themselves multilateral conventions based upon the Model Convention;
4. request Member countries to notify the Organisation of the text of any new or revised double taxation conventions concluded with each other and, where appropriate, the reasons why the provisions of the Model Convention have not been adopted in such conventions.

34.   The Committee on Fiscal Affairs also suggests that the Council may wish to instruct it to:

1. examine the notifications so supplied and to report to it as appropriate;
2. proceed to periodic reviews of situations where double taxation may occur, in the light of experience gained by Member countries, and to make appropriate proposals for its removal.

35.   The Committee on Fiscal Affairs recommends that the present report be published and given appropriate publicity by the OECD Secretariat.

ANNEX I

MODEL CONVENTION FOR THE AVOIDANCE OF DOUBLE TAXATION WITH RESPECT TO TAXES ON INCOME AND ON CAPITAL

SUMMARY OF THE CONVENTION

TITLE AND PREAMBLE

CHAPTER I
Scope of the Convention

CHAPTER II
Definitions

CHAPTER III
Taxation of income

CHAPTER IV
Taxation of Capital

CHAPTER V
Methods for elimination of double taxation

CHAPTER VI
Special provisions

CHAPTER VII
Final provisions

NOTE: In order to make it possible to compare the 1977 Model Convention with the 1963 Draft Convention, the text of the latter is reproduced at the end of this volume (Appendix III).

TITLE OF THE CONVENTION

Convention between (State A) and (State B) for the avoidance of double taxation with respect to taxes on income and on capital

PREAMBLE OF THE CONVENTION

NOTE: The Preamble of the Convention shall be drafted in accordance with the constitutional procedure of both Contracting States.

Chapter I

SCOPE OF THE CONVENTION

Article 1

PERSONAL SCOPE

This Convention shall apply to persons who are residents of one or both of the Contracting States.

Article 2

TAXES COVERED

1. This Convention shall apply to taxes on income and on capital imposed on behalf of a Contracting State or of its political subdivisions or local authorities, irrespective of the manner in which they are levied.

2. There shall be regarded as taxes on income and on capital all taxes imposed on total income, on total capital, or on elements of income or of capital, including taxes on gains from the alienation of movable or immovable property, taxes on the total amounts of wages or salaries paid by enterprises, as well as taxes on capital appreciation.

3. The existing taxes to which the Convention shall apply are in particular:
    a)   (in State A): ....
    b)   (in State B): ....

4. The Convention shall apply also to any identical or substantially similar taxes which are imposed after the date of signature of the Convention in addition to, or in place of, the existing taxes. At the end of each year, the competent authorities of the Contracting States shall notify each other of changes which have been made in their respective taxation laws.

24

CHAPTER II

DEFINITIONS

Article 3

GENERAL DEFINITIONS

1.   For the purposes of this Convention, unless the context otherwise requires:
  a)   the term "person" includes an individual, a company and any other body of persons;
  b)   the term "company" means any body corporate or any entity which is treated as a body corporate for tax purposes;
  c)   the terms "enterprise of a Contracting State" and "enterprise of the other Contracting State" mean respectively an enterprise carried on by a resident of a Contracting State and an enterprise carried on by a resident of the other Contracting State;
  d)   the term "international traffic" means any transport by a ship or aircraft operated by an enterprise which has its place of effective management in a Contracting State, except when the ship or aircraft is operated solely between places in the other Contracting State;
  e)   the term "competent authority" means:
    (*i*)   (in State A): ....
    (*ii*)   (in State B): ....

2.   As regards the application of the Convention by a Contracting State any term not defined therein shall, unless the context otherwise requires, have the meaning which it has under the law of that State concerning the taxes to which the Convention applies.

Article 4

RESIDENT

1.   For the purposes of this Convention, the term "resident of a Contracting State" means any person who, under the laws of that State, is liable to tax therein by reason of his domicile, residence, place of management or any other criterion of a similar nature. But this term does not include any person who is liable to tax in that State in respect only of income from sources in that State or capital situated therein.

25

2.   Where by reason of the provisions of paragraph 1 an individual is a resident of both Contracting States, then his status shall be determined as follows:

a)   he shall be deemed to be a resident of the State in which he has a permanent home available to him; if he has a permanent home available to him in both States, he shall be deemed to be a resident of the State with which his personal and economic relations are closer (centre of vital interests);

b)   if the State in which he has his centre of vital interests cannot be determined, or if he has not a permanent home available to him in either State, he shall be deemed to be a resident of the State in which he has an habitual abode;

c)   if he has an habitual abode in both States or in neither of them, he shall be deemed to be a resident of the State of which he is a national;

d)   if he is a national of both States or of neither of them, the competent authorities of the Contracting States shall settle the question by mutual agreement.

3.   Where by reason of the provisions of paragraph 1 a person other than an individual is a resident of both Contracting States, then it shall be deemed to be a resident of the State in which its place of effective management is situated.

Article 5

PERMANENT ESTABLISHMENT

1.   For the purposes of this Convention, the term "permanent establishment" means a fixed place of business through which the business of an enterprise is wholly or partly carried on.

2.   The term "permanent establishment" includes especially:
a)   a place of management;
b)   a branch;
c)   an office;
d)   a factory;
e)   a workshop, and
f)   a mine, an oil or gas well, a quarry or any other place of extraction of natural resources.

3.   A building site or construction or installation project constitutes a permanent establishment only if it lasts more than twelve months.

4.   Notwithstanding the preceding provisions of this Article, the term "permanent establishment" shall be deemed not to include:

a)   the use of facilities solely for the purpose of storage, display or delivery of goods or merchandise belonging to the enterprise;

b)   the maintenance of a stock of goods or merchandise belonging to the enterprise solely for the purpose of storage, display or delivery;

c)   the maintenance of a stock of goods or merchandise belonging to the enterprise solely for the purpose of processing by another enterprise;

d)   the maintenance of a fixed place of business solely for the purpose of purchasing goods or merchandise or of collecting information, for the enterprise;

e) the maintenance of a fixed place of business solely for the purpose of carrying on, for the enterprise, any other activity of a preparatory or auxiliary character;

f) the maintenance of a fixed place of business solely for any combination of activities mentioned in sub-paragraphs a) to e), provided that the overall activity of the fixed place of business resulting from this combination is of a preparatory or auxiliary character.

5.   Notwithstanding the provisions of paragraphs 1 and 2, where a person— other than an agent of an independent status to whom paragraph 6 applies—is acting on behalf of an enterprise and has, and habitually exercises, in a Contracting State an authority to conclude contracts in the name of the enterprise, that enterprise shall be deemed to have a permanent establishment in that State in respect of any activities which that person undertakes for the enterprise, unless the activities of such person are limited to those mentioned in paragraph 4 which, if exercised through a fixed place of business, would not make this fixed place of business a permanent establishment under the provisions of that paragraph.

6.   An enterprise shall not be deemed to have a permanent establishment in a Contracting State merely because it carries on business in that State through a broker, general commission agent or any other agent of an independent status, provided that such persons are acting in the ordinary course of their business.

7.   The fact that a company which is a resident of a Contracting State controls or is controlled by a company which is a resident of the other Contracting State, or which carries on business in that other State (whether through a permanent establishment or otherwise), shall not of itself constitute either company a permanent establishment of the other.

CHAPTER III

TAXATION OF INCOME

Article 6

INCOME FROM IMMOVABLE PROPERTY

1.   Income derived by a resident of a Contracting State from immovable property (including income from agriculture or forestry) situated in the other Contracting State may be taxed in that other State.

2.   The term "immovable property" shall have the meaning which it has under the law of the Contracting State in which the property in question is situated. The term shall in any case include property accessory to immovable property, livestock and equipment used in agriculture and forestry, rights to which the provisions of general law respecting landed property apply, usufruct of immovable property and rights to variable or fixed payments as consideration for the working of, or the right to work, mineral deposits, sources and other natural resources; ships, boats and aircraft shall not be regarded as immovable property.

3.   The provisions of paragraph 1 shall apply to income derived from the direct use, letting, or use in any other form of immovable property.

4.   The provisions of paragraphs 1 and 3 shall also apply to the income from immovable property of an enterprise and to income from immovable property used for the performance of independent personal services.

Article 7

BUSINESS PROFITS

1.   The profits of an enterprise of a Contracting State shall be taxable only in that State unless the enterprise carries on business in the other Contracting State through a permanent establishment situated therein. If the enterprise carries on business as aforesaid, the profits of the enterprise may be taxed in the other State but only so much of them as is attributable to that permanent establishment.

2.   Subject to the provisions of paragraph 3, where an enterprise of a Contracting State carries on business in the other Contracting State through a permanent establishment situated therein, there shall in each Contracting State be attributed to that permanent establishment the profits which it might be expected to make if it were a distinct and separate enterprise engaged in the same or similar activities under the same or similar conditions and dealing wholly independently with the enterprise of which it is a permanent establishment.

3.   In determining the profits of a permanent establishment, there shall be allowed as deductions expenses which are incurred for the purposes of the permanent establishment, including executive and general administrative expenses so incurred, whether in the State in which the permanent establishment is situated or elsewhere.

4.   Insofar as it has been customary in a Contracting State to determine the profits to be attributed to a permanent establishment on the basis of an apportionment of the total profits of the enterprise to its various parts, nothing in paragraph 2 shall preclude that Contracting State from determining the profits to be taxed by such an apportionment as may be customary; the method of apportionment adopted shall, however, be such that the result shall be in accordance with the principles contained in this Article.

5.   No profits shall be attributed to a permanent establishment by reason of the mere purchase by that permanent establishment of goods or merchandise for the enterprise.

6.   For the purposes of the preceding paragraphs, the profits to be attributed to the permanent establishment shall be determined by the same method year by year unless there is good and sufficient reason to the contrary.

7.   Where profits include items of income which are dealt with separately in other Articles of this Convention, then the provisions of those Articles shall not be affected by the provisions of this Article.

Article 8

SHIPPING, INLAND WATERWAYS TRANSPORT AND AIR TRANSPORT

1.   Profits from the operation of ships or aircraft in international traffic shall be taxable only in the Contracting State in which the place of effective management of the enterprise is situated.

2.   Profits from the operation of boats engaged in inland waterways transport shall be taxable only in the Contracting State in which the place of effective management of the enterprise is situated.

3.   If the place of effective management of a shipping enterprise or of an inland waterways transport enterprise is aboard a ship or boat, then it shall be deemed to be situated in the Contracting State in which the home harbour of the ship or boat is situated, or, if there is no such home harbour, in the Contracting State of which the operator of the ship or boat is a resident.

4.   The provisions of paragraph 1 shall also apply to profits from the participation in a pool, a joint business or an international operating agency.

Article 9
ASSOCIATED ENTERPRISES

1.   Where
   a)   an enterprise of a Contracting State participates directly or indirectly in the management, control or capital of an enterprise of the other Contracting State, or
   b)   the same persons participate directly or indirectly in the management, control or capital of an enterprise of a Contracting State and an enterprise of the other Contracting State,

and in either case conditions are made or imposed between the two enterprises in their commercial or financial relations which differ from those which would be made between independent enterprises, then any profits which would, but for those conditions, have accrued to one of the enterprises, but, by reason of those conditions, have not so accrued, may be included in the profits of that enterprise and taxed accordingly.

2.   Where a Contracting State includes in the profits of an enterprise of that State—and taxes accordingly—profits on which an enterprise of the other Contracting State has been charged to tax in that other State and the profits so included are profits which would have accrued to the enterprise of the first-mentioned State if the conditions made between the two enterprises had been those which would have been made between independent enterprises, then that other State shall make an appropriate adjustment to the amount of the tax charged therein on those profits.   In determining such adjustment, due regard shall be had to the other provisions of this Convention and the competent authorities of the Contracting States shall if necessary consult each other.

Article 10

DIVIDENDS

1.   Dividends paid by a company which is a resident of a Contracting State to a resident of the other Contracting State may be taxed in that other State.

2.   However, such dividends may also be taxed in the Contracting State of which the company paying the dividends is a resident and according to the laws of that State, but if the recipient is the beneficial owner of the dividends the tax so charged shall not exceed:

   a)   5 per cent of the gross amount of the dividends if the beneficial owner is a company (other than a partnership) which holds directly at least 25 per cent of the capital of the company paying the dividends;

   b)   15 per cent of the gross amount of the dividends in all other cases.

The competent authorities of the Contracting States shall by mutual agreement settle the mode of application of these limitations.

This paragraph shall not affect the taxation of the company in respect of the profits out of which the dividends are paid.

3.   The term "dividends" as used in this Article means income from shares, "jouissance" shares or "jouissance" rights, mining shares, founders' shares or other rights, not being debt-claims, participating in profits, as well as income from other corporate rights which is subjected to the same taxation treatment as income from shares by the laws of the State of which the company making the distribution is a resident.

4.   The provisions of paragraphs 1 and 2 shall not apply if the beneficial owner of the dividends, being a resident of a Contracting State, carries on business in the other Contracting State of which the company paying the dividends is a resident, through a permanent establishment situated therein, or performs in that other State independent personal services from a fixed base situated therein, and the holding in respect of which the dividends are paid is effectively connected with such permanent establishment or fixed base.   In such case the provisions of Article 7 or Article 14, as the case may be, shall apply.

5.   Where a company which is a resident of a Contracting State derives profits or income from the other Contracting State, that other State may not impose any tax on the dividends paid by the company, except insofar as such dividends are paid to a resident of that other State or insofar as the holding in respect of which the dividends are paid is effectively connected with a permanent establishment or a fixed base situated in that other State, nor subject the company's undistributed profits to a tax on the company's undistributed profits, even if the dividends paid or the undistributed profits consist wholly or partly of profits or income arising in such other State.

Article 11

INTEREST

1.   Interest arising in a Contracting State and paid to a resident of the other Contracting State may be taxed in that other State.

2.   However, such interest may also be taxed in the Contracting State in which it arises and according to the laws of that State, but if the recipient is the beneficial owner of the interest the tax so charged shall not exceed 10 per cent of the gross amount of the interest.   The competent authorities of the Contracting States shall by mutual agreement settle the mode of application of this limitation.

3.   The term "interest" as used in this Article means income from debt-claims of every kind, whether or not secured by mortgage and whether or not carrying a right to participate in the debtor's profits, and in particular, income from government securities and income from bonds or debentures, including premiums and prizes attaching to such securities, bonds or debentures.   Penalty charges for late payment shall not be regarded as interest for the purpose of this Article.

4.   The provisions of paragraphs 1 and 2 shall not apply if the beneficial owner of the interest, being a resident of a Contracting State, carries on business in the other Contracting State in which the interest arises, through a permanent establishment situated therein, or performs in that other State independent personal services from a fixed base situated therein, and the debt-claim in respect of which the interest is paid is effectively connected with such permanent establishment or fixed base.   In such case the provisions of Article 7 or Article 14, as the case may be, shall apply.

5.   Interest shall be deemed to arise in a Contracting State when the payer is that State itself, a political subdivision, a local authority or a resident of that State.   Where, however, the person paying the interest, whether he is a resident of a Contracting State or not, has in a Contracting State a permanent establishment or a fixed base in connection with which the indebtedness on which the interest is paid was incurred, and such interest is borne by such permanent establishment or fixed base, then such interest shall be deemed to arise in the State in which the permanent establishment or fixed base is situated.

6.   Where, by reason of a special relationship between the payer and the beneficial owner or between both of them and some other person, the amount of the interest, having regard to the debt-claim for which it is paid, exceeds the amount which would have been agreed upon by the payer and the beneficial owner in the absence of such relationship, the provisions of this Article shall apply only to the last-mentioned amount.   In such case, the excess part of the payments shall remain taxable according to the laws of each Contracting State, due regard being had to the other provisions of this Convention.

Article 12

ROYALTIES

1.   Royalties arising in a Contracting State and paid to a resident of the other Contracting State shall be taxable only in that other State if such resident is the beneficial owner of the royalties.

2.   The term "royalties" as used in this Article means payments of any kind received as a consideration for the use of, or the right to use, any copyright of literary, artistic or scientific work including cinematograph films, any patent, trade mark, design or model, plan, secret formula or process, or for the use of, or the right to use, industrial, commercial, or scientific equipment, or for information concerning industrial, commercial or scientific experience.

3.   The provisions of paragraph 1 shall not apply if the beneficial owner of the royalties, being a resident of a Contracting State, carries on business in the other Contracting State in which the royalties arise, through a permanent establishment situated therein, or performs in that other State independent personal services from a fixed base situated therein, and the right or property in respect of which the royalties are paid is effectively connected with such permanent establishment or fixed base. In such case the provisions of Article 7 or Article 14, as the case may be, shall apply.

4.   Where, by reason of a special relationship between the payer and the beneficial owner or between both of them and some other person, the amount of the royalties, having regard to the use, right or information for which they are paid, exceeds the amount which would have been agreed upon by the payer and the beneficial owner in the absence of such relationship, the provisions of this Article shall apply only to the last-mentioned amount. In such case, the excess part of the payments shall remain taxable according to the laws of each Contracting State, due regard being had to the other provisions of this Convention.

Article 13

CAPITAL GAINS

1.   Gains derived by a resident of a Contracting State from the alienation of immovable property referred to in Article 6 and situated in the other Contracting State may be taxed in that other State.

2.   Gains from the alienation of movable property forming part of the business property of a permanent establishment which an enterprise of a Contracting State has in the other Contracting State or of movable property pertaining to a fixed base available to a resident of a Contracting State in the other Contracting State for the purpose of performing independent personal services, including such gains from the alienation of such a permanent establishment (alone or with the whole enterprise) or of such fixed base, may be taxed in that other State.

3.   Gains from the alienation of ships or aircraft operated in international traffic, boats engaged in inland waterways transport or movable property pertaining to the operation of such ships, aircraft or boats, shall be taxable only in the Contracting State in which the place of effective management of the enterprise is situated.

4.   Gains from the alienation of any property other than that referred to in paragraphs 1, 2 and 3, shall be taxable only in the Contracting State of which the alienator is a resident.

Article 14

INDEPENDENT PERSONAL SERVICES

1.   Income derived by a resident of a Contracting State in respect of professional services or other activities of an independent character shall be taxable only in that State unless he has a fixed base regularly available to him in the other Contracting State for the purpose of performing his activities. If he has such a fixed base, the income may be taxed in the other State but only so much of it as is attributable to that fixed base.

2.   The term "professional services" includes especially independent scientific, literary, artistic, educational or teaching activities as well as the independent activities of physicians, lawyers, engineers, architects, dentists and accountants.

Article 15
DEPENDENT PERSONAL SERVICES

1.   Subject to the provisions of Articles 16, 18 and 19, salaries, wages and other similar remuneration derived by a resident of a Contracting State in respect of an employment shall be taxable only in that State unless the employment is exercised in the other Contracting State. If the employment is so exercised, such remuneration as is derived therefrom may be taxed in that other State.

2.   Notwithstanding the provisions of paragraph 1, remuneration derived by a resident of a Contracting State in respect of an employment exercised in the other Contracting State shall be taxable only in the first-mentioned State if:

a)   the recipient is present in the other State for a period or periods not exceeding in the aggregate 183 days in the fiscal year concerned, and

b)   the remuneration is paid by, or on behalf of, an employer who is not a resident of the other State, and

c)   the remuneration is not borne by a permanent establishment or a fixed base which the employer has in the other State.

3.   Notwithstanding the preceding provisions of this Article, remuneration derived in respect of an employment exercised aboard a ship or aircraft operated in international traffic, or aboard a boat engaged in inland waterways transport, may be taxed in the Contracting State in which the place of effective management of the enterprise is situated.

Article 16

DIRECTORS' FEES

Directors' fees and other similar payments derived by a resident of a Contracting State in his capacity as a member of the board of directors of a company which is a resident of the other Contracting State may be taxed in that other State.

Article 17

ARTISTES AND ATHLETES

1. Notwithstanding the provisions of Articles 14 and 15, income derived by a resident of a Contracting State as an entertainer, such as a theatre, motion picture, radio or television artiste, or a musician, or as an athlete, from his personal activities as such exercised in the other Contracting State, may be taxed in that other State.

2. Where income in respect of personal activities exercised by an entertainer or an athlete in his capacity as such accrues not to the entertainer or athlete himself but to another person, that income may, notwithstanding the provisions of Articles 7, 14 and 15, be taxed in the Contracting State in which the activities of the entertainer or athlete are exercised.

Article 18

PENSIONS

Subject to the provisions of paragraph 2 of Article 19, pensions and other similar remuneration paid to a resident of a Contracting State in consideration of past employment shall be taxable only in that State.

Article 19

GOVERNMENT SERVICE

1. *a)* Remuneration, other than a pension, paid by a Contracting State or a political subdivision or a local authority thereof to an individual in respect of services rendered to that State or subdivision or authority shall be taxable only in that State.

    b) However, such remuneration shall be taxable only in the other Contracting State if the services are rendered in that State and the individual is a resident of that State who:

        (i)   is a national of that State; or

        (ii) did not become a resident of that State solely for the purpose of rendering the services.

2. *a)* Any pension paid by, or out of funds created by, a Contracting State or a political subdivision or a local authority thereof to an individual in respect of services rendered to that State or subdivision or authority shall be taxable only in that State.

    b) However, such pension shall be taxable only in the other Contracting State if the individual is a resident of, and a national of, that State.

3. The provisions of Articles 15, 16 and 18 shall apply to remuneration and pensions in respect of services rendered in connection with a business carried on by a Contracting State or a political subdivision or a local authority thereof.

Article 20

STUDENTS

Payments which a student or business apprentice who is or was immediately before visiting a Contracting State a resident of the other Contracting State and who is present in the first-mentioned State solely for the purpose of his education or training receives for the purpose of his maintenance, education or training shall not be taxed in that State, provided that such payments arise from sources outside that State.

Article 21

OTHER INCOME

1. Items of income of a resident of a Contracting State, wherever arising, not dealt with in the foregoing Articles of this Convention shall be taxable only in that State.

2. The provisions of paragraph 1 shall not apply to income, other than income from immovable property as defined in paragraph 2 of Article 6, if the recipient of such income, being a resident of a Contracting State, carries on business in the other Contracting State through a permanent establishment situated therein, or performs in that other State independent personal services from a fixed base situated therein, and the right or property in respect of which the income is paid is effectively connected with such permanent establishment or fixed base. In such case the provisions of Article 7 or Article 14, as the case may be, shall apply.

CHAPTER IV

TAXATION OF CAPITAL

Article 22

CAPITAL

1.   Capital represented by immovable property referred to in Article 6, owned by a resident of a Contracting State and situated in the other Contracting State, may be taxed in that other State.

2.   Capital represented by movable property forming part of the business property of a permanent establishment which an enterprise of a Contracting State has in the other Contracting State or by movable property pertaining to a fixed base available to a resident of a Contracting State in the other Contracting State for the purpose of performing independent personal services, may be taxed in that other State.

3.   Capital represented by ships and aircraft operated in international traffic and by boats engaged in inland waterways transport, and by movable property pertaining to the operation of such ships, aircraft and boats, shall be taxable only in the Contracting State in which the place of effective management of the enterprise is situated.

4.   All other elements of capital of a resident of a Contracting State shall be taxable only in that State.

CHAPTER V

METHODS FOR ELIMINATION OF DOUBLE TAXATION

Article 23 A

EXEMPTION METHOD

1.   Where a resident of a Contracting State derives income or owns capital which, in accordance with the provisions of this Convention, may be taxed in the other Contracting State, the first-mentioned State shall, subject to the provisions of paragraphs 2 and 3, exempt such income or capital from tax.

2.   Where a resident of a Contracting State derives items of income which, in accordance with the provisions of Articles 10 and 11, may be taxed in the other Contracting State, the first-mentioned State shall allow as a deduction from the tax on the income of that resident an amount equal to the tax paid in that other State.   Such deduction shall not, however, exceed that part of the tax, as computed before the deduction is given, which is attributable to such items of income derived from that other State.

3.   Where in accordance with any provision of the Convention income derived or capital owned by a resident of a Contracting State is exempt from tax in that State, such State may nevertheless, in calculating the amount of tax on the remaining income or capital of such resident, take into account the exempted income or capital.

Article 23 B

CREDIT METHOD

1.   Where a resident of a Contracting State derives income or owns capital which, in accordance with the provisions of this Convention, may be taxed in the other Contracting State, the first-mentioned State shall allow:

    a)   as a deduction from the tax on the income of that resident, an amount equal to the income tax paid in that other State;

    b)   as a deduction from the tax on the capital of that resident, an amount equal to the capital tax paid in that other State.

Such deduction in either case shall not, however, exceed that part of the income tax or capital tax, as computed before the deduction is given, which is attributable, as the case may be, to the income or the capital which may be taxed in that other State.

39

2.   Where in accordance with any provision of the Convention income derived
or capital owned by a resident of a Contracting State is exempt from tax in that
State, such State may nevertheless, in calculating the amount of tax on the remaining income or capital of such resident, take into account the exempted income
or capital.

Chapter VI

SPECIAL PROVISIONS

Article 24

NON-DISCRIMINATION

1.   Nationals of a Contracting State shall not be subjected in the other Contracting State to any taxation or any requirement connected therewith, which is other or more burdensome than the taxation and connected requirements to which nationals of that other State in the same circumstances are or may be subjected. This provision shall, notwithstanding the provisions of Article 1, also apply to persons who are not residents of one or both of the Contracting States.

2.   The term "nationals" means:
   a)   all individuals possessing the nationality of a Contracting State;
   b)   all legal persons, partnerships and associations deriving their status as such from the laws in force in a Contracting State.

3.   Stateless persons who are residents of a Contracting State shall not be subjected in either Contracting State to any taxation or any requirement connected therewith, which is other or more burdensome than the taxation and connected requirements to which nationals of the State concerned in the same circumstances are or may be subjected.

4.   The taxation on a permanent establishment which an enterprise of a Contracting State has in the other Contracting State shall not be less favourably levied in that other State than the taxation levied on enterprises of that other State carrying on the same activities.   This provision shall not be construed as obliging a Contracting State to grant to residents of the other Contracting State any personal allowances, reliefs and reductions for taxation purposes on account of civil status or family responsibilities which it grants to its own residents.

5.   Except where the provisions of paragraph 1 of Article 9, paragraph 6 of Article 11, or paragraph 4 of Article 12, apply, interest, royalties and other disbursements paid by an enterprise of a Contracting State to a resident of the other Contracting State shall, for the purpose of determining the taxable profits of such enterprise, be deductible under the same conditions as if they had been paid to a resident of the first-mentioned State.   Similarly, any debts of an enterprise of a Contracting State to a resident of the other Contracting State shall, for the purpose of determining the taxable capital of such enterprise, be deductible under the same conditions as if they had been contracted to a resident of the first-mentioned State.

41

6.   Enterprises of a Contracting State, the capital of which is wholly or partly owned or controlled, directly or indirectly, by one or more residents of the other Contracting State, shall not be subjected in the first-mentioned State to any taxation or any requirement connected therewith which is other or more burdensome than the taxation and connected requirements to which other similar enterprises of the first-mentioned State are or may be subjected.

7.   The provisions of this Article shall, notwithstanding the provisions of Article 2, apply to taxes of every kind and description.

Article 25
MUTUAL AGREEMENT PROCEDURE

1.   Where a person considers that the actions of one or both of the Contracting States result or will result for him in taxation not in accordance with the provisions of this Convention, he may, irrespective of the remedies provided by the domestic law of those States, present his case to the competent authority of the Contracting State of which he is a resident or, if his case comes under paragraph 1 of Article 24, to that of the Contracting State of which he is a national. The case must be presented within three years from the first notification of the action resulting in taxation not in accordance with the provisions of the Convention.

2.   The competent authority shall endeavour, if the objection appears to it to be justified and if it is not itself able to arrive at a satisfactory solution, to resolve the case by mutual agreement with the competent authority of the other Contracting State, with a view to the avoidance of taxation which is not in accordance with the Convention. Any agreement reached shall be implemented notwithstanding any time limits in the domestic law of the Contracting States.

3.   The competent authorities of the Contracting States shall endeavour to resolve by mutual agreement any difficulties or doubts arising as to the interpretation or application of the Convention. They may also consult together for the elimination of double taxation in cases not provided for in the Convention.

4.   The competent authorities of the Contracting States may communicate with each other directly for the purpose of reaching an agreement in the sense of the preceding paragraphs. When it seems advisable in order to reach agreement to have an oral exchange of opinions, such exchange may take place through a Commission consisting of representatives of the competent authorities of the Contracting States.

Article 26
EXCHANGE OF INFORMATION

1.   The competent authorities of the Contracting States shall exchange such information as is necessary for carrying out the provisions of this Convention or of the domestic laws of the Contracting States concerning taxes covered by the Convention insofar as the taxation thereunder is not contrary to the Convention. The exchange of information is not restricted by Article 1. Any information received by a Contracting State shall be treated as secret in the same manner as information obtained under the domestic laws of that State and shall be disclosed

only to persons or authorities (including courts and administrative bodies) involved in the assessment or collection of, the enforcement or prosecution in respect of, or the determination of appeals in relation to, the taxes covered by the Convention. Such persons or authorities shall use the information only for such purposes. They may disclose the information in public court proceedings or in judicial decisions.

2.   In no case shall the provisions of paragraph 1 be construed so as to impose on a Contracting State the obligation:

   a)   to carry out administrative measures at variance with the laws and administrative practice of that or of the other Contracting State;
   b)   to supply information which is not obtainable under the laws or in the normal course of the administration of that or of the other Contracting State;
   c)   to supply information which would disclose any trade, business, industrial, commercial or professional secret or trade process, or information, the disclosure of which would be contrary to public policy (ordre public).

Article 27

DIPLOMATIC AGENTS AND CONSULAR OFFICERS

Nothing in this Convention shall affect the fiscal privileges of diplomatic agents or consular officers under the general rules of international law or under the provisions of special agreements.

Article 28

TERRITORIAL EXTENSION

1.   This Convention may be extended, either in its entirety or with any necessary modifications [to any part of the territory of (State A) or of (State B) which is specifically excluded from the application of the Convention or], to any State or territory for whose international relations (State A) or (State B) is responsible, which imposes taxes substantially similar in character to those to which the Convention applies. Any such extension shall take effect from such date and subject to such modifications and conditions, including conditions as to termination, as may be specified and agreed between the Contracting States in notes to be exchanged through diplomatic channels or in any other manner in accordance with their constitutional procedures.

2.   Unless otherwise agreed by both Contracting States, the termination of the Convention by one of them under Article 30 shall also terminate, in the manner provided for in that Article, the application of the Convention [to any part of the territory of (State A) or of (State B) or] to any State or territory to which it has been extended under this Article.

NOTE: The words between brackets are of relevance when, by special provision, a part of the territory of a Contracting State is excluded from the application of the Convention.

CHAPTER VII

FINAL PROVISIONS

Article 29

ENTRY INTO FORCE

1.   This Convention shall be ratified and the instruments of ratification shall be exchanged at .... as soon as possible.

2.   The Convention shall enter into force upon the exchange of instruments of ratification and its provisions shall have effect:

    a)   (in State A): ....
    b)   (in State B): ....

Article 30

TERMINATION

This Convention shall remain in force until terminated by a Contracting State.   Either Contracting State may terminate the Convention, through diplomatic channels, by giving notice of termination at least six months before the end of any calendar year after the year .... In such event, the Convention shall cease to have effect:

    a)   (in State A): ....
    b)   (in State B): ....

TERMINAL CLAUSE

NOTE: The terminal clause concerning the signing shall be drafted in accordance with the constitutional procedure of both Contracting States.

COMMENTARIES ON THE ARTICLES
OF THE MODEL CONVENTION

COMMENTARY ON ARTICLE 1
CONCERNING THE PERSONAL SCOPE
OF THE CONVENTION

1.   Whereas the earliest conventions in general were applicable to "citizens" of the Contracting States, more recent conventions usually apply to "residents" of one or both of the Contracting States without distinction of nationality. Some conventions were of even wider scope inasmuch as they apply more generally to "taxpayers" of the Contracting States; they are, therefore, also applicable to persons, who, although not residing in either State, are nevertheless liable to tax on part of their income or capital in each of them.   The Convention is intended to be applied between OECD Member countries and it has been deemed preferable for practical reasons to provide that the Convention is to apply to persons who are residents of one or both of the Contracting States.   It is recalled that the meaning of the term "resident" is defined in Article 4.

APPLICATION OF THE CONVENTION TO PARTNERSHIPS

2.   The domestic laws of the various OECD Member countries differ in the treatment of partnerships.   The main issue of such differences is founded on the fact that some countries treat partnerships as taxable units (sometimes even as companies) whereas other countries disregard the partnership and tax only the individual partners on their share of the partnership income.

3.   These differences in views have many effects on the application of the Convention in the case of partnerships, especially where one or more partners are not residents of the State in which the partnership was created or organised. First the question arises, whether a partnership as such may invoke the provisions of the Convention.   Where a partnership is treated as a company or taxed in the same way, it may reasonably be argued that the partnership is a resident of the Contracting State taxing the partnership on the grounds mentioned in paragraph 1 of Article 4 and therefore, falling under the scope of the Convention, is entitled to the benefits of the Convention.   In the other instances mentioned in paragraph 2 above, the application of the Convention to the partnership as such might be refused, at least if no special rule is provided for in the Convention covering partnerships.

4.   Moreover, different rules of the Convention may be applied in the Contracting States to income derived by a partner from the partnership, depending on the approach of such States.   In States, where partnerships are treated as companies, distributions of profits to the partners may be considered to be dividends (paragraph 3 of Article 10), whilst for other States all profits of a partnership, whether distributed or not, are considered as business profits of the partners (Article 7). In many States, business profits of partnerships include, for tax purposes, all or some special remuneration paid by a partnership to its partners (such as rents,

interest, royalties, remuneration for services), whilst in other States such payments are not dealt with as business profits (Article 7) but under other headings (in the above-mentioned examples: Articles 6, 11, 12, 14 or 15, respectively).

5.　　Finally the capital invested in a partnership or the alienation of a participation in a partnership may be treated, depending on the approach, under paragraph 2 of Articles 22 and 13 (permanent establishment) or paragraph 4 of Articles 22 and 13 (other movable property).

6.　　The concurrent application of different Articles of the Convention in the two Contracting States (or even the non-application of the Convention in one of them) may not only result in double taxation, but also in non-taxation. However, the practical application of double taxation conventions, whether or not based on the 1963 Draft Convention, and the discussions on the revision of the 1963 Draft Convention have shown that the opinions of the OECD Member countries differ too much and that it is extremely difficult to find a uniform solution which would be acceptable to all or even to the great majority of Member countries. The Convention does not, therefore, contain any special provisions relating to partnerships. Contracting States are however left free to examine the problems of partnerships in their bilateral negotiations and to agree upon such special provisions as they may find necessary and appropriate.

IMPROPER USE OF THE CONVENTION

7.　　The purpose of double taxation conventions is to promote, by eliminating international double taxation, exchanges of goods and services, and the movement of capital and persons; they should not, however, help tax avoidance or evasion. True, taxpayers have the possibility, double taxation conventions being left aside, to exploit the differences in tax levels as between States and the tax advantages provided by various countries' taxation laws, but it is for the States concerned to adopt provisions in their domestic laws to counter possible manoeuvres. Such States will then wish, in their bilateral double taxation conventions, to preserve the application of provisions of this kind contained in their domestic laws.

8.　　Moreover, the extension of the network of double taxation conventions still reinforces the impact of such manoeuvres as they make it possible, through the creation of usually artificial legal constructions, to benefit both from the tax advantages available under certain domestic laws and the reliefs from tax provided for in double taxation conventions.

9.　　This would be the case, for example, if a person (whether or not a resident of a Contracting State), acted through a legal entity created in a State essentially to obtain treaty benefits which would not be available directly to such person. Another case would be one of an individual having in a Contracting State both his permanent home and all his economic interests, including a substantial participation in a company of that State, and who, essentially in order to sell the participation and escape taxation in that State on the capital gains from the alienation (by virtue of paragraph 4 of Article 13), transferred his permanent home to the other Contracting State, where such gains were subject to little or no tax.

10.　　Some of these situations are dealt with in the Convention, e.g. by the introduction of the concept of "beneficial owner" (in Articles 10, 11 and 12) and of special provisions, for the so-called artiste-companies (paragraph 2 of Article

17). Such problems are also mentioned in the Commentaries on Article 10 (paragraphs 17 and 22), Article 11 (paragraph 12), Article 12 (paragraph 7). It may be appropriate for Contracting States to agree in bilateral negotiations that any relief from tax should not apply in certain cases, or to agree that the application of the provisions of domestic laws against tax avoidance should not be affected by the Convention.

RESERVATION ON THE ARTICLE

11. The *United States* reserves the right to tax its citizens and residents (with certain exceptions) without regard to the Convention.

COMMENTARY ON ARTICLE 2
CONCERNING TAXES COVERED
BY THE CONVENTION

1.   This Article is intended to make the terminology and nomenclature relating to the taxes covered by the Convention more acceptable and precise, to ensure identification of the Contracting States' taxes covered by the Convention, to widen as much as possible the field of application of the Convention by including, as far as possible, and in harmony with the domestic laws of the Contracting States, the taxes imposed by their political subdivisions or local authorities, and to avoid the necessity of concluding a new convention whenever the Contracting States' domestic laws are modified, by means of the periodical exchange of lists and through a procedure for mutual consultation.

Paragraph 1

2.   This paragraph defines the scope of application of the Convention: taxes on income and on capital; the term "direct taxes" which is far too imprecise has therefore been avoided.   It is immaterial on behalf of which authorities such taxes are imposed; it may be the State itself or its political subdivisions or local authorities (constituent States, regions, provinces, "départements", cantons, districts, "arrondissements", "Kreise", municipalities or groups of municipalities, etc.). The method of levying the taxes is equally immaterial: by direct assessment or by deduction at the source, in the form of surtaxes or surcharges, or as additional taxes ("centimes additionnels"), etc.

Paragraph 2

3.   This paragraph gives a definition of taxes on income and on capital.   Such taxes comprise taxes on total income and on elements of income, on total capital and on elements of capital.   They also include taxes on profits and gains derived from the alienation of movable or immovable property, as well as taxes on capital appreciation.   Finally, the definition extends to taxes on the total amounts of wages or salaries paid by undertakings ("payroll taxes"; in Germany "Lohn-summensteuer"; in France, "taxe sur les salaires").   Social security charges, or any other charges paid where there is a direct connection between the levy and the individual benefits to be received, shall not be regarded as "taxes on the total amount of wages".

4.   Clearly a State possessing taxing powers—and it alone—may levy the taxes imposed by its legislation together with any duties or charges accessory to them: increases, costs, interest, etc.   It has not been considered necessary to specify this in the Article, as it is obvious that in the levying of the tax the accessory duties or charges depend on the same rule as the principal duty.

5.   The Article does not mention "ordinary taxes" or "extraordinary taxes". Normally, it might be considered justifiable to include extraordinary taxes in a Model Convention, but experience has shown that such taxes are generally imposed in very special circumstances.   In addition, it would be difficult to define them. They may be extraordinary for various reasons; their imposition, the manner in which they are levied, their rates, their objects, etc.   This being so, it seems preferable not to include extraordinary taxes in the Article.   But, as it is not intended to exclude extraordinary taxes from all conventions, ordinary taxes have not been mentioned either.   The Contracting States are thus free to restrict the convention's field of application to ordinary taxes, to extend it to extraordinary taxes, or even to establish special provisions.

Paragraph 3

6.   This paragraph lists the taxes in force at the time of signature of the convention.   The list is not exhaustive.   It serves to illustrate the preceding paragraphs of the Article.   In principle, however, it will be a complete list of taxes imposed in each State at the time of signature and covered by the convention.

Paragraph 4

7.   This paragraph provides, since the list of taxes in paragraph 3 is purely declaratory, that the Convention is also to apply to all identical or substantially similar taxes which are imposed after the date of signature of the Convention in addition to, or in place of, the existing taxes.   This provision is necessary to prevent the Convention from becoming inoperative in the event of one of the States modifying its taxation laws.

8.   Each State undertakes to notify the other of any amendments made to its taxation laws by communicating to it at the end of each year, when necessary, a list of new or substituted taxes, imposed during that year.

OBSERVATION ON THE COMMENTARY

9.   In contexts such as limitations on the rate of tax or the granting of credits for foreign tax, *New Zealand* would wish to make it clear that the term "tax" does not include penalties.

RESERVATIONS ON THE ARTICLE

10.   *Australia, Canada* and the *United States* reserve their positions on that part of paragraph 1 which states that the Convention should apply to taxes of political subdivisions or local authorities.

11.   *Japan* reserves its position on that part of paragraph 1 which states that the Convention shall apply to taxes on capital.

COMMENTARY ON ARTICLE 3
CONCERNING GENERAL DEFINITIONS

1.   This Article groups together a number of general provisions required for the interpretation of the terms used in the Convention.   It should be observed, however, that the meaning of some important terms is explained elsewhere in the Convention.   Thus, the terms "resident" and "permanent establishment" are defined in Articles 4 and 5 respectively, while the interpretation of certain terms appearing in the Articles on special categories of income ("immovable property", "dividends", etc.) is clarified by provisions embodied in those Articles.   In addition to the definitions contained in the Article, Contracting States are free to agree bilaterally on definitions of the terms "a Contracting State" and "the other Contracting State".   Furthermore, Contracting States are free to agree bilaterally to include in the possible definitions of "Contracting States" a reference to continental shelves.

Paragraph 1

THE TERM "PERSON"

2.   The definition of the term "person" given in sub-paragraph *a*) is not exhaustive and should be read as indicating that the term "person" is used in a very wide sense (cf. especially Articles 1 and 4).   The definition explicitly mentions individuals, companies and other bodies of persons.   From the meaning assigned to the term "company" by the definition contained in sub-paragraph *b*) it follows that, in addition, the term "person" includes any entity which, although itself not a body of persons, is treated as a body corporate for tax purposes.   Thus, e.g. a foundation ("fondation", "Stiftung") may fall within the meaning of the term "person".   Special considerations for the application of the Convention to partnerships are found in paragraphs 2 to 6 of the Commentary on Article 1.

THE TERM "COMPANY"

3.   The term "company" means in the first place any body corporate.   In addition, the term covers any other taxable unit which is treated as a body corporate according to the tax laws of the Contracting State in which it is organised.   The definition is drafted with special regard to the Article on dividends.   It should be noted that the term "company" has a bearing only on that Article, paragraph 7 of Article 5 and Article 16.

THE TERM "ENTERPRISE"

4.   The question whether an activity is performed within the framework of an enterprise or is deemed to constitute in itself an enterprise has always been

51

interpreted according to the provisions of the domestic laws of the Contracting States. No definition, properly speaking, of the term "enterprise" has therefore been attempted in this Article.

THE TERM "INTERNATIONAL TRAFFIC"

5.   The definition of the term "international traffic" is based on the principle as set forth in paragraph 1 of Article 8 that the right to tax profits from the operation of ships or aircraft in international traffic resides only in the Contracting State in which the place of effective management is situated in view of the special nature of the international traffic business.   However, as stated in the Commentary on paragraph 1 of Article 8, the Contracting States are free on a bilateral basis to insert in sub-paragraph d) the reference to residence, in order to be consistent with the general pattern of the other Articles.   In such a case, the words "an enterprise which has its place of effective management in a Contracting State" should be replaced, by "an enterprise of a Contracting State" or "a resident of a Contracting State".

6.   It is to be noted that the definition of the term "international traffic" is broader than the term normally signifies.   However, this has been deliberate in order to preserve for the State of the place of effective management the right to tax purely domestic traffic as well as international traffic between third States, and to allow the other Contracting State to tax traffic solely within its borders. This intention may be clarified by the following illustration.   Suppose an enterprise of a Contracting State or an enterprise which has its place of effective management in a Contracting State, through an agent in the other Contracting State, sells tickets for a passage which is confined wholly within the first-mentioned State or, alternatively, within a third State.   The Article does not permit the other State to tax the profits of either voyage.   The other State is allowed to tax such an enterprise of the first-mentioned State only where the operations are confined solely to places in that other State.

THE TERM "COMPETENT AUTHORITY"

7.   The definition of the term "competent authority" has regard to the fact that in some OECD Member countries the execution of double taxation conventions does not exclusively fall within the competence of the highest tax authorities but that some matters are reserved or may be delegated to other authorities.   The present definition enables each Contracting State to nominate one or more authorities as being competent.

Paragraph 2

8.   This paragraph provides a general rule of interpretation in respect of terms used in the Convention but not defined therein.

OBSERVATION ON THE COMMENTARY

9.   For the purposes of Articles 10, 11 and 12 *New Zealand* would wish to treat dividends, interest and royalties in respect of which a trustee is subject to tax in the State of which he is a resident as being beneficially owned by that trustee.

RESERVATION ON THE ARTICLE

10.   *Belgium* reserves the right to vary, in its conventions, sub-paragraph *b*) of paragraph 1 of Article 3, and paragraph 1 of Article 4, so as to make it clear that partnerships constituted under Belgian law must be treated as residents of Belgium, in view of the twofold fact that they are legal persons and that their world income is in all cases subject to tax in Belgium.

COMMENTARY ON ARTICLE 4
CONCERNING THE DEFINITION OF RESIDENT

I. PRELIMINARY REMARKS

1.   The concept of "resident of a Contracting State" has various functions and is of importance in three cases:

  a)   in determining a convention's personal scope of application;
  b)   in solving cases where double taxation arises in consequence of double residence;
  c)   in solving cases where double taxation arises as a consequence of taxation in the State of residence and in the State of source or situs.

2.   The Article is intended to define the meaning of the term "resident of a Contracting State" and to solve cases of double residence. To clarify the scope of the Article some general comments are made below referring to the two typical cases of conflict, i.e. between two residences and between residence and source or situs. In both cases the conflict arises because, under their domestic laws, one or both Contracting States claim that the person concerned is resident in their territory.

3.   Generally the domestic laws of the various States impose a comprehensive liability to tax—"full tax liability"—based on the taxpayers' personal attachment to the State concerned (the "State of residence"). This liability to tax is not imposed only on persons who are "domiciled" in a State in the sense in which "domicile" is usually taken in the legislations (private law). The cases of full liability to tax are extended to comprise also, for instance, persons who stay continually, or maybe only for a certain period, in the territory of the State. Some legislations impose full liability to tax on individuals who perform services on board ships which have their home harbour in the State.

4.   Conventions for the avoidance of double taxation do not normally concern themselves with the domestic laws of the Contracting States laying down the conditions under which a person is to be treated fiscally as "resident" and, consequently, is fully liable to tax in that State. They do not lay down standards which the provisions of the domestic laws on "residence" have to fulfil in order that claims for full tax liability can be accepted between the Contracting States. In this respect the States take their stand entirely on the domestic laws.

5.   This manifests itself quite clearly in the cases where there is no conflict at all between two residences, but where the conflict exists only between residence and source or situs. But the same view applies in conflicts between two residences. The special point in these cases is only that no solution of the conflict can be arrived at by reference to the concept of residence adopted in the domestic laws of the States concerned. In these cases special provisions must be established in the Convention to determine which of the two concepts of residence is to be given preference.

6.   An example will elucidate the case.   An individual has his permanent home in State A, where his wife and children live. He has had a stay of more than six months in State B and according to the legislation of the latter State he is, in consequence of the length of the stay, taxed as being a resident of that State.   Thus, both States claim that he is fully liable to tax.   This conflict has to be solved by the Convention.

7.   In this particular case the Article (under paragraph 2) gives preference to the claim of State A.   This does not, however, imply that the Article lays down special rules on "residence" and that the domestic laws of State B are ignored because they are incompatible with such rules.   The fact is quite simply that in the case of such a conflict a choice must necessarily be made between the two claims, and it is on this point that the Article proposes special rules.

II.   COMMENTARY ON THE PROVISIONS OF THE ARTICLE

Paragraph 1

8.   Paragraph 1 provides a definition of the expression "resident of a Contracting State" for the purposes of the Convention. The definition refers to the concept of residence adopted in the domestic laws (cf. Preliminary Remarks). As criteria for the taxation as a resident the definition mentions: domicile, residence, place of management or any other criterion of a similar nature. As far as individuals are concerned, the definition aims at covering the various forms of personal attachment to a State which, in the domestic taxation laws, form the basis of a comprehensive taxation (full liability to tax). It also covers cases where a person is deemed, according to the taxation laws of a State, to be a resident of that State and on account thereof is fully liable to tax therein (e.g. diplomats or other persons in government service). In accordance with the provisions of the second sentence of paragraph 1, however, a person is not to be considered a "resident of a Contracting State" in the sense of the Convention if, although not domiciled in that State, he is considered to be a resident according to the domestic laws but is subject only to a taxation limited to the income from sources in that State or to capital situated in that State. That situation exists in some States in relation to individuals, e.g. in the case of foreign diplomatic and consular staff serving in their territory.

Paragraph 2

9.   This paragraph relates to the case where, under the provisions of paragraph 1, an individual is a resident of both Contracting States.

10.   To solve this conflict special rules must be established which give the attachment to one State a preference over the attachment to the other State.   As far as possible, the preference criterion must be of such a nature that there can be no question but that the person concerned will satisfy it in one State only, and at the same time it must reflect such an attachment that it is felt to be natural that the right to tax devolves upon that particular State.

11.   The Article gives preference to the Contracting State in which the individual has a permanent home available to him.   This criterion will frequently be sufficient to solve the conflict, e.g. where the individual has a permanent home in one Contracting State and has only made a stay of some length in the other Contracting State.

12.   Sub-paragraph *a*) means, therefore, that in the application of the Convention (that is, where there is a conflict between the laws of the two States) it is considered that the residence is that place where the individual owns or possesses a home; this home must be permanent, that is to say, the individual must have arranged and retained it for his permanent use as opposed to staying at a particular place under such conditions that it is evident that the stay is intended to be of short duration.

13.   As regards the concept of home, it should be observed that any form of home may be taken into account (house of apartment belonging to or rented by the individual, rented furnished room). But the permanence of the home is essential; this means that the individual has arranged to have the dwelling available to him at all times continuously, and not occasionally for the purpose of a stay which, owing to the reasons for it, is necessarily of short duration (travel for pleasure, business travel, educational travel, attending a course at a school, etc.).

14.   If the individual has a permanent home in both Contracting States, paragraph 2 gives preference to the State with which the personal and economic relations of the individual are closer, this being understood as the centre of vital interests.   In the cases where the residence cannot be determined by reference to this rule, paragraph 2 provides as subsidiary criteria, first, habitual abode, and then nationality.   If the individual is a national of both States or of neither of them, the question shall be solved by mutual agreement between the States concerned according to the procedure laid down in Article 25.

15.   If the individual has a permanent home in both Contracting States, it is necessary to look at the facts in order to ascertain with which of the two States his personal and economic relations are closer.   Thus, regard will be had to his family and social relations, his occupations, his political, cultural or other activities, his place of business, the place from which he administers his property, etc. The circumstances must be examined as a whole, but it is nevertheless obvious that considerations based on the personal acts of the individual must receive special attention.   If a person who has a home in one State sets up a second in the other State while retaining the first, the fact that he retains the first in the environment where he has always lived, where he has worked, and where he has his family and possessions, can, together with other elements, go to demonstrate that he has retained his centre of vital interests in the first State.

16.   Sub-paragraph *b*) establishes a secondary criterion for two quite distinct and different situations:

   a)   the case where the individual has a permanent home available to him in both Contracting States and it is not possible to determine in which one he has his centre of vital interests;
   b)   the case where the individual has a permanent home available to him in neither Contracting State.

Preference is given to the Contracting State where the individual has an habitual abode.

17.   In the first situation, the case where the individual has a permanent home available to him in both States, the fact of having an habitual abode in one State rather than in the other appears therefore as the circumstance which, in case of doubt as to where the individual has his centre of vital interests, tips the balance towards the State where he stays more frequently.   For this purpose regard must

be had to stays made by the individual not only at the permanent home in the State in question but also at any other place in the same State.

18.   The second situation is the case of an individual who has a permanent home available to him in neither Contracting State, as for example, a person going from one hotel to another.   In this case also all stays made in a State must be considered without it being necessary to ascertain the reasons for them.

19.   In stipulating that in the two situations which it contemplates preference is given to the Contracting State where the individual has an habitual abode, sub-paragraph *b*) does not specify over what length of time the comparison must be made.   The comparison must cover a sufficient length of time for it to be possible to determine whether the residence in each of the two States is habitual and to determine also the intervals at which the stays take place.

20.   Where, in the two situations referred to in sub-paragraph *b*) the individual has an habitual abode in both Contracting States or in neither, preference is given to the State of which he is a national.   If, in these cases still, the individual is a national of both Contracting States or of neither of them the sub-paragraph *d*) assigns to the competent authorities the duty of resolving the difficulty by mutual agreement according to the procedure established in Article 25.

Paragraph 3

21.   This paragraph concerns companies and other bodies of persons, irrespective of whether they are or not legal persons.   It may be rare in practice for a company, etc. to be subject to tax as a resident in more than one State, but it is, of course, possible if, for instance, one State attaches importance to the registration and the other State to the place of effective management.   So, in the case of companies, etc., also, special rules as to the preference must be established.

22.   It would not be an adequate solution to attach importance to a purely formal criterion like registration.   Therefore paragraph 3 attaches importance to the place where the company, etc. is actually managed.

23.   The formulation of the preference criterion in the case of persons other than individuals was considered in particular in connection with the taxation of income from shipping, inland waterways transport and air transport.   A number of conventions for the avoidance of double taxation on such income accord the taxing power to the State in which the "place of management" of the enterprise is situated; other conventions attach importance to its "place of effective management", others again to the "fiscal domicile of the operator".   Concerning conventions concluded by the United Kingdom which provide that a company shall be regarded as resident in the State in which "its business is managed and controlled", it has been made clear, on the United Kingdom side, that this expression means the "effective management" of the enterprise.

24.   As a result of these considerations, the "place of effective management" has been adopted as the preference criterion for persons other than individuals.

OBSERVATION ON THE COMMENTARY

25.   *New Zealand's* interpretation of the term "effective management" is practical day to day management, irrespective of where the overriding control is exercised.

RESERVATIONS ON THE ARTICLE

26.   *Canada* and the *United States* reserve the right to use as the test for paragraph 3 the place of incorporation or organisation with respect to a company.

27.   *Japan* wishes to be free to conclude a bilateral convention which provides that the fiscal domicile of a resident of both Contracting States is to be determined through consultation between competent authorities.   When entering into such consultation, Japan is prepared to take into consideration the rules set out in paragraph 2 of this Article as far as practicable.

28.   *Japan* also reserves its position on the provisions in this and other Articles in the Model Convention which refer directly or indirectly to the place of effective management.

COMMENTARY ON ARTICLE 5
CONCERNING THE DEFINITION OF PERMANENT ESTABLISHMENT

1.   The main use of the concept of a permanent establishment is to determine the right of a Contracting State to tax the profits of an enterprise of the other Contracting State.   Under Article 7 a Contracting State cannot tax the profits of an enterprise of the other Contracting State unless it carries on its business through a permanent establishment situated therein.

Paragraph 1

2.   Paragraph 1 gives a general definition of the term "permanent establish-ment" which brings out its essential characteristics of a permanent establishment in the sense of the Convention, i.e. a distinct "situs", a "fixed place of business". The paragraph defines the term "permanent establishment" as a fixed place of business, through which the business of an enterprise is wholly or partly carried on.   This definition, therefore, contains the following conditions:

— the existence of a "place of business", i.e. a facility such as premises or, in certain instances, machinery or equipment;

— this place of business must be "fixed", i.e. it must be established at a distinct place with a certain degree of permanence;

— the carrying on of the business of the enterprise through this fixed place of business.   This means usually that persons who, in one way or another, are dependent on the enterprise (personnel) conduct the business of the enterprise in the State in which the fixed place is situated.

3.   It could perhaps be argued that in the general definition some mention should also be made of the other characteristic of a permanent establishment to which some importance has sometimes been attached in the past, namely that the establishment must have a productive character—i.e. contribute to the profits of the enterprise.   In the present definition this course has not been taken.   Within the framework of a well-run business organisation it is surely axiomatic to assume that each part contributes to the productivity of the whole.   It does not, of course, follow in every case that because in the wider context of the whole organisation a particular establishment has a "productive character" it is consequently a permanent establishment to which profits can properly be attributed for the purpose of tax in a particular territory (cf. Commentary on paragraph 4).

4.   The term "place of business" covers any premises, facilities or installations used for carrying on the business of the enterprise whether or not they are used exclusively for that purpose.   A place of business may also exist where no premises are available or required for carrying on the business of the enterprise and it simply has a certain amount of space at its disposal.   It is immaterial whether the premises, facilities or installations are owned or rented by or are otherwise at the disposal of the enterprise.   A place of business may thus be constituted

by a pitch in a market place, or by a certain permanently used area in a Customs depot (e.g., for the storage of dutiable goods). Again the place of business may be situated in the business facilities of another enterprise. This may be the case, for instance where the foreign enterprise has at its constant disposal certain premises or a part thereof owned by the other enterprise.

5.　　According to the definition, the place of business has to be a "fixed" one. Thus in the normal way there has to be a link between the place of business and a specific geographical point. It is immaterial how long an enterprise of a Contracting State operates in the other Contracting State if it does not do so at a distinct place, but this does not mean that the equipment constituting the place of business has to be actually fixed to the soil on which it stands. It is enough that the equipment remains on a particular site (but cf. paragraph 19 below).

6.　　Since the place of business must be fixed, it also follows that a permanent establishment can be deemed to exist only if the place of business has a certain degree of permanency, i.e. if it is not of a purely temporary nature. If the place of business was not set up merely for a temporary purpose, it can constitute a permanent establishment, even though it existed, in practice, only for a very short period of time because of the special nature of the activity of the enterprise or because, as a consequence of special circumstances (e.g. death of the taxpayer, investment failure), it was prematurely liquidated. Where a place of business which was, at the outset, designed for a short temporary purpose only, is maintained for such a period that it cannot be considered as a temporary one, it becomes a fixed place of business and thus—retrospectively—a permanent establishment.

7.　　For a place of business to constitute a permanent establishment the enterprise using it must carry on its business wholly or partly through it. As stated in paragraph 3 above, the activity need not be of a productive character. Furthermore, the activity need not be permanent in the sense that there is no interruption of operation, but operations must be carried out on a regular basis.

8.　　Where tangible property such as facilities, equipment, buildings, or intangible property such as patents, procedures and similar property, are let or leased to third parties through a fixed place of business maintained by an enterprise of a Contracting State in the other State, this activity will, in general, render the place of business a permanent establishment. The same applies if capital is made available through a fixed place of business. If an enterprise of a State lets or leases facilities, equipment, buildings or intangible property to an enterprise of the other State without maintaining for such letting or leasing activity a fixed place of business in the other State, the leased facility, equipment, building or intangible property, as such, will not constitute a permanent establishment of the lessor provided the contract is limited to the mere leasing of the equipment, etc. This remains the case even when, for example, the lessor supplies personnel after installation to operate the equipment provided that their responsibility is limited solely to the operation or maintenance of the equipment under the direction, responsibility and control of the lessee. If the personnel have wider responsibilities, for example, participation in the decisions regarding the work for which the equipment is used, the activity of the lessor may go beyond the mere leasing of equipment and may constitute an entrepreneurial activity. In such a case a permanent establishment could be deemed to exist if the criterion of permanency is met. When such activity is connected with, or is similar in character to, those mentioned in paragraph 3, the time limit of twelve months applies. Other cases have to be determined according to the circumstances.

9.   The business of an enterprise is carried on mainly by the entrepreneur or persons who are in a paid-employment relationship with the enterprise (personnel). This personnel includes employees and other persons receiving instructions from the enterprise (e.g. dependent agents).   The powers of such personnel in its relationship with third parties are irrelevant. It makes no difference whether or not the dependent agent is authorised to conclude contracts if he works at the fixed place of business (cf. paragraph 34 below). But a permanent establishment may nevertheless exist if the business of the enterprise is carried on mainly through automatic equipment, the activities of the personnel being restricted to setting up, operating, controlling and maintaining such equipment. Whether or not gaming and vending machines and the like set up by an enterprise of a State in the other State constitute a permanent establishment thus depends on whether or not the enterprise carries on a business activity besides the initial setting up of the machines. A permanent establishment does not exist if the enterprise merely sets up the machines and then leases the machines to other enterprises. A permanent establishment may exist, however, if the enterprise which sets up the machines also operates and maintains them for its own account. This also applies if the machines are operated and maintained by an agent dependent on the enterprise.

10.   A permanent establishment begins to exist as soon as the enterprise commences to carry on its business through a fixed place of business. This is the case once the enterprise prepares, at the place of business, the activity for which the place of business is to serve permanently. The period of time during which the fixed place of business itself is being set up by the enterprise should not be counted, provided that this activity differs substantially from the activity for which the place of business is to serve permanently. The permanent establishment ceases to exist with the disposal of the fixed place of business or with the cessation of any activity through it, that is when all acts and measures connected with the former activities of the permanent establishment are terminated (winding up current business transactions, maintenance and repair of facilities). A temporary interruption of operations, however, cannot be regarded as a closure. If the fixed place of business is leased to another enterprise, it will normally only serve the activities of that enterprise instead of the lessor's; in general, the lessor's permanent establishment ceases to exist, except where he continues carrying on a business activity of his own through the fixed place of business.

Paragraph 2

11.   This paragraph contains a list, by no means exhaustive, of examples, each of which can be regarded, prima facie, as constituting a permanent establishment. As these examples are to be seen against the background of the general definition given in paragraph 1, it is assumed that the Contracting States interpret the terms listed, "a place of management", "a branch", "an office", etc. in such a way that such places of business constitute permanent establishments only if they meet the requirements of paragraph 1.

12.   The term "place of management" has been mentioned separately because it is not necessarily an "office". However, where the laws of the two Contracting States do not contain the concept of "a place of management" as distinct from an "office", there will be no need to refer to the former term in their bilateral convention.

13.   Sub-paragraph *f*) provides that mines, oil or gas wells, quarries or any other place of extraction of natural resources are permanent establishments. The

term "any other place of extraction of natural resources" should be interpreted broadly. It includes, for example, all places of extraction of hydrocarbons whether on or off-shore.

14.   Sub-paragraph *f*) refers to the extraction of natural resources, but does not mention the exploration of such resources, whether on or off-shore. Therefore, whenever income from such activities is considered to be business profits, the question whether these activities are carried on through a permanent establishment is governed by paragraph 1. Since, however, it has not been possible to arrive at a common view on the basic questions of the attribution of taxation rights and of the qualification of the income from exploration activities, the Contracting States may agree upon the insertion of specific provisions. They may agree, for instance, that an enterprise of a Contracting State, as regards its activities of exploration of natural resources in a place or area in the other Contracting State:

  a)   shall be deemed not to have a permanent establishment in that other State; or
  b)   shall be deemed to carry on such activities through a permanent establishment in that other State; or
  c)   shall be deemed to carry on such activities through a permanent establishment in that other State if such activities last longer than a specified period of time.

The Contracting States may moreover agree to submit the income from such activities to any other rule.

Paragraph 3

15.   This paragraph provides expressly that a building site or construction or installation project constitutes a permanent establishment only if it lasts more than twelve months. Any of those items which does not meet this condition does not of itself constitute a permanent establishment, even if there is within it an installation, for instance an office or a workshop within the meaning of paragraph 2, associated with the construction activity.

16.   The term "building site or construction or installation project" includes not only the construction of buildings but also the construction of roads, bridges or canals, the laying of pipe-lines and excavating and dredging. Planning and supervision of the erection of a building are covered by this term, if carried out by the building contractor. However, planning and supervision is not included if carried out by another enterprise whose activities in connection with the construction concerned are restricted to planning and supervising the work. If that other enterprise has an office which it uses only for planning or supervision activities relating to a site or project which does not constitute a permanent establishment, such office does not constitute a fixed place of business within the meaning of paragraph 1, because its existence has not a certain degree of permanence.

17.   The twelve month test applies to each individual site or project. In determining how long the site or project has existed, no account should be taken of the time previously spent by the contractor concerned on other sites or projects which are totally unconnected with it. A building site should be regarded as a single unit, even if it is based on several contracts, provided that it forms a coherent whole commercially and geographically. Subject to this proviso, a

building site forms a single unit even if the orders have been placed by several persons (e.g. for a row of houses).

18.   A site exists from the date on which the contractor begins his work, including any preparatory work, in the country where the construction is to be established, e.g. if he installs a planning office for the construction. In general, it continues to exist until the work is completed or permanently abandoned. A site should not be regarded as ceasing to exist when work is temporarily discontinued. Seasonal or other temporary interruptions should be included in determining the life of a site. Seasonal interruptions include interruptions due to bad weather. Temporary interruption could be caused, for example, by shortage of material or labour difficulties. Thus, for example, if a contractor started work on a road on 1st May, stopped on 1st November because of bad weather conditions or a lack of materials but resumed work on 1st February the following year, completing the road on 1st June, his construction project should be regarded as a permanent establishment because thirteen months elapsed between the date he first commenced work (1st May) and the date he finally finished (1st June of the following year). If an enterprise (general contractor) which has undertaken the performance of a comprehensive project sub-contracts parts of such a project to other enterprises (sub-contractors), the period spent by a sub-contractor working on the building site must be considered as being time spent by the general contractor on the building project. The sub-contractor himself has a permanent establishment at the site if his activities there last more than twelve months.

19.   The very nature of a construction or installation project may be such that the contractor's activity has to be relocated continuously or at least from time to time, as the project progresses. This would be the case for instance where roads or canals were being constructed, waterways dredged, or pipe-lines laid. In such a case, the fact that the work force is not present for twelve months in one particular place is immaterial. The activities performed at each particular spot are part of a single project, and that project must be regarded as a permanent establishment if, as a whole, it lasts more than twelve months.

Paragraph 4

20.   This paragraph lists a number of business activities which are treated as exceptions to the general definition laid down in paragraph 1 and which are not permanent establishments, even if the activity is carried on through a fixed place of business. The common feature of these activities is that they are, in general, preparatory or auxiliary activities. This is laid down explicitly in the case of the exception mentioned in sub-paragraph *e)*, which actually amounts to a general restriction of the scope of the definition contained in paragraph 1. Moreover sub-paragraph *f)* provides that combinations of activities mentioned in sub-paragraphs *a)* to *e)* in the same fixed place of business shall be deemed not to be a permanent establishment, provided that the overall activity of the fixed place of business resulting from this combination is of a preparatory or auxiliary character. Thus the provisions of paragraph 4 are designed to prevent an enterprise of one State from being taxed in the other State, if it carries on in that other State, activities of a purely preparatory or auxiliary character.

21.   Sub-paragraph *a)* relates only to the case in which an enterprise acquires the use of facilities for storing, displaying or delivering its own goods or merchandise. Sub-paragraph *b)* relates to the stock of merchandise itself and provides that the stock, as such, shall not be treated as a permanent establishment if it is

maintained for the purpose of storage, display or delivery. Sub-paragraph *c)* covers the case in which a stock of goods or merchandise belonging to one enterprise is processed by a second enterprise, on behalf of, or for the account of, the first-mentioned enterprise. The reference to the collection of information in sub-paragraph *d)* is intended to include the case of the newspaper bureau which has no purpose other than to act as one of many "tentacles" of the parent body; to exempt such a bureau is to do no more than to extend the concept of "mere purchase".

22.   Sub-paragraph *e)* provides that a fixed place of business through which the enterprise exercises solely an activity which has for the enterprise a preparatory or auxiliary character, is deemed not to be a permanent establishment. The wording of this sub-paragraph makes it unnecessary to produce an exhaustive list of exceptions. Furthermore, this sub-paragraph provides a generalised exception to the general definition in paragraph 1 and, when read with that paragraph, provides a more selective test, by which to determine what constitutes a permanent establishment. To a considerable degree it limits that definition and excludes from its rather wide scope a number of forms of business organisations which, although they are carried on through a fixed place of business, should not be treated as permanent establishments. It is recognised that such a place of business may well contribute to the productivity of the enterprise, but the services it performs are so remote from the actual realisation of profits that it is difficult to allocate any profit to the fixed place of business in question. Examples are fixed places of business solely for the purpose of advertising or for the supply of information or for scientific research or for the servicing of a patent or a know-how contract, if such activities have a preparatory or auxiliary character.

23.   It is often difficult to distinguish between activities which have a preparatory or auxiliary character and those which have not. The decisive criterion is whether or not the activity of the fixed place of business in itself forms an essential and significant part of the activity of the enterprise as a whole. Each individual case will have to be examined on its own merits. In any case, a fixed place of business whose general purpose is one which is identical to the general purpose of the whole enterprise, does not exercise a preparatory or auxiliary activity. Where, for example, the servicing of patents and know-how is the purpose of an enterprise, a fixed place of business of such enterprise exercising such an activity cannot get the benefits of sub-paragraph *e)*. A fixed place of business which has the function of managing an enterprise or even only a part of an enterprise or of a group of the concern cannot be regarded as doing a preparatory or auxiliary activity, for such a managerial activity exceeds this level. If enterprises with international ramifications establish a so-called "management office" in States in which they maintain subsidiaries, permanent establishments, agents or licensees, such office having supervisory and co-ordinating functions for all departments of the enterprise located within the region concerned, a permanent establishment will normally be deemed to exist, because the management office may be regarded as an office within the meaning of paragraph 2. Where a big international concern has delegated all management functions to its regional management offices so that the functions of the head office of the concern are restricted to general supervision (so-called polycentric enterprises), the regional management offices even have to be regarded as a "place of management" within the meaning of sub-paragraph *a)* of paragraph 2. The function of managing an enterprise, even if it only covers a certain area of the operations of the concern, constitutes an essential part of the business operations of the enterprise and there-

fore can in no way be regarded as an activity which has a preparatory or auxiliary character within the meaning of sub-paragraph *e*) of paragraph 4.

24. A permanent establishment could also be constituted if an enterprise maintains a fixed place of business in order to supply spare parts to customers for the machinery supplied to such customers, and to maintain and repair such machinery, as this goes beyond the pure delivery mentioned in sub-paragraph *a*) of paragraph 4. Since these after-sale organisations perform an essential and significant part of the services of an enterprise vis-à-vis its customers, their activities are not merely auxiliary ones. Sub-paragraph *e*) applies only if the activity of the fixed place of business is limited to a preparatory or auxiliary one. This would not be the case where, for example, the fixed place of business does not only give information but also furnishes plans etc. specially developed for the purposes of the individual customer. Nor would it be the case if a research establishment were to concern itself with manufacture.

25. Moreover, sub-paragraph *e*) makes it clear that the activities of the fixed place of business must be carried on for the enterprise. A fixed place of business which renders services not only to its enterprise but also directly to other enterprises, for example to other companies of a group to which the company owning the fixed place belongs, would not fall within the scope of sub-paragraph *e*).

26. As already mentioned in paragraph 20 above, paragraph 4 is designed to provide for exceptions to the general definition of paragraph 1 in respect of fixed places of business which are engaged in activities having a preparatory or auxiliary character. Therefore, according to sub-paragraph *f*) of paragraph 4, the fact that one fixed place of business combines any of the activities mentioned in the sub-paragraphs *a*) to *e*) of paragraph 4 does not mean of itself that a permanent establishment exists. As long as the combined activity of such a fixed place of business is merely preparatory or auxiliary a permanent establishment should be deemed not to exist. Such combinations should not be viewed on rigid lines, but should be considered in the light of the particular circumstances. The criterion "preparatory or auxiliary character" is to be interpreted in the same way as is set out for the same criterion of sub-paragraph *e*) (cf. paragraphs 23 and 24 above). Sub-paragraph *f*) is of no importance in a case where an enterprise maintains several fixed places of business within the meaning of the sub-paragraphs *a*) to *e*) provided that they are separated from each other locally and organisationally, as in such a case each place of business has to be viewed separately and in isolation for deciding the question whether or not a permanent establishment exists. States which want to allow any combination of the items mentioned in sub-paragraphs *a*) to *e*), disregarding whether or not the criterion of the preparatory or auxiliary character of such a combination is met, are free to do so by deleting the words "provided" to "character" in sub-paragraph *f*).

27. The fixed places of business mentioned in paragraph 4 cannot be deemed to constitute permanent establishments so long as their activities are restricted to the functions which are the prerequisite for assuming that the fixed place of business is not a permanent establishment. This will be the case even if the contracts necessary for establishing and carrying on the business are concluded by those in charge of the places of business themselves. The employees of places of business within the meaning of paragraph 4 who are authorised to conclude such contracts should not be regarded as agents within the meaning of paragraph 5. A case in point would be a research institution the manager of which is authorised to con-

clude the contracts necessary for maintaining the institution and who exercises this authority within the framework of the functions of the institution. A permanent establishment, however, exists if the fixed place of business exercising any of the functions listed in paragraph 4 were to exercise them not only on behalf of the enterprise to which it belongs but also on behalf of other enterprises. If, for instance, an advertising agency maintained by an enterprise were also to engage in advertising for other enterprises, it would be regarded as a permanent establishment of the enterprise by which it is maintained.

28.   If a fixed place of business under paragraph 4 is deemed not to be a permanent establishment, this exception applies likewise to the disposal of movable property forming part of the business property of the place of business at the termination of the enterprise's activity in such installation (cf. paragraph 10 above and paragraph 2 of Article 13).   Since, for example, the display of merchandise is excepted under sub-paragraphs *a*) and *b*), the sale of the merchandise at the termination of a trade fair or convention is covered by this exception.   The exception does not, of course, apply to sales of merchandise not actually displayed at the trade fair or convention.

29.   A fixed place of business used both for activities which rank as exceptions (paragraph 4) and for other activities would be regarded as a single permanent establishment and taxable as regards both types of activities.   This would be the case, for instance, where a store maintained for the delivery of goods also engaged in sales.

Paragraph 5

30.   It is a generally accepted principle that an enterprise should be treated as having a permanent establishment in a State if there is under certain conditions a person acting for it, even though the enterprise may not have a fixed place of business in that State within the meaning of paragraphs 1 and 2.   This provision intends to give that State the right to tax in such cases.   Thus paragraph 5 stipulates the conditions under which an enterprise is deemed to have a permanent establishment in respect of any activity of a person acting for it.   The paragraph has been redrafted to clarify the intention of the corresponding provision of the 1963 Draft Convention without altering its substance apart from an extension of the excepted activities of the person.

31.   Persons whose activities may create a permanent establishment for the enterprise are so-called dependent agents i.e. persons, whether employees or not, who are not independent agents falling under paragraph 6.   Such persons may be either individuals or companies.   It would not have been in the interest of international economic relations to provide that the maintenance of any dependent person would lead to a permanent establishment for the enterprise.   Such treatment is to be limited to persons who in view of the scope of their authority or the nature of their activity involve the enterprise to a particular extent in business activities in the State concerned.   Therefore, paragraph 5 proceeds on the basis that only persons having the authority to conclude contracts can lead to a permanent establishment for the enterprise maintaining them.   In such a case the person has sufficient authority to bind the enterprise's participation in the business activity in the State concerned.   The use of the term "permanent establishment" in this context presupposes, of course, that that person makes use of this authority repeatedly and not merely in isolated cases.

32.   The authority to conclude contracts must cover contracts relating to operations which constitute the business proper of the enterprise.   It would be irrelevant, for instance, if the person had authority to engage employees for the enterprise to assist that person's activity for the enterprise or if the person were authorised to conclude, in the name of the enterprise, similar contracts relating to internal operations only.   Moreover the authority has to be habitually exercised in the other State; whether or not this is the case should be determined on the basis of the commercial realities of the situation.   A person who is authorised to negotiate all elements and details of a contract in a way binding on the enterprise can be said to exercise this authority "in that State", even if the contract is signed by another person in the State in which the enterprise is situated.   Since, by virtue of paragraph 4, the maintenance of a fixed place of business solely for purposes listed in that paragraph is deemed not to constitute a permanent establishment, a person whose activities are restricted to such purposes does not create a permanent establishment either.

33.   Where the requirements set out in paragraph 5 are met, a permanent establishment of the enterprise exists to the extent that the person acts for the latter, i.e. not only to the extent that such a person exercises the authority to conclude contracts in the name of the enterprise.

34.   Under paragraph 5, only those persons who meet the specific conditions, may create a permanent establishment; all other persons are excluded.   It should be borne in mind, however, that paragraph 5 simply provides an alternative test of whether an enterprise has a permanent establishment in a State.   If it can be shown that the enterprise has a permanent establishment within the meaning of paragraphs 1 and 2 (subject to the provisions of paragraph 4), it is not necessary to show that the person in charge is one who would fall under paragraph 5.

Paragraph 6

35.   Where an enterprise of a Contracting State carries on business dealings through a broker, general commission agent or any other agent of an independent status, it cannot be taxed in the other Contracting State in respect of those dealings if the agent is acting in the ordinary course of his business (cf. paragraph 31 above).   Although it stands to reason that such an agent, representing a separate enterprise, cannot constitute a permanent establishment of the foreign enterprise, paragraph 6 has been inserted in the Article for the sake of clarity and emphasis.

36.   A person will come within the scope of paragraph 6—i.e. he will not constitute a permanent establishment of the enterprise on whose behalf he acts—only if

  a)   he is independent of the enterprise both legally and economically, and
  b)   he acts in the ordinary course of this business when acting on behalf of the enterprise.

37.   Whether a person is independent of the enterprise represented depends on the extent of the obligations which this person has vis-à-vis the enterprise. Where the person's commercial activities for the enterprise are subject to detailed instructions or to comprehensive control by it, such person cannot be regarded as independent of the enterprise.   Another important criterion will be whether the entrepreneurial risk has to be borne by the person or by the enterprise the person represents.   A subsidiary is not to be considered dependent on its parent company solely because of the parent's ownership of the share capital.   Persons cannot be

said to act in the ordinary course of their own business if, in place of the enterprise, such persons perform activities which, economically, belong to the sphere of the enterprise rather than to that of their own business operations. Where, for example, a commission agent not only sells the goods or merchandise of the enterprise in his own name but also habitually acts, in relation to that enterprise, as a permanent agent having an authority to conclude contracts, he would be deemed in respect of this particular activity to be a permanent establishment, since he is thus acting outside the ordinary course of his own trade or business (namely that of a commission agent), unless his activities are limited to those mentioned at the end of paragraph 5.

38.   According to the definition of the term "permanent establishment" an insurance company of one State may be taxed in the other State on its insurance business, if it has a fixed place of business within the meaning of paragraph 1 or if it carries on business through a person within the meaning of paragraph 5. Since agencies of foreign insurance companies sometimes do not meet either of the above requirements, it is conceivable that these companies do large-scale business in a State without being taxed in that State on their profits arising from such business. In order to obviate this possibility, various conventions concluded by OECD Member countries include a provision which stipulates that insurance companies of a State are deemed to have a permanent establishment in the other State if they collect premiums in that other State through an agent established there—other than an agent who already constitutes a permanent establishment by virtue of paragraph 5—or insure risks situated in that territory through such an agent. The decision as to whether or not a provision along these lines should be included in a convention will depend on the factual and legal situation prevailing in the Contracting States concerned. Frequently, therefore, such a provision will not be comtemplated. In view of this fact, it did not seem advisable to insert a provision along these lines in the Model Convention.

Paragraph 7

39.   It is generally accepted that the existence of a subsidiary company does not, of itself, constitute that subsidiary company a permanent establishment of its parent company. This follows from the principle that, for the purpose of taxation, such a subsidiary company constitutes an independent legal entity. Even the fact that the trade or business carried on by the subsidiary company is managed by the parent company does not constitute the subsidiary company a permanent establishment of the parent company.

40.   However, a subsidiary company will constitute a permanent establishment for its parent company under the same conditions stipulated in paragraph 5 as are valid for any other unrelated company, i.e. if it cannot be regarded as an independent agent in the meaning of paragraph 6, and if it has and habitually exercises an authority to conclude contracts in the name of the parent company. And the effects would be the same as for any other unrelated company to which paragraph 5 applies.

41.   The same rules should apply to activities which one subsidiary carries on for any other subsidiary of the same company.

OBSERVATIONS ON THE COMMENTARY

42.   Treatment in Irish tax law of non-resident operators in *Ireland* and in the Irish continental shelf area. Profits arising to a person not resident in Ireland

from exploration or exploitation activities in Ireland or in the Irish continental shelf area as well as profits from exploration or exploitation rights are treated as the profits of a trade carried on in Ireland through a branch or agency and are, in consequence, taxable in Ireland. This includes non-resident contractors who supply well-drilling, pipe-laying and similar services in Ireland or in the Irish continental shelf area.   In addition, capital gains accruing on the disposal of exploration or exploitation rights in Ireland or in the Irish continental shelf area are treated as gains accruing on the disposal of assets situated in Ireland.   When negotiating conventions with other Member countries, Ireland would wish sub-paragraph *f)* of paragraph 2 to be so drafted and interpreted as to reflect the Irish position.

43.   *Italy* does not adhere to the interpretation given in paragraph 11 above concerning the list of examples of paragraph 2.   In its opinion, these examples can always be regarded as constituting "a priori" permanent establishments.

44.   While, subject to its reservations in relation to this Article, *New Zealand,* for the purpose of negotiating conventions with other Member countries, accepts, in general, the principles of this Article, it would wish to be free to negotiate for the addition of specific provisions deeming an enterprise in some particular situations to have a permanent establishment in New Zealand.

RESERVATIONS ON THE ARTICLE

45.   *Australia* reserves the right to treat an enterprise as having a permanent establishment in a State if the enterprise carries on designated supervisory activities in that State for more than twelve months, if substantial equipment is used in that State for more than twelve months by, for or under contract with the enterprise in the exploration for or exploitation of natural resources, or if a person acting in that State on behalf of the enterprise—manufactures or processes there goods or merchandise belonging to the enterprise.

46.   *Greece, New Zealand, Portugal* and *Turkey* reserve their positions on paragraph 3, and consider that any building site or construction or installation project which lasts more than six months should be regarded as a permanent establishment.

47.   *New Zealand* also reserves its position so as to be able to tax an enterprise which carries on supervisory activities for more than six months in connection with a building site or construction or installation project lasting more than six months, and also an enterprise where substantial equipment or machinery is for more than six months being used by, for or under contract with the enterprise.

48.   *Spain* reserves its position on paragraph 3 so as to be able to tax an enterprise having a permanent establishment in Spain, even if the site of the construction or installation project does not last for more than twelve months, where the activity of this enterprise in Spain presents a certain degree of permanency within the meaning of paragraphs 1 and 2.

COMMENTARY ON ARTICLE 6
CONCERNING THE TAXATION OF INCOME
FROM IMMOVABLE PROPERTY

1.   Paragraph 1 gives the right to tax income from immovable property to the State of source, that is, the State in which the property producing such income is situated.   This is due to the fact that there is always a very close economic connection between the source of this income and the State of source.   Although income from agriculture or forestry is included in Article 6, Contracting States are free to agree in their bilateral conventions to treat such income under Article 7.   Article 6 deals only with income which a resident of a Contracting State derives from immovable property situated in the other Contracting State.   It does not, therefore, apply to income from immovable property situated in the Contracting State of which the recipient is a resident within the meaning of Article 4 or situated in a third State; the provisions of paragraph 1 of Article 21 shall apply to such income.

2.   Defining the concept of immovable property by reference to the law of the State in which the property is situated, as is provided in paragraph 2, will help to avoid difficulties of interpretation over the question whether an asset or a right is to be regarded as immovable property or not.   The paragraph, however, specifically mentions the assets and rights which must always be regarded as immovable property.   In fact such assets and rights are already treated as immovable property according to the laws or the taxation rules of most OECD Member countries. Conversely, the paragraph stipulates that ships, boats and aircraft shall never be considered as immovable property.   No special provision has been included as regards income from indebtedness secured by immovable property, as this question is settled by Article 11.

3.   Paragraph 3 indicates that the general rule applies irrespective of the form of exploitation of the immovable property.   Paragraph 4 makes it clear that the provisions of paragraphs 1 and 3 apply also to income from immovable property of industrial, commercial and other enterprises and to income from immovable property used for the performance of independent personal services.

4.   It should be noted in this connection that the right to tax of the State of source has priority over the right to tax of the other State and applies also where, in the case of an enterprise or of non-industrial and non-commercial activities, income is only indirectly derived from immovable property.   This does not prevent income from immovable property, when derived through a permanent establishment, from being treated as income of an enterprise, but secures that income from immovable property will be taxed in the State in which the property is situated also in the case where such property is not part of a permanent establishment situated in that State.   It should further be noted that the provisions of the Article

do not prejudge the application of domestic law as regards the manner in which income from immovable property is to be taxed.

RESERVATIONS ON THE ARTICLE

5.　　*Finland* reserves the right to tax income of shareholders in Finnish companies from the direct use, letting, or use in any other form of the right to enjoyment of immovable property situated in Finland and owned by the company, where such right is based on the ownership of shares or other corporate rights in the company.

6.　　*France* wishes to retain the possibility of applying the provisions in its domestic laws relative to the taxation of income from shares or rights, which are treated therein as income from immovable property.

COMMENTARY ON ARTICLE 7
CONCERNING THE TAXATION OF BUSINESS PROFITS

I. PRELIMINARY REMARKS

1.   This Article is in many respects a continuation of, and a corollary to, Article 5 on the definition of the concept of permanent establishment. The permanent establishment criterion is commonly used in international double taxation conventions to determine whether a particular kind of income shall or shall not be taxed in the country from which it originates but the criterion does not of itself provide a complete solution to the problem of the double taxation of business profits; in order to prevent such double taxation it is necessary to supplement the definition of permanent establishment by adding to it an agreed set of rules of reference to which the profits made by the permanent establishment, or by an enterprise trading with a foreign member of the same group of enterprises, are to be calculated. To put the matter in a slightly different way, when an enterprise of a Contracting State carries on business in the other Contracting State the authorities of that second State have to ask themselves two questions before they levy tax on the profits of the enterprise: the first question is whether the enterprise has a permanent establishment in their country; if the answer is in the affirmative the second question is what, if any, are the profits on which that permanent establishment should pay tax. It is with the rules to be used in determining the answer to this second question that Article 7 is concerned. Rules for ascertaining the profits of an enterprise of a Contracting State which is trading with an enterprise of the other Contracting State when both enterprises are members of the same group of enterprises or are under the same effective control are dealt with in Article 9.

2.   It should perhaps be said at this point that neither Article is strikingly novel or particularly detailed. The question of what criteria should be used in attributing profits to a permanent establishment, and of how to allocate profits from transactions between enterprises under common control, has had to be dealt with in a large number of double taxation conventions and it is fair to say that the solutions adopted have generally conformed to a standard pattern. It is generally recognised that the essential principles on which this standard pattern is based are well founded, and it has been thought sufficient to restate them with some slight amendments and modifications primarily aimed at producing greater clarity. The two Articles incorporate a number of directives. They do not, nor in the nature of things could they be expected to, lay down a series of precise rules for dealing with every kind of problem that may arise when an enterprise of one State makes profits in another. Modern commerce organises itself in an infinite variety of ways, and it would be quite impossible within the fairly narrow limits of an Article in a double taxation convention to specify an exhaustive set of rules for dealing with every kind of problem that may arise. This, however, is a matter of relatively minor importance, if there is agreement on general lines.

Special cases may require special consideration, but it should not be difficult to find an appropriate solution if the problem is approached within the framework of satisfactory rules based on agreed principles.

II. COMMENTARY ON THE PROVISIONS OF THE ARTICLE

Paragraph 1

3.   This paragraph is concerned with two questions. First, it restates the generally accepted principle of double taxation conventions that an enterprise of one State shall not be taxed in the other State unless it carries on business in that other State through a permanent establishment situated therein.   It is hardly necessary to argue here the merits of this principle.   It is perhaps sufficient to say that it has come to be accepted in international fiscal matters that until an enterprise of one State sets up a permanent establishment in another State it should not properly be regarded as participating in the economic life of that other State to such an extent that it comes within the jurisdiction of that other State's taxing rights.

4.   The second and more important point is that it is laid down—in the second sentence—that when an enterprise carries on business through a permanent establishment in another State that State may tax the profits of the enterprise but only so much of them as is attributable to the permanent establishment; in other words that the right to tax does not extend to profits that the enterprise may derive from that State otherwise than through the permanent establishment.   This is a question on which there may be differences of view.   Some countries have taken the view that when a foreign enterprise has set up a permanent establishment within their territory it has brought itself within their fiscal jurisdiction to such a degree that they can properly tax all profits that the enterprise derives from their territory, whether the profits come from the permanent establishment or from other activities in that territory.   But it is thought that it is preferable to adopt the principle contained in the second sentence of paragraph 1, namely that the test that business profits should not be taxed unless there is a permanent establishment is one that should properly be applied not to the enterprise itself but to its profits.   To put the matter another way, the principle laid down in the second sentence of paragraph 1 is based on the view that in taxing the profits that a foreign enterprise derives from a particular country, the fiscal authorities of that country should look at the separate sources of profit that the enterprise derives from their country and should apply to each the permanent establishment test. This is of course without prejudice to other Articles.

5.   On this matter, naturally, there is room for differences of view, and since it is an important question it may be useful to set out the arguments for each point of view.

6.   Apart from the background question of fiscal jurisdiction, the main argument commonly put forward against the solution advocated above is that there is a risk that it might facilitate avoidance of tax.   This solution, the argument runs, might leave it open to an enterprise to set up in a particular country a permanent establishment which made no profits, was never intended to make profits, but existed solely to supervise a trade, perhaps of an extensive nature, that the enterprise carried on in that country through independent agents and the like. Moreover, the argument goes, although the whole of this trade might be directed

and arranged by the permanent establishment, it might be difficult in practice to prove that that was the case. If the rates of tax are higher in that country than they are in the country in which the head office is situated, then the enterprise has a strong incentive to see that it pays as little tax as possible in the other territory; the main criticism of the solution advocated above is that it might conceivably provide the enterprise with a means of ensuring that result.

7. Apart again from the question of the proper extent of fiscal jurisdiction, the main argument in favour of the proposed solution is that it is conducive to simple and efficient administration, and that it is more closely adapted to the way in which business is commonly transacted. The organisation of modern business is highly complex. In OECD Member countries, there are a considerable number of companies each of which is engaged in a wide diversity of activities and is carrying on business extensively in many countries. It may be that such a company may have set up a permanent establishment in a second country and may be transacting a considerable amount of business through that permanent establishment in one particular kind of manufacture; that a different part of the same company may be selling quite different goods or manufactures in that second country through independent agents; and that the company may have perfectly genuine reasons for taking this course—reasons based, for example, either on the historical pattern of its business or on commercial convenience. Is it desirable that the fiscal authorities should go so far as to insist on trying to search out the profit element of each of the transactions carried on through independent agents, with a view to aggregating that profit with the profits of the permanent establishment? Such an Article might interfere seriously with ordinary commercial processes, and so be out of keeping with the aims of the Convention.

8. It is no doubt true that evasion of tax could be practised by undisclosed channelling of profits away from a permanent establishment and that this may sometimes need to be watched, but it is necessary in considering this point to preserve a sense of proportion and to bear in mind what is said above. It is not, of course, sought in any way to sanction any such malpractice, or to shelter any concern thus evading tax from the consequences that would follow from detection by the fiscal authorities concerned. It is fully recognised that Contracting States should be free to use all methods at their disposal to fight fiscal evasion.

9. For the reasons given above, it is thought that the argument that the solution advocated might lead to increased avoidance of tax by foreign enterprises should not be given undue weight. Much more importance is attached to the desirability of interfering as little as possible with existing business organisation and of refraining from inflicting demands for information on foreign enterprises which are unnecessarily onerous.

Paragraph 2

10. This paragraph contains the central directive on which the allocation of profits to a permanent establishment is intended to be based. The paragraph incorporates the view, which is generally contained in bilateral conventions, that the profits to be attributed to a permanent establishment are those which that permanent establishment would have made if, instead of dealing with its head office, it had been dealing with an entirely separate enterprise under conditions and at prices prevailing in the ordinary market. Normally, these would be the same profits that one would expect to be determined by the ordinary processes

of good business accountancy. This principle also extends to the allocation of profits which the permanent establishment may derive from transactions with other permanent establishments of the enterprise and with associated companies and their permanent establishments; but Contracting States which consider that the existing paragraph does not in fact cover these more general transactions may, in their bilateral negotiations, agree upon more detailed provisions.

11.   In the great majority of cases, trading accounts of the permanent establishment—which are commonly available if only because a well-run business organisation is normally concerned to know what is the profitability of its various branches—will be used by the taxation authorities concerned to ascertain the profit properly attributable to that establishment. Exceptionally there may be no separate accounts (cf. paragraphs 23 to 27 below). But where there are such accounts they will naturally form the starting point for any processes of adjustment in case adjustment is required to produce the amount of properly attributable profits. It should perhaps be emphasized that the directive contained in paragraph 2 is no justification for tax administrations to construct hypothetical profit figures in vacuo; it is always necessary to start with the real facts of the situation as they appear from the business records of the permanent establishment and to adjust as may be shown to be necessary the profit figures which those facts produce. It should also be noted that the principle set out in paragraph 2 is subject to the provisions contained in paragraph 3, especially as regards the treatment of payments which, under the name of interest, royalties, etc. are made by a permanent establishment to its head office in return for money loaned, or patent rights conceded by the latter to the permanent establishment (cf. paragraphs 16 below and following).

12.   Even where a permanent establishment is able to produce proper accounts which purport to show the profits arising from its activities, it may still be necessary for the taxation authorities of the country concerned to rectify those accounts, in accordance with the general directive laid down in paragraph 2. Adjustment of this kind may be necessary, for example, because goods have been invoiced from the head office to the permanent establishment at prices which are not consistent with this directive, and profits have thus been diverted from the permanent establishment to the head office, or vice versa.

13.   In such cases, it will usually be appropriate to substitute for the prices used ordinary market prices for the same or similar goods supplied on the same or similar conditions. Clearly the price at which goods can be bought on open market terms varies with the quantity required and the period over which they will be supplied; such factors would have to be taken into account in deciding the open market price to be used. It is perhaps only necessary to mention at this point that there may sometimes be perfectly good commercial reasons for an enterprise invoicing its goods at prices less than those prevailing in the ordinary market; this may, for example, be a perfectly normal commercial method of establishing a competitive position in a new market and should not then be taken as evidence of an attempt to divert profits from one country to another. Difficulties may also occur in the case of proprietary goods produced by an enterprise, all of which are sold through its permanent establishments; if in such circumstances there is no open market price, and it is thought that the figures in the accounts are unsatisfactory, it may be necessary to calculate the permanent establishment's profits by other methods, for example, by applying an average ratio of gross profit to the turnover of the permanent establishment and then deducting

from the figure so obtained the proper amount of expenses incurred. Clearly many special problems of this kind may arise in individual cases but the general rule should always be that the profits attributed to a permanent establishment should be based on that establishment's accounts insofar as accounts are available which represent the real facts of the situation. If available accounts do not represent the real facts then new accounts will have to be constructed, or the original ones rewritten, and for this purpose the figures to be used will be those prevailing in the open market.

14.   Some States consider that there is a realisation of a taxable profit when an asset, other than trading stock, forming part of the business property of a permanent establishment situated within their territory is transferred to a permanent establishment or the head office of the same enterprise situated in another State. Article 7 allows such States to tax profits deemed to arise in connection with such a transfer. Such profits may be determined as indicated in paragraphs 10 to 13 above.

Paragraph 3

15.   This paragraph clarifies, in relation to the expenses of a permanent establishment, the general directive laid down in paragraph 2. The paragraph specifically recognises that in calculating the profits of a permanent establishment allowance is to be made for expenses, wherever incurred, that were incurred for the purposes of the permanent establishment. Clearly in some cases it will be necessary to estimate or to calculate by conventional means the amount of expenses to be taken into account. In the case, for example, of general administrative expenses incurred at the head office of the enterprise, it may be appropriate to take into account a proportionate part based on the ratio that the permanent establishment's turnover (or perhaps gross profits) bears to that of the enterprise as a whole. Subject to this, it is considered that the amount of expenses to be taken into account as incurred for the purposes of the permanent establishment should be the actual amount so incurred. The deduction allowable to the permanent establishment for any of the expenses of the enterprise attributed to it does not depend upon the actual reimbursement of such expenses by the permanent establishment.

16.   Apart from what may be regarded as ordinary expenses, there are some classes of payments between permanent establishments and head offices which give rise to special problems, and it is convenient to deal with them at this point. The next paragraphs discuss three specific cases of this kind and give solutions for them. It should not, of course, be inferred that it is only in relation to the three classes of payments mentioned in these paragraphs that problems may arise; there may well be payments of other kinds to which similar considerations apply.

17.   The first of these cases relates to payments which under the name of interest, royalties, etc. are made by a permanent establishment to its head office in return for money loaned, or patent rights conceded, by the latter to the permanent establishment. In such a case, it is considered that the payments should not be allowed as deductions in computing the permanent establishment's taxable profits. Equally, such payments made to a permanent establishment by the head office should be excluded from the computation of the permanent establishment's taxable profits. It is, however, recognised that special considerations apply to payments of interest made by different parts of a financial enterprise (e.g. a bank) to each other on advances etc. (as distinct from capital allotted to them), in view

of the fact that making and receiving advances is narrowly related to the ordinary business of such enterprises. Furthermore, if an enterprise makes payments of interest, etc. to a third party and these payments in part relate to the activities of the permanent establishment, then a proportionate part of them should naturally be taken into account in calculating the permanent establishment's profits insofar as they can properly be regarded as expenses incurred for the purposes of the permanent establishment.

18.   The second case relates to the performance of ancillary services by a permanent establishment on behalf of its head office or vice versa. Consider, for example, the case of a large company with a varied business, part of which it carries on in another country through a permanent establishment. In addition, that permanent establishment advertises on behalf of its head office goods which that enterprise produces but which the permanent establishment itself does not handle. Clearly, in calculating for tax purposes the profits of the permanent establishment, the profits should be increased by the amount of the expense it has incurred on behalf of the head office (unless, of course, such an adjustment has already been made in drawing up the accounts of the permanent establishment). In fact if the permanent establishment and its head office were entirely separate and independent, the permanent establishment would ordinarily carry out services for the head office only if it were paid a commission as well as reimbursed the actual expenses incurred. It is, therefore, necessary to decide whether the calculation should be made on the basis of account being taken not only of any expenses borne by a permanent establishment by reason of services performed for the head office but also of a notional commission increasing the profits of the permanent establishment.

19.   After consideration of this question, it is thought that in such circumstances the profits of the permanent establishment should not be increased by the addition of a "commission" figure. While, on one view, to include a "commission" figure in the profits of every permanent establishment that has performed services otherwise than for its own purposes could be looked at in theory as a consequential application of the fiction of separate enterprise, it would inevitably be found exceedingly cumbersome in practice. There would be scope for lengthy argument about, and usually no concrete basis for determining, the percentage to be used in calculating the amount of notional "commission". In the great majority of cases the accounts of the permanent establishment would doubtless take into consideration actual expenses incurred; in other words they would not normally include any credit for "commission". If as a general rule the "separate enterprise" test were to be applied to services performed by a permanent establishment on behalf of its head office and a notional "commission" profit were to be included in the profits of the permanent establishment, it would, therefore, be necessary in the great majority of cases first to settle how the "commission" element was to be calculated and then re-write the accounts of the permanent establishment. Considerations of practical administration weigh heavily against such a course. Therefore no "commission" element should in such cases be included in the profits of the permanent establishment. Similarly, in the converse case where the head office undertakes services on behalf of the permanent establishment, no "commission" element should be deducted in determining the profits of the permanent establishment.

20.   The third case is related to the question whether any part of the total profits of an enterprise should be deemed to arise from the exercise of good

management. Consider the case of a company that has its head office in one country but carries on all its business through a permanent establishment situated in another country. In the extreme case it might well be that only the directors' meetings were held at the head office and that all other activities of the company, apart from purely formal legal activities, were carried on in the permanent establishment. In such a case there is something to be said for the view that at least part of the profits of the whole enterprise arose from the skilful management and business acumen of the directors and that part of the profits of the enterprise ought, therefore, to be attributed to the country in which the head office was situated. If the company has been managed by a managing agency, then that agency would doubtless have charged a fee for its services and the fee might well have been a simple percentage participation in the profits of the enterprise. But, once again, whatever the theoretical merits of such a course, practical considerations weigh heavily against it. In the kind of case quoted the expenses of management would, of course, be set against the profits of the permanent establishment in accordance with the provisions of paragraph 3, but when the matter is looked at as a whole, it is thought that it would not be right to go further by deducting and taking into account some notional figure for "profits of management". In cases identical to the extreme case mentioned above, no account should therefore be taken in determining taxable profits of the permanent establishment of any notional figure such as profits of management.

21.   It may be, of course, that countries where it has been customary to allocate some proportion of the total profits of an enterprise to the head office of the enterprise to represent the profits of good management will wish to continue to make such an allocation. Nothing in the Article is designed to prevent this. Nevertheless it follows from what is said in paragraph 20 above that a country in which a permanent establishment is situated is in no way required to deduct when calculating the profits attributable to that permanent establishment an amount intended to represent a proportionate part of the profits of management attributable to the head office.

22.   It might well be that if the country in which the head office of an enterprise is situated allocates to the head office some percentage of the profits of the enterprise only in respect of good management, while the country in which the permanent establishment is situated does not, the resulting total of the amounts charged to tax in the two countries would be greater than it should be. In any such case the country in which the head office of the enterprise is situated should take the initiative in arranging for such adjustments to be made in computing the taxation liability in that country as may be necessary to ensure that any double taxation is eliminated.

23.   It is usually found that there are, or there can be constructed, adequate accounts for each part or section of an enterprise so that profits and expenses, adjusted as may be necessary, can be allocated to a particular part of the enterprise with a considerable degree of precision. This method of allocation is, it is thought, to be preferred in general wherever it is reasonably practicable to adopt it. There are, however, circumstances in which this may not be the case and paragraphs 2 and 3 are in no way intended to imply that other methods cannot properly be adopted where appropriate in order to arrive at the profits of a permanent establishment on a "separate enterprise" footing. It may well be, for example, that profits of insurance enterprises can most conveniently be ascertained by special methods of computation, e.g. by applying appropriate co-efficients to gross premiums received from policy holders in the country concerned. Again,

in the case of a relatively small enterprise operating on both sides of the border between two countries, there may be no proper accounts for the permanent establishment nor means of constructing them. There may, too, be other cases where the affairs of the permanent establishment are so closely bound up with those of the head office that it would be impossible to disentangle them on any strict basis of branch accounts. Where it has been customary in such cases to estimate the arm's length profit of a permanent establishment by reference to suitable criteria, it may well be reasonable that that method should continue to be followed, notwithstanding that the estimate thus made may not achieve as high a degree of accurate measurement of the profit as adequate accounts. Even where such a course has not been customary, it may, exceptionally, be necessary for practical reasons to estimate the arm's length profits.

Paragraph 4

24.   It has in some cases been the practice to determine the profits to be attributed to a permanent establishment not on the basis of separate accounts or by making an estimate of arm's length profit, but simply by apportioning the total profits of the enterprise by reference to various formulae. Such a method differs from those envisaged in paragraph 2, since it contemplates not an attribution of profits on a separate enterprise footing, but an apportionment of total profits; and indeed it might produce a result in figures which would differ from that which would be arrived at by a computation based on separate accounts. Paragraph 4 makes it clear that such a method may continue to be employed by a Contracting State if it has been customary in that State to adopt it, even though the figure arrived at may at times differ to some extent from that which would be obtained from separate accounts, provided that the result can fairly be said to be in accordance with the principles contained in the Article. It is emphasized, however, that in general the profits to be attributed to a permanent establishment should be determined by reference to the establishment's accounts if these reflect the real facts. It is considered that a method of allocation which is based on apportioning total profits is generally not as appropriate as a method which has regard only to the activities of the permanent establishment and should be used only where, exceptionally, it has as a matter of history been customary in the past and is accepted in the country concerned both by the taxation authorities and taxpayers generally there as being satisfactory. It is understood that paragraph 4 may be deleted where neither State uses such a method. Where, however, Contracting States wish to be able to use a method which has not been customary in the past the paragraph should be amended during the bilateral negotiations to make this clear.

25.   It would not, it is thought, be appropriate within the framework of this Commentary to attempt to discuss at length the many various methods involving apportionment of total profits that have been adopted in particular fields for allocating profits. These methods have been well documented in treatises on international taxation. It may, however, not be out of place to summarise briefly some of the main types and to lay down some very general directives for their use.

26.   The essential character of a method involving apportionment of total profits is that a proportionate part of the profits of the whole enterprise is allocated to a part thereof, all parts of the enterprise being assumed to have contributed on the basis of the criterion or criteria adopted to the profitability of the whole.

The difference between one such method and another arises for the most part from the varying criteria used to determine what is the correct proportion of the total profits. It is fair to say that the criteria commonly used can be grouped into three main categories, namely those which are based on the receipts of the enterprise, its expenses or its capital structure. The first category covers allocation methods based on turnover or on commission, the second on wages and the third on the proportion of the total working capital of the enterprise allocated to each branch or part. It is not, of course, possible to say in vacuo that any of these methods is intrinsically more accurate than the others; the appropriateness of any particular method will depend on the circumstances to which it is applied. In some enterprises, such as those providing services or producing proprietary articles with a high profit margin, net profits will depend very much on turnover. For insurance enterprises it may be appropriate to make an apportionment of total profits by reference to premiums received from policy holders in each of the countries concerned. In the case of an enterprise manufacturing goods with a high cost raw material or labour content, profits may be found to be related more closely to expenses. In the case of banking and financial concerns the proportion of total working capital may be the most relevant criterion. It is considered that the general aim of any method involving apportionment of total profits ought to be to produce figures of taxable profit that approximate as closely as possible to the figures that would have been produced on a separate accounts basis, and that it would not be desirable to attempt in this connection to lay down any specific directive other than that it should be the responsibility of the taxation authority, in consultation with the authorities of other countries concerned, to use the method which in the light of all the known facts seems most likely to produce that result.

27.   The use of any method which allocates to a part of an enterprise a proportion of the total profits of the whole does, of course, raise the question of the method to be used in computing the total profits of the enterprise. This may well be a matter which will be treated differently under the laws of different countries. This is not a problem which it would seem practicable to attempt to resolve by laying down any rigid rule. It is scarcely to be expected that it would be accepted that the profits to be apportioned should be the profits as they are computed under the laws of one particular country; each country concerned would have to be given the right to compute the profits according to the provisions of its own laws.

Paragraph 5

28.   In paragraph 4 of Article 5 there are listed a number of examples of activities which, even though carried on at a fixed place of business, are deemed not to be included in the term "permanent establishment". In considering rules for the allocation of profits to a permanent establishment the most important of these examples is the activity mentioned in paragraph 5 of this Article, i.e. the purchasing office.

29.   Paragraph 5 is not, of course, concerned with the organisation established solely for purchasing; such an organisation is not a permanent establishment and the profits allocation provisions of this Article would not therefore come into play. The paragraph is concerned with a permanent establishment which although carrying on other business also carries on purchasing for its head office. In such a case the paragraph provides that the profits of the permanent establishment shall not be increased by adding to them a notional figure for profits from purchasing. It follows, of course, that any expenses that arise from the purchasing activities

will also be excluded in calculating the taxable profits of the permanent establishment.

Paragraph 6

30.   This paragraph is intended to lay down clearly that a method of allocation once used should not be changed merely because in a particular year some other method produces more favourable results.   One of the purposes of a double taxation convention is to give an enterprise of a Contracting State some degree of certainty about the tax treatment that will be accorded to its permanent establishment in the other Contracting State as well as to the part of it in its home State which is dealing with the permanent establishment; for this reason, paragraph 6 gives an assurance of continuous and consistent tax treatment.

Paragraph 7

31.   Although it has not been found necessary in the Convention to define the term "profits", it should nevertheless be understood that the term when used in this Article and elsewhere in the Convention has a broad meaning including all income derived in carrying on an enterprise.   Such a broad meaning corresponds to the use of the term made in the tax laws of most OECD Member countries.

32.   This interpretation of the term "profits", however, may give rise to some uncertainty as to the application of the Convention.   If the profits of an enterprise include categories of income which are treated separately in other Articles of the Convention, e.g. dividends, it may be asked whether the taxation of those profits is governed by the special Article on dividends etc., or by the provisions of this Article.

33.   To the extent that an application of this Article and the special Article concerned would result in the same tax treatment, there is little practical significance to this question.   Further, it should be noticed that some of the special Articles contain specific provisions giving priority to a specific Article (cf. paragraph 4 of Article 6, paragraph 4 of Articles 10 and 11, paragraph 3 of Article 12, and paragraph 2 of Article 21).

34.   It has seemed desirable, however, to lay down a rule of interpretation in order to clarify the field of application of the present Article in relation to the other Articles dealing with a specific category of income.   In conformity with the practice generally adhered to in existing bilateral conventions, paragraph 7 gives first preference to the special Articles on dividends, interest etc.   It follows from the rule that this Article will be applicable to industrial and commercial income which does not belong to categories of income covered by the special Articles, and, in addition, to dividends, interest etc. which under paragraph 4 of Articles 10 and 11, paragraph 3 of Article 12 and paragraph 2 of Article 21, fall within this Article.   It is understood that the items of income covered by the special Articles may, subject to the provisions of the Convention, be taxed either separately, or as industrial and commercial profits, in conformity with the tax laws of the Contracting States.

35.   It is open to Contracting States to agree bilaterally upon special explanations or definitions concerning the term "profits" with a view to clarifying the distinction between this term and e.g. the concept of dividends.   It may in particular be found appropriate to do so where in a convention under negotiation a deviation has been made from the definitions in the special Articles on dividends, interest

and royalties. It may also be deemed desirable if the Contracting States wish to place on notice, that, in agreement with the domestic tax laws of one or both of the States, the term "profits" includes special classes of receipts such as income from the alienation or the letting of a business or of movable property used in a business. In this connection it may have to be considered whether it would be useful to include also additional rules for the allocation of such special profits.

OBSERVATIONS ON THE COMMENTARY

36. *Australia* and *New Zealand* would wish to be free to propose in bilateral negotiations a provision to the effect that, if the information available to the competent authority of a Contracting State is inadequate to determine the profits to be attributed to the permanent establishment of an enterprise, the competent authority may apply to that enterprise for that purpose the provisions of the taxation law of that State, subject to the qualification that such law will be applied, so far as the information available to the competent authority permits, in accordance with the principles of this Article.

37. *Australia* would wish that in this Article there be provision that will permit resort to domestic law in relation to the taxation of the profit of an insurance enterprise.

38. While *New Zealand,* for the purpose of negotiating conventions with other Member countries, accepts, in general, the principles of this Article relating to the attribution of profits to a permanent establishment, it would wish to be free to negotiate for the inclusion of specific provision governing the basis of attribution in some particular situations.

RESERVATIONS ON THE ARTICLE

39. *New Zealand* reserves the right to exclude from the scope of this Article income from the business of any form of insurance.

40. The *United States* believes it appropriate to provide in paragraph 2 for arm's length treatment not only with the head office of the enterprise, but also with any person controlling, controlled by, or subject to the same common control as, the enterprise. This can be accomplished by changing the phrase "separate enterprise" to "independent enterprise" and by deleting the last fourteen words.

COMMENTARY ON ARTICLE 8
CONCERNING THE TAXATION OF PROFITS
FROM SHIPPING, INLAND WATERWAYS TRANSPORT
AND AIR TRANSPORT

Paragraph 1

1.   The object of paragraph 1 concerning profits from the operation of ships or aircraft in international traffic is to secure that such profits will be taxed in one State alone.   The provision is based on the principle that the taxing right shall be left to the Contracting State in which the place of effective management of the enterprise is situated.   The term "international traffic" is defined in sub-paragraph *d*) of paragraph 1 of Article 3.

2.   In certain circumstances the Contracting State in which the place of effective management is situated may not be the State of which an enterprise operating ships or aircraft is a resident, and some States therefore prefer to confer the exclusive taxing right on the State of residence.   Such States are free to substitute a rule on the following lines:

> "Profits of an enterprise of a Contracting State from the operation of ships or aircraft in international traffic shall be taxable only in that State."

3.   Some other States, on the other hand, prefer to use a combination of the residence criterion and the place of effective management criterion by giving the primary right to tax to the State in which the place of effective management is situated while the State of residence eliminates double taxation in accordance with Article 23, so long as the former State is able to tax the total profits of the enterprise, and by giving the primary right to tax to the State of residence when the State of effective management is not able to tax total profits.   States wishing to follow that principle are free to substitute a rule on the following lines:

> "Profits of an enterprise of a Contracting State from the operation of ships or aircraft, other than those from transport by ships or aircraft, operated solely between places in the other Contracting State, shall be taxable only in the first-mentioned State.   However, where the place of effective management of the enterprise is situated in the other State and that other State imposes tax on the whole of the profits of the enterprise from the operation of ships or aircraft, the profits from the operation of ships or aircraft, other than those from transport by ships or aircraft operated solely between places in the first-mentioned State, may be taxed in that other State."

4.   The profits covered consist in the first place of the profits obtained by the enterprise from the carriage of passengers or cargo.   With this definition, however the provision would be unduly restrictive, in view of the development of shipping and air transport, and for practical considerations also.   The provision therefore covers other classes of profits as well, i.e. those which by reason of their nature

or their close relationship with the profits directly obtained from transport may all be placed in a single category. Some of these classes of profits are mentioned in the following paragraphs.

5.   Profits obtained by leasing a ship or aircraft on charter fully equipped, manned and supplied must be treated like the profits from the carriage of passengers or cargo. Otherwise, a great deal of business of shipping or air transport would not come within the scope of the provision. The Article does not apply to profits from leasing a ship or aircraft on a bare boat charter basis except when it is an occasional source of income for an enterprise engaged in the international operation of ships or aircraft.

6.   The principle that the taxing right should be left to one Contracting State alone makes it unnecessary to devise detailed rules, e.g. for defining the profits covered, this being rather a question of appying general principles of interpretation.

7.   Shipping and air transport enterprises—particularly the latter—often engage in additional activities more or less closely connected with the direct operation of ships and aircraft. Although it would be out of the question to list here all the auxiliary activities which could properly be brought under the provision, nevertheless a few examples may usefully be given.

8.   The provision applies, inter alia, to the following activities:

   a)   the sale of passage tickets on behalf of other enterprises;
   b)   the operation of a bus service connecting a town with its airport;
   c)   advertising and commercial propaganda;
   d)   transportation of goods by truck connecting a depot with a port or airport.

9.   If an enterprise engaged in international transport undertakes to see to it that, in connection with such transport, goods are delivered directly to the consignee in the other Contracting State, such inland transportation is considered to fall within the scope of the international operation of ships or aircraft and, therefore, is covered by the provisions of this Article.

10.   Recently, "containerisation" has come to play an increasing role in the field of international transport. Such containers frequently are also used in inland transport. Profits derived by an enterprise engaged in international transport from the lease of containers which is supplementary or incidental to its international operation of ships or aircraft fall within the scope of this Article.

11.   On the other hand, the provision does not cover a clearly separate activity, such as the keeping of a hotel as a separate business; the profits from such an establishment are in any case easily determinable. In certain cases, however, circumstances are such that the provision must apply even to a hotel business, e.g. the keeping of a hotel for no other purpose than to provide transit passengers with night accommodation, the cost of such a service being included in the price of the passage ticket. In such a case, the hotel can be regarded as a kind of waiting room.

12.   There is another activity which is excluded from the field of application of the provision, namely a shipbuilding yard operated in one country by a shipping enterprise having its place of effective management in another country.

13.　　It may be agreed bilaterally that profits from the operation of vessels engaged in fishing, dredging or hauling activities on the high seas be treated as income falling under this Article.

14.　　Investment income of shipping, inland waterways or air transport enterprises (e.g. income from stocks, bonds, shares or loans) is to be subjected to the treatment ordinarily applied to this class of income.

Paragraph 2

15.　　The rules with respect to the taxing right of the State of residence as set forth in paragraphs 2 and 3 above apply also to this paragraph of the Article.

16.　　The object of this paragraph is to apply the same treatment to transport on rivers, canals and lakes as to shipping and air transport in international traffic. The provision applies not only to inland waterways transport between two or more countries, but also to inland waterways transport carried on by an enterprise of one country between two points in another country.

17.　　The provision does not prevent specific tax problems which may arise in connection with inland waterways transport, in particular between adjacent countries, from being settled specially by bilateral agreement.

ENTERPRISES NOT EXCLUSIVELY ENGAGED IN SHIPPING,
INLAND WATERWAYS TRANSPORT OR AIR TRANSPORT

18.　　It follows from the wording of paragraphs 1 and 2 that enterprises not exclusively engaged in shipping, inland waterways transport or air transport nevertheless come within the provisions of these paragraphs as regards profits arising to them from the operation of ships, boats or aircraft belonging to them.

19.　　If such an enterprise has in a foreign country permanent establishments exclusively concerned with the operation of its ships or aircraft, there is no reason to treat such establishments differently from the permanent establishments of enterprises engaged exclusively in shipping, inland waterways transport or air transport.

20.　　Nor does any difficulty arise in applying the provisions of paragraphs 1 and 2 if the enterprise has in another State a permanent establishment which is not exclusively engaged in shipping, inland waterways transport or air transport. If its goods are carried in its own ships to a permanent establishment belonging to it in a foreign country, it is right to say that none of the profit obtained by the enterprise through acting as its own carrier can properly be attributed to the permanent establishment.　The same must be true even if the permanent establishment maintains installations for operating the ships or aircraft (e.g. consignment wharves) or incurs other costs in connection with the carriage of the enterprise's goods (e.g. staff costs).　In this case, the permanent establishment's expenditure in respect of the operation of the ships, boats or aircraft should be attributed not to the permanent establishment but to the enterprise itself, since none of the profit obtained through the carrying benefits the permanent establishment.

21.　　Where the enterprise's ships or aircraft are operated by a permanent establishment which is not the place of effective management of the whole enterprise (e.g. ships or aircraft put into service by the permanent establishment and figuring on its balance sheet), then the effective management for the purposes of paragraphs 1 and 2 must be considered, as regards the operation of the ships or aircraft, as being in the Contracting State in which the permanent establishment is situated.

Paragraph 3

22.   This paragraph deals with the particular case where the place of effective management of the enterprise is aboard a ship or a boat. In this case tax will only be charged by the State where the home harbour of the ship or boat is situated.   It is provided that if the home harbour cannot be determined, tax will be charged only in the Contracting State of which the operator of the ship or boat is a resident.

Paragraph 4

23.   Various forms of international co-operation exist in shipping or air transport. In this field international co-operation is secured through pooling agreements or other conventions of a similar kind which lay down certain rules for apportioning the receipts (or profits) from the joint business.

24.   In order to clarify the taxation position of the participant in a pool, joint business or in an international operating agency and to cope with any difficulties which may arise the Contracting States may bilaterally add the following, if they find it necessary:

> "but only to so much of the profits so derived as is attributable to the participant in proportion to its share in the joint operation."

SPECIAL DEROGATION

25.   In view of its particular situation in relation to shipping, *Greece* will retain its freedom of action with regard to the provisions in the Convention relating to profits from the operation of ships in international traffic, to remuneration of crews of such ships, to capital represented by ships in international traffic and by movable property pertaining to the operation of such ships, and to capital gains from the alienation of such ships and assets.

OBSERVATIONS ON THE COMMENTARY

26.   While agreeing in principle to abide by the provisions of Article 8 in bilateral conventions, *Turkey* intends in exceptional cases to apply the permanent establishment rule in taxing international transport profits.

27.   *Portugal, Spain* and *Turkey* reserve the right, in the course of negotiations for concluding conventions with other Member countries, to propose that the part of inland transport (cf. paragraph 9 above) carried out by means other than that employed for international transport be excluded from the scope of the Article, whether or not the means of transport belong to the transporting enterprise.

28.   These countries also reserve the right, in the course of such negotiations, to propose that the leasing of containers (cf. paragraph 10 above) even if supplementary or incidental be regarded as an activity separate from international shipping or aircraft operations, and consequently be excluded from the scope of the Article.

29.   *Germany* reserves its position as to the application of the Article to income from inland transportation and container services (cf. paragraphs 9 and 10 above).

RESERVATIONS ON THE ARTICLE

30.   *Australia and Canada* reserve the right to tax as profits from internal traffic profits from the carriage of passengers or cargo taken on board at one place in a respective country for discharge at another place in the same country. *Australia* also reserves the right to tax as profits from internal traffic profits from other coastal and continental shelf activities.

31.   *Canada, Turkey and the United States* reserve the right not to extend the scope of the Article to cover inland transportation in bilateral conventions (paragraph 2 of the Article).

COMMENTARY ON ARTICLE 9
CONCERNING THE TAXATION OF ASSOCIATED ENTERPRISES

Paragraph 1

1.   This Article deals with associated enterprises (parent and subsidiary companies and companies under common control) and its paragraph 1 provides that in such cases the taxation authorities of a Contracting State may for the purpose of calculating tax liabilities re-write the accounts of the enterprises if as a result of the special relations between the enterprises the accounts do not show the true taxable profits arising in that State. It is evidently appropriate that adjustment should be sanctioned in such circumstances, and this paragraph seems to call for very little comment. It should perhaps be mentioned that the provisions of this paragraph apply only if special conditions have been made or imposed between the two enterprises. No re-writing of the accounts of associated enterprises is authorised if the transactions between such enterprises have taken place on normal open market commercial terms (on an arm's length basis).

Paragraph 2

2.   The re-writing of transactions between associated enterprises in the situation envisaged in paragraph 1 may give rise to economic double taxation (taxation of the same income in the hands of different persons), insofar as an enterprise of State A whose profits are revised upwards will be liable to tax on an amount of profit which has already been taxed in the hands of its associated enterprise in State B. Paragraph 2 provides that in these circumstances, State B shall make an appropriate adjustment so as to relieve the double taxation.

3.   It should be noted, however, that an adjustment is not automatically to be made in State B simply because the profits in State A have been increased; the adjustment is due only if State B considers that the figure of adjusted profits correctly reflects what the profits would have been if the transactions had been at arm's length. In other words, the paragraph does not seek to avoid a double charge to tax which arises where the profits of one associated enterprise are increased to a level which exceeds what they would have been if they had been correctly computed on an arm's length basis. State B is therefore committed to make an adjustment of the profits of the affiliated company only if it considers that the adjustment made in State A is justified both in principle and as regards the amount.

4.   The paragraph does not specify the method by which an adjustment is to be made. OECD Member countries use different methods to provide relief in these circumstances and it is therefore left open for Contracting States to agree bilaterally on any specific rules which they wish to add to the Article. Some States, for example, would prefer the system under which, where the profits of enterprise X in State A are increased to what they would have been on an arm's

length basis, the adjustment would be made by re-opening the assessment on the associated enterprise Y in State B containing the doubly taxed profits in order to reduce the taxable profit by an appropriate amount. Some other States, on the other hand, would prefer to provide that, for the purposes of Article 23, the doubly taxed profits should be treated in the hands of enterprise Y of State B as if they may be taxed in State A; accordingly, the enterprise of State B is entitled to relief in State B, under Article 23, in respect of tax paid by its associate enterprise in State A.

5.   It is not the purpose of the paragraph to deal with what might be called "secondary adjustments". Suppose that an upward revision of taxable profits of enterprise X in State A has been made in accordance with the principle laid down in paragraph 1; and suppose also that an adjustment is made to the profits of enterprise Y in State B in accordance with the principle laid down in paragraph 2. The position has still not been restored exactly to what it would have been had the transactions taken place at arm's length prices because, as a matter of fact, the money representing the profits which are the subject of the adjustment is found in the hands of enterprise Y instead of in those of enterprise X. It can be argued that if arm's length pricing had operated and enterprise X had subsequently wished to transfer these profits to enterprise Y, it would have done so in the form of, for example, a dividend or a royalty (if enterprise Y were the parent of enterprise X) or in the form of, for example, a loan (if enterprise X were the parent of enterprise Y); and that in those circumstances there could have been other tax consequences (e.g. the operation of a withholding tax) depending upon the type of income concerned and the provisions of the Article dealing with such income.

6.   These secondary adjustments, which would be required to establish the situation exactly as it would have been if transactions had been at arm's length, depend on the facts of the individual case. It should be noted that nothing in paragraph 2 prevents such secondary adjustments from being made where they are permitted under the domestic laws of Contracting States.

7.   The paragraph also leaves open the question whether there should be a period of time after the expiration of which State B would not be obliged to make an appropriate adjustment to the profits of enterprise Y following an upward revision of the profits of enterprise X in State A. Some States consider that State B's commitment should be open-ended—in other words, that however many years State A goes back to revise assessments, enterprise Y should in equity be assured of an appropriate adjustment in State B. Other States consider that an open-ended commitment of this sort is unreasonable as a matter of practical administration. In the circumstances, therefore, this problem has not been dealt with in the text of the Article; but Contracting States are left free in bilateral conventions to include, if they wish, provisions dealing with the length of time during which State B is to be under obligation to make an appropriate adjustment.

8.   If there is a dispute between the interested parties over the character and amount of the appropriate adjustment, the matter will be dealt with in the same way as any other question of fact; if necessary the competent authorities may consult each other.

OBSERVATIONS ON THE COMMENTARY

9.   In negotiating conventions with other Member countries, *Australia* and *New Zealand* would wish to be free to propose a provision to the effect that, if

the information available to the competent authority of a Contracting State is inadequate to determine the profits to be attributed to an enterprise, the competent authority may apply to that enterprise for that purpose the provisions of the taxation law of that State, subject to the qualification that such law will be applied, as far as the information available to the competent authority permits, in accordance with the principles of this Article.

10.   *Australia* would wish that, in this Article, there be provision that will permit resort to domestic law in relation to the taxation of the profits of an insurance enterprise.

RESERVATIONS ON THE ARTICLE

11.   *Belgium, Finland, Germany, Italy, Japan, Portugal and Switzerland* reserve the right not to insert paragraph 2 in their conventions.

12.   The *United States* believes that this Article should apply to all related persons, not just an enterprise of one Contracting State and a related enterprise of the other Contracting State, and that it should apply to "income, deductions, credits or allowances", not just to "profits".

COMMENTARY ON ARTICLE 10
CONCERNING THE TAXATION OF DIVIDENDS

I. PRELIMINARY REMARKS

1. By "dividends" is generally meant the distribution of profits to the shareholders by companies limited by shares[1], limited partnerships with share capital[2], limited liability companies[3] or other joint stock companies[4]. Under the laws of the OECD Member countries, such joint stock companies are legal entities with a separate juridical personality distinct from all their shareholders. On this point, they differ from partnerships insofar as the latter do not have juridical personality in most countries.

2. The profits of a business carried on by a partnership are the partners' profits derived from their own exertions; for them they are industrial or commercial profits. So the partner is ordinarily taxed personally on his share of the partnership capital and partnership profits.

3. The position is different for the shareholder; he is not a trader and the company's profits are not his; so they cannot be attributed to him. He is personally taxable only on those profits which are distributed by the company (apart from the provisions in certain countries' laws relating to the taxation of undistributed profits in special cases). From the shareholders' standpoint, dividends are income from the capital which they have made available to the company as its shareholders.

II. COMMENTARY ON THE PROVISIONS OF THE ARTICLE

Paragraph 1

4. Paragraph 1 does not prescribe the principle of taxation of dividends either exclusively in the State of the beneficiary's residence or exclusively in the State of which the company paying the dividends is a resident.

5. Taxation of dividends exclusively in the State of source is not acceptable as a general rule. Furthermore, there are some States which do not have taxation of dividends at the source, while as a general rule, all the States tax residents in respect of dividends they receive from non-resident companies.

6. On the other hand, taxation of dividends exclusively in the State of the beneficiary's residence is not feasible as a general rule. It would be more in keeping with the nature of dividends, which are investment income, but it would be unrea-

---

1. « Sociétés anonymes ».
2. « Sociétés en commandite par actions ».
3. « Sociétés à responsabilité limitée ».
4. « Sociétés de capitaux ».

listic to suppose that there is any prospect of it being agreed that all taxation of dividends at the source should be relinquished.

7.   For this reason, paragraph 1 states simply that dividends may be taxed in the State of the beneficiary's residence. The term "paid" has a very wide meaning, since the concept of payment means the fulfilment of the obligation to put funds at the disposal of the shareholder in the manner required by contract or by custom.

8.   The Article deals only with dividends paid by a company which is a resident of a Contracting State to a resident of the other Contracting State. It does not, therefore, apply to dividends paid by a company which is a resident of a third State or to dividends paid by a company which is a resident of a Contracting State which are attributable to a permanent establishment which an enterprise of that State has in the other Contracting State (for these cases, cf. paragraphs 4 to 6 of the Commentary on Article 21).

Paragraph 2

9.   Paragraph 2 reserves a right to tax to the State of source of the dividends, i.e. to the State of which the company paying the dividends is a resident; this right to tax, however, is limited considerably. The rate of tax is limited to 15 per cent, which appears to be a reasonable maximum figure. A higher rate could hardly be justified since the State of source can already tax the company's profits.

10.   On the other hand, a lower rate (5 per cent) is expressly provided in respect of dividends paid by a subsidiary company to its parent company. If a company of one of the States owns directly a holding of at least 25 per cent in a company of the other State, it is reasonable that payments of profits by the subsidiary to the foreign parent company should be taxed less heavily to avoid recurrent taxation and to facilitate international investment. The realisation of this intention depends on the fiscal treatment of the dividends in the State of which the parent company is a resident (cf. paragraphs 49 to 54 of the Commentary on Articles 23 A and 23 B).

11.   If a partnership is treated as a body corporate under the domestic laws applying to it, the two Contracting States may agree to modify sub-paragraph *a)* of paragraph 2 in a way to give the benefits of the reduced rate provided for parent companies also to such partnership.

12.   Under paragraph 2, the limitation of tax in the State of source is not available when an intermediary, such as an agent or nominee, is interposed between the beneficiary and the payer, unless the beneficial owner is a resident of the other Contracting State. States which wish to make this more explicit are free to do so during bilateral negotiations.

13.   The tax rates fixed by the Article for the tax in the State of source are maximum rates. The States may agree, in bilateral negotiations, on lower rates or even on taxation exclusively in the State of the beneficiary's residence. The reduction of rates provided for in paragraph 2 refers solely to the taxation of dividends and not to the taxation of the profits of the company paying the dividends.

14.   The two Contracting States may also, during bilateral negotiations, agree to a holding percentage lower than that fixed in the Article. A lower percentage

is, for instance, justified in cases where the State of residence of the parent company, in accordance with its domestic law, grants exemption to such a company for dividends derived from a holding of less than 25 per cent in a non-resident subsidiary.

15.   In sub-paragraph *a*) of paragraph 2, the term "capital" is used in relation to the taxation treatment of dividends, i.e. distributions of profits to shareholders. The use of this term in this context implies that, for the purposes of sub-paragraph *a*), it should be used in the sense in which it is used for the purposes of distribution to the shareholder (in the particular case, the parent company).

- *a*) As a general rule, therefore, the term "capital" in sub-paragraph *a*) should be understood as it is understood in company law. Other elements, in particular the reserves, are not to be taken into account.
- *b*) Capital, as understood in company law, should be indicated in terms of par value of all shares which in the majority of cases will be shown as capital in the company's balance sheet.
- *c*) No account need be taken of differences due to the different classes of shares issued (ordinary shares, preference shares, plural voting shares, non-voting shares, bearer shares, registered shares, etc.), as such differences relate more to the nature of the shareholder's right than to the extent of his ownership of the capital.
- *d*) When a loan or other contribution to the company does not, strictly speaking, come as capital under company law but when on the basis of internal law or practice ("thin capitalisation", or assimilation of a loan to share capital), the income derived in respect thereof is treated as dividend under Article 10, the value of such loan or contribution is also to be taken as "capital" within the meaning of sub-paragraph *a*).
- *e*) In the case of bodies which do not have a capital within the meaning of company law, capital for the purpose of sub-paragraph *a*) is to be taken as meaning the total of all contributions to the body which are taken into account for the purpose of distributing profits.

In bilateral negotiations, Contracting States may depart from the criterion of "capital" used in sub-paragraph *a*) of paragraph 2 and use instead the criterion of "voting power".

16.   Sub-paragraph *a*) of paragraph 2 does not require that the company receiving the dividends must have owned at least 25 per cent of the capital for a relatively long time before the date of the distribution. This means that all that counts regarding the holding is the situation prevailing at the time material for the coming into existence of the liability to the tax to which paragraph 2 applies, i.e. in most cases the situation existing at the time when the dividends become legally available to the shareholders. The primary reason for this resides in the desire to have a provision which is applicable as broadly as possible. To require the parent company to have possessed the minimum holding for a certain time before the distribution of the profits could involve extensive inquiries. Internal laws of certain OECD Member countries provide for a minimum period during which the recipient company must have held the shares to qualify for exemption or relief in respect of dividends received. In view of this, Contracting States may include a similar condition in their conventions.

17.   The reduction envisaged in sub-paragraph *a*) of paragraph 2 should not be granted in cases of abuse of this provision, for example, where a company with a holding of less than 25 per cent has, shortly before the dividends become

payable, increased its holding primarily for the purpose of securing the benefits of the above-mentioned provision, or otherwise, where the qualifying holding was arranged primarily in order to obtain the reduction. To counteract such manoeuvres Contracting States may find it appropriate to add to sub-paragraph *a*) a provision along the following lines:

"provided that this holding was not acquired primarily for the purpose of taking advantage of this provision".

18. Paragraph 2 lays down nothing about the mode of taxation in the State of source. It therefore leaves that State free to apply its own laws and, in particular, to levy the tax either by deduction at source or by individual assessment.

19. The paragraph does not settle procedural questions. Each State should be able to use the procedure provided in its own laws. It can either forthwith limit its tax to the rates given in the Article or tax in full and make a refund.

20. It does not specify whether or not the relief in the State of source should be conditional upon the dividends being subject to tax in the State of residence. This question can be settled by bilateral negotiations.

21. The Article contains no provisions as to how the State of the beneficiary's residence should make allowance for the taxation in the State of source of the dividends. This question is dealt with in Articles 23 A and 23 B.

22. Attention is drawn generally to the following case: the beneficial owner of the dividends arising in a Contracting State is a company resident of the other Contracting State; all or part of its capital is held by shareholders resident outside that other State; its practice is not to distribute its profits in the form of dividends; and it enjoys preferential taxation treatment (private investment company, base company). The question may arise whether in the case of such a company it is justifiable to allow in the State of source of the dividends the limitation of tax which is provided in paragraph 2. It may be appropriate, when bilateral negotiations are being conducted, to agree upon special exceptions to the taxing rule laid down in this Article, in order to define the treatment applicable to such companies.

Paragraph 3

23. In view of the great differences between the laws of OECD Member countries, it is impossible to define "dividends" fully and exhaustively. Consequently, the definition merely mentions examples which are to be found in the majority of the Member countries' laws and which, in any case, are not treated differently in them. The enumeration is followed up by a general formula. In the course of the revision of the 1963 Draft Convention, a thorough study has been undertaken to find a solution which does not refer to domestic laws. This study has led to the conclusion that, in view of the still remaining dissimilarities between Member countries in the field of company law and taxation law, it does not yet appear to be possible to work out a definition of the concept of dividends that would be independent of domestic laws. It is open to the Contracting States, through bilateral negotiations, to make allowance for peculiarities of their laws and to agree to bring under the definition of "dividends" other payments by companies falling under the Article.

24. The notion of dividends basically concerns distributions by companies within the meaning of sub-paragraph *b*) of paragraph 1 of Article 3. Therefore

the definition relates, in the first instance, to distributions of profits the title to which is constituted by shares, that is holdings in a company limited by shares (joint stock company). The definition assimilates to shares all securities issued by companies which carry a right to participate in the companies' profits without being debt-claims; such are, for example, "jouissance" shares or "jouissance" rights, founders' shares or other rights participating in profits. In bilateral conventions, of course, this enumeration may be adapted to the legal situation in the Contracting States concerned. This may be necessary in particular, as regards income from "jouissance" shares and founders' shares. On the other hand, debt-claims participating in profits do not come into this category; (cf. paragraph 18 of the Commentary on Article 11); likewise interest on convertible debentures is not a dividend.

25.   The laws of many of the States put participations in a "Société à responsabilité limitée" (limited liability company) on the same footing as shares. Likewise, distributions of profits by co-operative societies are generally regarded as dividends.

26.   Distributions of profits by partnerships are not dividends within the meaning of the definition, unless the partnerships are subject, in the State where their place of effective management is situated, to a fiscal treatment substantially similar to that applied to companies limited by shares (for instance, in Belgium, Portugal and Spain, also in France as regards distributions to "commanditaires" in the "sociétés en commandite simple"). On the other hand, clarification in bilateral conventions may be necessary in cases where the taxation law of a Contracting State gives the owner of holdings in a company a right to opt, under certain conditions, for being taxed as a partner of a partnership, or, vice versa, gives the partner of a partnership the right to opt for taxation as the owner of holdings in a company.

27.   Payments regarded as dividends may include not only distributions of profits decided by annual general meetings of shareholders, but also other benefits in money or money's worth, such as bonus shares, bonuses, profits on a liquidation and disguised distributions of profits. The reliefs provided in the Article apply so long as the State of which the paying company is a resident taxes such benefits as dividends. It is immaterial whether any such benefits are paid out of current profits made by the company or are derived, for example, from reserves, i.e. profits of previous financial years. Normally, distributions by a company which have the effect of reducing the membership rights, for instance, payments constituting a reimbursement of capital in any form whatever are not regarded as dividends.

28.   The benefits to which a holding in a company confer entitlement are, as a general rule, available solely to the shareholders themselves. Should, however, certain of such benefits be made available to persons who are not shareholders within the meaning of company law, they may constitute dividends if:
—   the legal relations between such persons and the company are assimilated to a holding in a company ("concealed holdings") and
—   the persons receiving such benefits are closely connected with a shareholder; this is the case, for example, where the recipient is a relative of the shareholder or is a company belonging to the same group as the company owning the shares.

29.   When the shareholder and the person receiving such benefits are residents of two different States with which the State of source has concluded conventions,

differences of views may arise as to which of these conventions is applicable. A similar problem may arise when the State of source has concluded a convention with one of the States but not with the other. This, however, is a conflict which may affect other types of income, and the solution to it can be found only through an arrangement under the mutual agreement procedure.

Paragraph 4

30.   Certain States consider that dividends, interest and royalties arising from sources in their territory and payable to individuals or legal persons who are residents of other States fall outside the scope of the arrangement made to prevent them from being taxed both in the State of source and in the State of the beneficiary's residence when the beneficiary has a permanent establishment in the former State. Paragraph 4 is not based on such a conception which is sometimes referred to as "the force of attraction of the permanent establishment". It does not stipulate that dividends flowing to a resident of a Contracting State from a source situated in the other State must, by a kind of legal presumption, or fiction even, be related to a permanent establishment which that resident may have in the latter State, so that the said State would not be obliged to limit its taxation in such a case. The paragraph merely provides that in the State of source the dividends are taxable as part of the profits of the permanent establishment there owned by the beneficiary which is a resident of the other State, if they are paid in respect of holdings forming part of the assets of the permanent establishment or otherwise effectively connected with that establishment. In that case, paragraph 4 relieves the State of source of the dividends from any limitations under the Article. The foregoing explanations accord with those in the Commentary on Article 7.

31.   The rules set out above also apply where the beneficiary of the dividends has in the other Contracting State, for the purpose of performing any of the kinds of independent personal services mentioned in Article 14, a fixed base with which the holding in respect of which the dividends are paid is effectively connected.

Paragraph 5

32.   The Article deals only with dividends paid by a company which is a resident of a Contracting State to a resident of the other State. Certain States, however, tax not only dividends paid by companies resident therein—but even distributions by non-resident companies of profits arising within their territory. Each State, of course, is entitled to tax profits arising in its territory which are made by non-resident companies, to the extent provided in the Convention (in particular in Article 7). The shareholders of such companies should not be taxed as well at any rate, unless they are residents of the State and so naturally subject to its fiscal sovereignty.

33.   Paragraph 5 rules out the extra-territorial taxation of dividends, i.e. the practice by which States tax dividends distributed by a non-resident company solely because the corporate profits from which the distributions are made originated in their territory (for example, realised through a permanent establishment situated therein). There is, of course, no question of extra-territorial taxation when the country of source of the corporate profits taxes the dividends because they are paid to a shareholder who is a resident of that State or to a permanent establishment or fixed base situated in that State.

34.   Moreover, it can be argued that such a provision does not aim at, or cannot result in, preventing a State from subjecting the dividends to a withholding

tax when distributed by foreign companies if they are cashed in its territory. Indeed, in such a case, the criterion for tax liability is the fact of the payment of the dividends, and not the origin of the corporate profits allotted for distribution. But if the person cashing the dividends in a Contracting State is a resident of the other Contracting State (of which the distributing company is a resident), he may under Article 21 obtain exemption from, or refund of, the withholding tax of the first-mentioned State. Similarly, if the beneficiary of the dividends is a resident of a third State which had concluded a double taxation convention with the State where the dividends are cashed, he may, under Article 21 of that convention, obtain exemption from, or refund of, the withholding tax of the last-mentioned State.

35.   Paragraph 5 further provides that non-resident companies are not to be subjected to special taxes on undistributed profits.

III.   Effects of Special Features of the Domestic Tax Laws of Certain Countries[1]

36.   Certains countries' laws seek to avoid or mitigate economic double taxation, i.e. the simultaneous taxation of the company's profits at the level of the company and of the dividends at the level of the shareholder. There are various ways of achieving this:

— company tax in respect of distributed profits is charged at a lower rate than that on retained profits (Austria, Finland, Germany, Iceland, Japan, Norway);
— the tax paid by the company on the distributed profits is partly set off against the shareholder's personal tax (Belgium; Canada; Denmark, from 1977; France; Germany, from 1977; Ireland, from 1976; Turkey; United Kingdom);
— dividends bear only one tax, the distributed profits not being taxed at the level of the company (Greece).

The Committee on Fiscal Affairs has examined the question whether the special features of the tax laws of such countries would justify solutions other than those contained in the Model Convention.

A.   Dividends Distributed to Individuals

37.   In contrast to the notion of juridical double taxation, which has, generally, a quite precise meaning, the concept of economic double taxation is less certain. Some States do not accept the validity of this concept and others, more numerously, do not consider it necessary to relieve economic double taxation at the national level (dividends distributed by resident companies to resident shareholders). Consequently, as the concept of economic double taxation was not sufficiently well defined to serve as a basis for the analysis, it seemed appropriate to study the problem from a more general economic standpoint, i.e. from the point of view of the effects which the various systems for alleviating such double taxation can have on the international flow of capital. For this purpose, it was necessary to see, among other things, what distortions and discriminations the various national systems could create; but it was necessary to have regard also to the implications for States' budgets and for effective fiscal verification, without losing sight of the principle of reciprocity that underlies every convention. In

---

1.   This Section reflects the position as of 1st Juanary, 1977.

considering all these aspects, it became apparent that the burden represented by company tax could not be wholly left out of account.

1. *States with the classical system*
(no relief of economic double taxation: All Member countries not referred to in paragraph 36 above[1]; hereinafter called type A States)

38. The Committee has recognised that economic double taxation need not be relieved at the international level when such double taxation remains unrelieved at the national level. It therefore considers that in relations between two States with the classical system, i.e. States which do not relieve economic double taxation, the respective levels of company tax in the Contracting States should have no influence on the rate of withholding tax on the dividend in the State of source (rate limited to 15 per cent by sub-paragraph *b*) of paragraph 2 of Article 10). Consequently, the solution recommended in 1963 remains fully applicable in the present case.

2. *States applying a split rate company tax*
(Austria; Finland; Germany; Iceland[2]; Japan; Norway; hereinafter called type B States)

39. These States levy company tax at different rates according to what the company does with its profits: the high rate is charged on any profits retained and the lower rate on those distributed. These rates are, respectively, in Austria, 55 and 27.5 per cent (maximum rates); in Germany, 56 and 36 per cent; in Japan, 40 and 30 percent (maximum rates) and in Norway 50.8 and 23 per cent. Finland should be considered among the split rate countries as it grants in the state income taxation a deduction calculated at 40 per cent on profits distributed. While undistributed profits are taxed at the rate of 43 per cent distributed profits are taxed at a correspondingly lower effective rate. Therefore, the effects of this deduction are similar to those of the normal split rate system.

40. None of these States, in negotiating double taxation conventions, has obtained, on the grounds of its split rate of company tax, the right to levy withholding tax of more than 15 per cent (cf. sub-paragraph *b*) of paragraph 2 of Article 10) on dividends paid by its companies to a shareholder who is an individual resident in the other State.

41. The Committee considered whether States in that group should not be recognised as being entitled to levy withholding tax exceeding 15 per cent on dividends distributed by their companies to residents of the other State (type A), with the proviso that the excess over 15 per cent, which would be designed to offset, in relation to the shareholder concerned, the effects of the lower rate of company tax on distributed profits of companies of State B, would not be creditable against the tax payable by the shareholder in the type A State of which he is a resident.

---

1. The Italian system in force as from 1st January, 1974, may be considered as close to the classical system although it will be noted that economic double taxation is mitigated to a certain extent by the fact that the shareholder is not subject to local tax on the income he receives.

2. The effects of the Icelandic corporation tax system are similar to those of a split-rate system, insofar as dividends paid out during the fiscal year are deductible from net income in that year, to a maximum of 10 per cent of the nominal value of capital stock.

42.   Most members considered that in a type B State regard should be had to the average level of company tax, and that such average level should be considered as the counterpart to the charge levied in the form of a single-rate tax on companies resident of State A. The levy by State B of an additional withholding tax not credited in State A would, moreover, create twofold discrimination: on the one hand, dividends, distributed by a company resident of State B would be more heavily taxed when distributed to residents of State A than when distributed to residents of State B, and, on the other hand, the resident of State A would pay higher personal tax on his dividends from State B than on his dividends from State A. The idea of a "balancing tax" was not, therefore, adopted by the Committee.

3.   *States which allow a part of company tax against the shareholter's tax* (Belgium; Canada; Denmark, from 1977; France; Germany, from 1977; Ireland, from 1976; Turkey; the United Kingdom; hereinafter called type C States)

43.   In these States, the company is taxed on its total profits, whether distributed or not, and the dividends are taxed in the hands of the resident shareholder (an individual); the latter, however, is entitled to a tax credit against his personal tax, on the grounds that—in the normal course at least—the dividend has borne company tax as part of the company's profits.

44.   The rate of this tax credit, in terms of the dividend declared, is 46 per cent in Belgium (where it is called the "crédit d'impôt"), 33 1/3 per cent in Canada, about 15 per cent in Denmark, 50 per cent in France (where it is called the "avoir fiscal"), 9/16 in Germany, 7/13 in Ireland, 15/60 in Turkey and 35/65 in the United Kingdom. Internal law of States in this group does not provide for the extension of the tax credit to the international field. This credit is allowed only to residents and only in respect of dividends of domestic sources[1]. However, in recent conventions, some States extended the right to the tax credit to residents of the other Contracting States.

Case of France and the United Kingdom

45.   Under the French "avoir fiscal" system and the United Kingdom tax credit system, the resident shareholder receives a credit in recognition of the fact that the profits out of which the dividends are paid have already been taxed in the hands of the company. The resident shareholder is taxed on his dividend grossed up by the "avoir fiscal" or tax credit; this "avoir fiscal" or tax credit is set against the tax payable and can possibly give rise to refund. These imputation systems differ in structure from the split rate systems of type B States, but both these types of systems may, if the conditions are comparable, have a similar result, provided that the shareholder of the company in the type B State reports his dividends. In double taxation conventions France and the United Kingdom have respectively given the "avoir fiscal" and the tax credit to shareholders who are residents of the other Contracting States.

Case of Turkey

46.   Certain features of the Turkish system suggest that it should be regarded as analogous to the French and British systems. The Turkish Delegation has

---

1. In Ireland and in the United Kingdom, however, the right to the tax credit is given to shareholders who are not residents of those States but are nationals of the States.

pointed out that account ought to be taken of the requirements of Turkey's economic and fiscal policy; for this reason, Turkey would not consider extending in a bilateral convention the tax credit (set off for additional withholding tax levy) to non-resident shareholders. The Turkish Delegation furthermore considers that this problem can be dealt with only in bilateral negotiations where the sacrifices and advantages which the convention entails for each Contracting State may be best appreciated.

Case of Belgium and Canada

47.   These States claim that under their systems the company tax remains in its entirety a true company tax, in that it is charged by reference solely to the company's own situation, without any regard to the person and the residence of the shareholder, and in that, having been so charged, it remains appropriated to the Treasury. The tax credit given to the shareholder is designed to relieve his personal tax liability and in no way constitutes an adjustment of the company's tax. No refund, therefore, is given if the tax credit exceeds that personal tax.

48.   The Committee could not reach a general agreement on whether these two countries' systems and the French or British system display a fundamental difference that could justify different solutions at the international level.

49.   Some members were of the opinion that such a fundamental difference does not exist. This opinion leaves room for the conclusion that the two countries concerned should—like France and the United Kingdom (paragraph 45 above)—extend the tax credit to non-resident shareholders. Such a solution tends to ensure neutrality as regards dividends distributed by companies of these countries, the same treatment being given to resident and non-resident shareholders. On the other hand, it would in relation to shareholders who are residents of a Contracting State (a type A State in particular) encourage investment in a type C State; residents of State A receive a tax credit (in fact a refund of company tax) for dividends from State C while they do not receive one for dividends from their own country. However, these effects, which also occur in the case of France and the United Kingdom, are similar to those which present themselves between a type B and a type A State or between two type A States one of which has a lower company tax rate than the other (paragraphs 38 and 39 to 42 above).

50.   On the other hand, many members stressed the fact that a determination of the true nature of the tax relief given under these two countries' systems, reveals a mere alleviation of the shareholder's personal income tax in recognition of the fact that his dividend will normally have borne company tax. The tax credit is given once and for all (forfaitaire) and is therefore not in exact relation to the actual company tax appropriate to the profits out of which the dividend is paid. There is no refund if the tax credit exceeds the personal income tax.

51.   As the relief in essence is not a refund of company tax but an alleviation of the personal income tax, the extension of the relief to non-resident shareholders who are not subject to personal income tax in the countries concerned does not come into consideration. On the other hand, however, on this line of reasoning, the question whether a type C State should give relief against personal income tax levied from resident shareholders on foreign dividends deserves attention. In this respect it should be observed that the answer is in the affirmative if the question is looked at from the standpoint of neutrality as regards the source of the dividends; otherwise, residents of State C will be encouraged to acquire shares

in their own country rather than abroad. But such an extension of the tax credit would be contrary to the principle of reciprocity: not only would the State concerned thereby be making a unilateral budgetary sacrifice (allowing the tax credit over and above the withholding tax levied in the other State), but it would do so without receiving any economic compensation, since it would not be encouraging residents of the other State to acquire shares in its own territory.

52.   To overcome these objections, it might be a conceivable proposition, amongst other possibilities, that State A—which will have collected company tax on dividends distributed by resident companies—should bear the cost of the tax credit that State C would allow, by transferring funds to that State. As, however, such transfers are hardly favoured by the States this might be more simply achieved by means of a "compositional" arrangement under which State A would relinquish all withholding tax on dividends paid to residents of State C, and the latter would then allow against its own tax, not the 15 per cent withholding tax (abolished in State A) but a tax credit similar to that which it gives on dividends of domestic source.

53.   When exerything is fully considered, it seems that the problem can be solved only in bilateral negotiations, where one is better placed to evaluate the sacrifices and advantages which the Convention must bring for each Contracting State.

Case of Denmark, Germany and Ireland

54.   Denmark and Ireland have company tax systems similar to the French and British ones. The German company tax system as it is in effect from 1977, differs from the other systems insofar as it combines the economic effects of a split rate system and a credit system. The rate of tax on company profits is 56 per cent, but it is reduced by 20 percentage points in respect to profits distributed, which are therefore taxed at a rate of 36 per cent (cf. paragraph 39 above). Moreover, resident shareholders of a German company (individuals and companies) are entitled to a tax credit of 9/16 of the cash dividends received from the company with the effect that the whole company tax on profits distributed to such shareholders is credited against the latter's tax on income. If the tax on income is lower than the credit to be given the excess part is reimbursed. As their systems have been introduced very recently, these countries wish to leave to bilateral negotiations the question whether the special features of their tax laws would justify solutions other than those contained in the Model Convention.[1]

4.   State with a special system
(Greece)

55.   Under the Greek system, a company's profits are taxed at the level of the company, but any part of them which is distributed—whether immediately or subsequently—to the shareholders is taxed once only, the tax paid by the company on this part of its profits being refunded to it.

56.   Since Greece does not tax distributed profits at the level of the company, the Committee recognises this State's right to tax at source profits distributed by

---

1. Since the introduction in Ireland of the imputation system of company taxation, that country has concluded only one double taxation convention, namely, that with the United Kingdom. The convention provides for giving the tax credit to United Kingdom portfolio investors but this is not regarded by Ireland as constituting a guideline for future conventions.

its companies at a higher rate than those specified in paragraph 2. The maximum rate must in this case be fixed by bilateral negotiations, regard being had to the special features of each situation, e.g. the respective levels of the taxes in the two States, the budgetary sacrifices accepted by the two States, etc.

B.   DIVIDENDS DISTRIBUTED TO COMPANIES

57.   Comments above relating to dividends paid to individuals are generally applicable to dividends paid to companies which hold less than 25 per cent of the capital of the company paying the dividends. Moreover, the Committee on Fiscal Affairs has not covered in the Commentary the special problem of dividends paid to collective investment institutions (investment companies or investment funds).[1]

58.   In respect of dividends paid to companies which hold at least 25 per cent of the capital of the company paying the dividends, the Committee has examined the incidence which the particular company taxation systems quoted in paragraphs 39 and following have on the tax treatment of dividends paid by the subsidiary.

59.   Various opinions were expressed in the course of the discussion. Opinions diverge even when the discussion is limited to the taxation of subsidiaries and parent companies. They diverge still more if the discussion takes into account more general economic considerations and extends to the taxation of shareholders of the parent company.

60.   In their bilateral conventions States have adopted different solutions, which were motivated by the economic objectives and the peculiarities of the legal situation of those States, by budgetary considerations, and by a whole series of other factors. Accordingly, no generally accepted principles have emerged. The Committee did nevertheless consider the situation for the more common systems of company taxation.

1. *Classical system in the State of the subsidiary*
   (Type A States—paragraph 38 above)

61.   The provisions of the Convention have been drafted to apply when the State of which the distributing company is a resident has a so-called "classical" system of company taxation, namely one under which distributed profits are not entitled to any benefit at the level either of the company or of the shareholder (except for the purpose of avoiding recurrent taxation of inter-company dividends).

2. *Split-rate company tax system in the State of the subsidiary*
   (Type B States—paragraphs 39 to 42 above)

62.   States of this kind collect company tax on distributed profits at a lower rate than on retained profits which results in a lower company tax burden on profits distributed by a subsidiary to its parent company. In view of this situation, most of these States have obtained, in their conventions, rates of tax at source of 10 or 15 per cent, and in some cases even above 15 per cent. It has not been possible in the Committee to get views to converge on this question, the solution of which is left to bilateral negotiations.

---

1.   This problem is the subject of other work by the Committee on Fiscal Affairs.

3. *Imputation system in the State of the subsidiary*
(Type C States—paragraphs 43 and following)

63.   In such States, a company is liable to tax on the whole of its profits, whether distributed or not; the shareholders resident of the State of which the distributing company is itself a resident are subject to tax on dividends distributed to them, but receive a tax credit in consideration of the fact that the profits distributed have been taxed at company level.

64.   The question has been considered whether States of this kind should extend the benefit of the tax credit to the shareholders of parent companies resident of another State[1], or even to grant the tax credit directly to such parent companies. It has not been possible in the Committee to get views to converge on this question, the solution of which is left to bilateral negotiations.

65.   If, in such a system, profits, whether distributed or not, are taxed at the same rate, the system is not different from a "classical" one at the level of the distributing company.   Consequently, the State of which the subsidiary is a resident can only levy a tax at source at the rate provided in sub-paragraph *a*) of paragraph 2.

OBSERVATIONS ON THE COMMENTARY

66.   *Portugal* makes the following observations as regards paragraph 27 above. Indeed gains from the increase in capital of companies with a head office or place of effective management in Portugal, when the increase results from the capitalisation of reserves or the issue of shares, are taxed under the Portuguese domestic law as capital gains.   In bilateral conventions, Portugal usually inserts in Article 13 a provision allowing it to tax such gains.

67.   The *United Kingdom* does not adhere to paragraph 24 above.   Under United Kingdom law, certain interest payments are treated as distributions, and are therefore included by the United Kingdom in the definition of dividends.

RESERVATIONS ON THE ARTICLE

Paragraph 2

68.   *Australia* reserves the right always to tax, at a rate of not less than 15 per cent, dividends paid by a company which is a resident of Australia for purposes of its tax.

69.   *Belgium, Japan* and *New Zealand* reserve their positions on sub-paragraph *a*) because they wish to retain their freedom of action with regard to the treatment of holding (parent companies and subsidiaries).

70.   *Canada* reserves the right to apply a 15 per cent rate of tax at source on dividends paid to non-residents without regard to the relation between the company paying the dividends and the beneficial owner.

---

1. This solution is provided for in a Draft Directive presented on 1st August, 1975 by the Commission of the European Communities.   According to this draft, the State in which the parent company is resident should, when shareholders resident in its territory are taxed, wholly or partly offset the company tax levied in the State in which the subsidiary is a resident.   The draft also provides for compensation for the tax burden resulting from offsetting between the State in which the parent company is a resident and that in which the subsidiary is a resident.

71.   *Germany,* with a view to its system of company taxation, reserves its position on paragraph 2.

72.   *Italy* reserves its position concerning the percentage envisaged for the holding (25 per cent) and can only agree to a rate of tax of 5 per cent for a direct holding of more than 50 per cent.

73.   *The Netherlands* reserves its position on the rate of 5 per cent, since it considers that transfers of profits within a group of enterprises should be entirely exempted from tax at the source.

74.   *Portugal* reserves its position on the rates of tax in paragraph 2.

75.   *Spain* reserves its position on the rate of tax of 5 per cent and the determination of the minimum percentage for the holding.

76.   *Turkey* cannot accept a rate of tax which is lower than 20 per cent.

Paragraph 3

77.   *Belgium* reserves the right to amplify the definition of dividends in paragraph 3 so as to cover expressly income—even when paid in the form of interest—which is taxable as income from capital invested by partners in Belgian partnerships which have not opted for their profits to be charged to personal income tax in the names of such partners individually.

78.   In view, moreover, of the fact that Belgian law excludes distributions of liquidation surpluses from the movable capital income category ("revenus mobiliers") and subjects them to a compositional charge to company tax which relieves the individual shareholders or partners from any liability to personal tax, *Belgium* reserves the right to levy, in accordance with its internal law, such "special contributions", either in the case of the redemption of its own shares or partnership shares by a company or partnership resident in Belgium or on the division of its assets by such a company or partnership among its shareholders or members. Such special contributions fall neither under the restrictions provided in paragraph 2, as regards distribution tax charged on dividends, nor under any other restrictive provision whatever of the Convention (paragraph 4 of Article 13; paragraph 1 of Article 21, etc.).

Paragraph 4

79.   *Italy* reserves the right to subject dividends to the taxes imposed by its law whenever the recipient thereof has a permanent establishment in Italy, even if the holding on which the dividends are paid is not effectively connected with such permanent establishment.

Paragraph 5

80.   *Australia* reserves the right to impose tax on the undistributed Australian income of a private (close) company which is a resident of the other State.

81.   *France* cannot adhere to the provisions of this paragraph. France wishes to retain the possibility of applying the provisions in its laws according to which profits made in France by foreign companies are deemed to be distributed to non-resident shareholders and are taxed accordingly. France is prepared, however, to reduce in bilateral conventions the rate provided for in its domestic laws.

104

82.   *Spain* cannot adhere without a reservation to the provisions of this paragraph owing to the structure of its fiscal law which provides that permanent establishments in Spain of foreign companies are to be taxed under the same conditions as Spanish companies.

83.   *The United States* believes that the text should clarify that the prohibition of paragraph 5 will apply regardless of whether the company derives profits or income from the other Contracting State.

84.   *The United States* reserves the right to impose its accumulated earnings tax and personal holding company tax, to prevent tax avoidance.

85.   *The United States* reserves the right to apply its dividend withholding tax to dividends paid by a company which is incorporated outside the United States, if at least one-half of the company's income consists of profits attributable to a permanent establishment in the United States.

COMMENTARY ON ARTICLE 11
CONCERNING THE TAXATION OF INTEREST

I. PRELIMINARY REMARKS

1.   "Interest" is generally taken to mean remuneration on money lent, being remuneration coming within the category of "income from movable capital" (revenus de capitaux mobiliers).   Unlike dividends, interest does not suffer economic double taxation, that is, it is not taxed both in the hands of the debtor and in the hands of the creditor.   Unless it is provided to the contrary by the contract, payment of the tax charged on interest falls on the recipient.   If it happens that the debtor undertakes to bear any tax chargeable at the source, this is as though he had agreed to pay his creditor additional interest corresponding to such tax.

2.   But, like dividends, interest on bonds or debentures or loans usually attracts tax charged by deduction at the source when the interest is paid.   This method is, in fact, commonly used for practical reasons, as the tax charged at the source can constitute an advance of the tax payable by the recipient in respect of his total income or profits.   If in such a case the recipient is a resident of the country which practises deduction at the source, any double taxation he suffers is remedied by internal measures.   But the position is different if he is a resident of another country: he is then liable to be taxed twice on the interest, first by the State of source and then by the State of which he is a resident.   It is clear that his double charge of tax can reduce considerably the interest on the money lent and so hamper the movement of capital and the development of international investment.

3.   A formula reserving the exclusive taxation of interest to one State, whether the State of the beneficiary's residence or the State of source, could not be sure of receiving general approval.   Therefore a compromise solution was adopted. It provides that interest may be taxed in the State of residence—but leaves to the State of source the right to impose a tax if its laws so provide, it being implicit in this right that the State of source is free to give up all taxation on interest paid to non-residents.   Its exercise of this right will however be limited by a ceiling which its tax cannot exceed but, it goes without saying, the Contracting States can agree to adopt an even lower rate of taxation in the State of source.   The sacrifice that the latter would accept in such conditions will be matched by a relief to be given by the State of residence, in order to take into a account the tax levied in the State of source (cf. Article 23 A or 23 B).

4.   Certain countries do not allow interest paid to be deducted for the purposes of the payer's tax unless the recipient also resides in the same State or is taxable in that State.   Otherwise they forbid the deduction.   The question whether the deduction should also be allowed in cases where the interest is paid by a resident of a Contracting State to a resident of the other State, is dealt with in paragraph 5 of Article 24.

II. Commentary on the Provisions of the Article

Paragraph 1

5.   Paragraph 1 lays down the principle that interest arising in a Contracting State and paid to a resident of the other Contracting State may be taxed in the latter.   In doing so, it does not stipulate an exclusive right to tax in favour of the State of residence.   The term "paid" has a very wide meaning, since the concept of payment means the fulfilment of the obligation to put funds at the disposal of the creditor in the manner required by contract or by custom.

6.   The Article deals only with interest arising in a Contracting State and paid to a resident of the other Contracting State.   It does not, therefore, apply to interest arising in a third State or to interest arising in a Contracting State which is attributable to a permanent establishment which an enterprise of that State has in the other Contracting State (for these cases, cf. paragraphs 4 to 6 of the Commentary on Article 21).

Paragraph 2

7.   Paragraph 2 reserves a right to tax interest to the State in which the interest arises; but it limits the exercise of that right by determining a ceiling for the tax, which may not exceed 10 per cent.   This rate may be considered a reasonable maximum bearing in mind that the State of source is already entitled to tax profits or income produced on its territory by investments financed out of borrowed capital.   The Contracting States may agree in bilateral negotiations upon a lower tax or even on exclusive taxation in the State of the beneficiary's residence.

8.   Under paragraph 2, the limitation of tax in the State of source is not available when an intermediary, such as an agent or nominee, is interposed between the beneficiary and the payer, unless the beneficial owner is a resident of the other Contracting State.   States which wish to make this more explicit are free to do so during bilateral negotiations.

9.   The paragraph lays down nothing about the mode of taxation in the State of source.   It therefore leaves that State free to apply its own laws and, in particular, to levy the tax either by deduction at source or by individual assessment.

10.   It does not specify whether or not the relief in the State of source should be conditional upon the interest being subject to tax in the State of residence.   This question can be settled by bilateral negotiations.

11.   The Article contains no provisions as to how the State of the beneficiary's residence should make allowance for the taxation in the State of source of the interest.   This question is dealt with in Articles 23 A and 23 B.

12.   Attention is drawn generally to the following case: the beneficial owner of interest arising in a Contracting State is a company resident in the other Contracting State; all or part of its capital is held by shareholders resident outside that other State; its practice is not to distribute its profits in the form of dividends; and it enjoys preferential taxation treatment (private investment company, base company).   The question may arise whether, in the case of such a company, it is justifiable to allow in the State of source of the interest the limitation of tax which is provided in paragraph 2.   It may be appropriate, when bilateral negotiations are being conducted, to agree upon special exceptions to the taxing

rule laid down in this Article, in order to define the treatment applicable to such companies.

13.   It should, however, be pointed out that the solution adopted, given the combined effect of the right to tax accorded to the State of source and the allowance to be made for the tax levied there against that due in the State of residence, could, in certain cases, result in maintaining partial double taxation and lead to adverse economic consequences.. In fact, when the beneficiary of the interest has himself had to borrow in order to finance the operation which earns him interest the profit he will realise by way of interest will be much smaller than the nominal amount of interest he receives; if the interest he pays and that which he receives balance, there will be no profit at all. In such a case, the allowance to be made under paragraph 2 of Article 23 A, or paragraph 1 of Article 23 B, raises a difficult and sometimes insoluble problem in view of the fact that the tax levied in the State where the interest arises is calculated on the gross amount thereof, whereas the same interest is reflected in the beneficiary's business results at its net amount only. The result of this is that part, or sometimes even the whole amount, of the tax levied in the State where the interest arises cannot be allowed as a credit in the beneficiary's State of residence and so constitutes an excess charge for the beneficiary, who, to that extent, suffers double taxation. Moreover, the latter, in order to avoid the disadvantage just mentioned, will tend to increase the rate of interest he charges his debtor, whose financial burden would then be increased to a corresponding extent. Thus in certain cases the practice of taxation at the source can constitute an obstacle to international trade. Furthermore, if the payer of the interest happens to be the State itself, a public sector institution, or an enterprise guaranteed by the State, the end result may well be that the tax levied at source is actually borne by the Treasury of the debtor's State, which latter thus derives no real benefit from its own taxation.

14.   The disadvantages just mentioned arise in business, particularly with the sale on credit of equipment, other commercial credit sales, and loans granted by banks. The supplier in such cases very often merely passes on to the customer, without any additional charge, the price he will himself have had to pay to a bank or an export finance agency to finance the credit; similarly, the banker generally finances the loan which he grants with funds lent to his bank and, in particular, funds accepted by him on deposit. In the case especially of the person selling equipment on credit, the interest is more an element of the selling price than income from invested capital.

15.   If two Contracting States, in order to eliminate all risks of double taxation, should desire to avoid the imposition of a tax in the State of source on interest arising from the above-mentioned categories of debts, their common intention can be expressed by an additional paragraph which would follow paragraph 2 of the Article, and which might be in the following terms:

"3.   Notwithstanding the provisions of paragraph 2, any such interest as is mentioned in paragraph 1 shall be taxable only in the Contracting State of which the recipient is a resident, if such recipient is the beneficial owner of the interest and if such interest is paid:

a)   in connection with the sale on credit of any industrial, commercial or scientific equipment,

b)   in connection with the sale on credit of any merchandise by one enterprise to another enterprise, or

c)   on any loan of whatever kind granted by a bank."

16. As regards, more particularly, the types of credit sale referred to in sub-paragraph *a*) of the text suggested above, they comprise not only sales of complete units, but also sales of separate components thereof. Furthermore, as regards credit sales of the types referred to in sub-paragraphs *a*) and *b*) of the suggested text, it is immaterial whether the interest is stipulated separately and as additional to the sale price, or is included from the outset in the price payable by instalments.

17. Contracting States may add to the categories of interest enumerated in the text suggested in paragraph 15 above, other categories in regard to which the imposition of a tax in the State of source might appear to them to be undesirable. They may also agree that the exclusion of a right to tax in the State of source shall be limited to certain of the categories of interest mentioned.

Paragraph 3

18. Paragraph 3 specifies the meaning to be attached to the term "interest" for the application of the taxation treatment defined by the Article. The term designates, in general, income from debt-claims of every kind, whether or not secured by mortgage and whether or not carrying a right to participate in profits. The term "debt-claims of every kind" obviously embraces cash deposits and security in the form of money, as well as Government securities, and bonds and debentures, although the three latter are specially mentioned because of their importance and of certain peculiarities that they may present. It is recognised, on the one hand, that mortgage interest comes within the category of income from movable capital ("revenus de capitaux mobiliers"), even though certain countries assimilate it to income from immovable property. On the other hand, debt-claims, and bonds and debentures in particular, which carry a right to participate in the debtor's profits are nonetheless regarded as loans if the contract by its general character clearly evidences a loan at interest. In the contrary case, where the participation in profits rests upon a provision of funds that is subject to the hazards of the enterprise's business, the operation is not in the nature of a loan and Article 11 does not apply. As regards, more particularly, Government securities, and bonds and debentures, the text specifies that premiums or prizes attaching thereto constitute interest. Generally speaking, what constitutes interest yielded by a loan security, and may properly be taxed as such in the State of source, is all that the institution issuing the loan pays over and above the amount paid by the subscriber, that is to say, the interest accruing plus any premium paid at redemption or at issue. It follows that when a bond or debenture has been issued at a premium, the excess of the amount paid by the subscriber over that repaid to him may constitute negative interest which should be deducted from the interest that is taxable. On the other hand, any profit or loss which a holder of such a security realises by the sale thereof to another person does not enter into the concept of interest. Such profit or loss may, depending on the case, constitute either a business profit or a loss, a capital gain or a loss, or income falling under Article 21.

19. Moreover, the definition of interest in the first sentence of paragraph 3 is, in principle, exhaustive. It has seemed preferable not to include a subsidiary reference to domestic laws in the text; this is justified by the following considerations:

    a)   the definition covers practically all the kinds of income which are regarded as interest in the various domestic laws;

    b)   the formula employed offers greater security from the legal point of view and ensures that conventions would be unaffected by future changes in any country's domestic laws;

c) in the Model Convention references to domestic laws should as far as possible be avoided.

It nevertheless remains understood that in a bilateral convention two Contracting States may widen the formula employed so as to include in it any income which is taxed as interest under either of their domestic laws but which is not covered by the definition and in these circumstances may find it preferable to make reference to their domestic laws.

20. The second sentence of paragraph 3 excludes from the definition of interest penalty charges for late payment but Contracting States are free to omit this sentence and treat penalty charges as interest in their bilateral conventions. Penalty charges, which may be payable under the contract, or by customs or by virtue of a judgement, consist either of payments calculated pro rata temporis or else of fixed sums; in certain cases they may combine both forms of payment. Even if they are determined pro rata temporis they constitute not so much income from capital as a special form of compensation for the loss suffered by the creditor through the debtor's delay in meeting his obligations. Moreover, considerations of legal security and practical convenience make it advisable to place all penalty charges of this kind, in whatever form they be paid, on the same footing for the purposes of their taxation treatment. On the other hand, two Contracting States may exclude from the application of Article 11 any kinds of interest which they intend to be treated as dividends.

21. Finally, the question arises whether annuities ought to be assimilated to interest; it is considered that they ought not to be. On the one hand, annuities granted in consideration of past employment are referred to in Article 18 and are subject to the rules governing pensions. On the other hand, although it is true that instalments of purchased annuities include an interest element on the purchase capital as well as return of capital, such instalments thus constituting "fruits civils" which accrue from day to day, it would be difficult for many countries to make a distinction between the element representing income from capital and the element representing a return of capital in order merely to tax the income element under the same category as income from movable capital. Taxation laws often contain special provisions classifying annuities in the category of salaries, wages and pensions, and taxing them accordingly.

Paragraph 4

22. Certain States consider that dividends, interest and royalties arising from sources in their territory and payable to individuals or legal persons who are residents of other States fall outside the scope of the arrangement made to prevent them from being taxed both in the State of source and in the State of the beneficiary's residence when the beneficiary has a permanent establishment in the former State Paragraph 4 is not based on such a conception which is sometimes referred to as "the force of attraction of the permanent establishment". It does not stipulate that interest arising to a resident of a Contracting State from a source situated in the other State must, by a kind of legal presumption, or fiction even, be related to a permanent establishment which that resident may have in the latter State, so that the said State would not be obliged to limit its taxation in such a case. The paragraph merely provides that in the State of source the interest is taxable as part of the profits of the per-

manent establishment there owned by the beneficiary which is a resident in the other State, if it is paid in respect of debt-claims forming part of the assets of the permanent establishment or otherwise effectively connected with that establishment. In that case, paragraph 4 relieves the State of source of the interest from any limitation under the Article. The foregoing explanations accord with those in the Commentary on Article 7.

23.   The rules set out above also apply where the beneficiary of the interest has in the other Contracting State, for the purpose of performing any of the kinds of independent personal services mentioned in Article 14, a fixed base with which the debt-claim in respect of which the interest is paid is effectively connected.

Paragraph 5

24.   This paragraph lays down the principle that the State of source of the interest is the State of which the payer of the interest is a resident, who may, moreover, be that State itself or one of its political subdivisions or local authorities. It provides, however, for an exception to this rule in the case of interest-bearing loans which have an obvious economic link with a permanent establishment owned in the other Contracting State by the payer of the interest. If the loan was contracted for the requirements of that establishment and the interest is borne by the latter, the paragraph determines that the source of the interest is in the Contracting State in which the permanent establishment is situated, leaving aside the place of residence of the owner of the permanent establishment, even when he resides in a third State.

25.   In the absence of an economic link between the loan on which the interest arises and the permanent establishment, the State where the latter is situated cannot on that account be regarded as the State where the interest arises; it is not entitled to tax such interest, not even within the limits of a "taxable quota" proportional to the importance of the permanent establishment. Such a practice would be incompatible with paragraph 5. Moreover, any departure from the rule fixed in the first sentence of paragraph 5 is justified only where the economic link between the loan and the permanent establishment is sufficiently clear-cut. In this connection, a number of possible cases may be distinguished:

  a)   The management of the permanent establishment has contracted a loan which it uses for the specific requirements of the permanent establishment; it shows it among its liabilities and pays the interest thereon directly to the creditor.

  b)   The head office of the enterprise has contracted a loan the proceeds of which are used solely for the purposes of a permanent establishment situated in another country. The interest is serviced by the head office but is ultimately borne by the permanent establishment.

  c)   The loan is contracted by the head office of the enterprise and its proceeds are used for several permanent establishments situated in different countries.

In cases a) and b) the conditions laid down in the second sentence of paragraph 5 are fulfilled, and the State where the permanent establishment is situated is to be regarded as the State where the interest arises. Case c), however, falls outside the provisions of paragraph 5, the text of which precludes the attribution of more than one source to the same loan. Such a solution, moreover, would give rise to considerable administrative complications and make it impossible for lenders to calculate in advance the taxation that interest would attract. It is, however, open to two Contracting States to restrict the application of the final provision in paragraph 5 to case *a*) or to extend it to case *c*).

26.   Paragraph 5 provides no solution for the case, which it excludes from its provisions, where both the beneficiary and the payer are indeed residents of the Contracting States, but the loan was borrowed for the requirements of a permanent establishment owned by the payer in a third State and the interest is borne by that establishment.   As paragraph 5 now stands, therefore, only its first sentence will apply in such a case.   The interest will be deemed to arise in the Contracting State of which the payer is a resident and not in the third State in whose territory is situated the permanent establishment for the account of which the loan was effected and by which the interest is payable.   Thus the interest will be taxed both in the Contracting State of which the payer is a resident and in the Contracting State of which the beneficiary is a resident.   But, although double taxation will be avoided between these two States by the arrangements provided in the Article, it will not be avoided between them and the third State if the latter taxes the interest on the loan at the source when it is borne by the permanent establishment in its territory.

27.   It has not, however, been considered possible to refer to such a case in a bilateral convention and provide for it a solution consisting, for example, in obliging the Contracting State of the payer's residence to relinquish its tax at the source in favour of the third State in which is situated the permanent establishment for the account of which the loan was effected and by which the interest is borne. The risk of double taxation just referred to can only be fully avoided through a bilateral convention containing a similar provision to that in paragraph 5, between the Contracting State of which the payer of the interest is a resident and the third State in which the permanent establishment paying the interest is situated, or through a multilateral convention containing such a provision.

28.   Moreover, in the case—not settled in paragraph 5—where whichever of the two Contracting States is that of the payer's residence and the third State in which is situated the permanent establishment for the account of which the loan is effected and by which the interest is borne, together claim the right to tax the interest at the source, there would be nothing to prevent those two States— together with, where appropriate, the State of the beneficiary's residence—from concerting measures to avoid the double taxation that would result from such claims.   The proper remedy, it must be said again, would be the establishment between these different States of bilateral conventions, or a multilateral convention, containing a provision similar to that in paragraph 5.   Another solution would be for two Contracting States to word the second sentence of paragraph 5 in the following way:

> "Where, however, the person paying the interest, whether he is a resident of a Contracting State or not, has in a State other than that of which he is a resident a permanent establishment or a fixed base in connection with which the indebtedness on which the interest is paid was incurred, and such interest is borne by such permanent establishment or fixed base, then such interest shall be deemed to arise in the State in which the permanent establishment or fixed base is situated."

29.   If two Contracting States agree in bilateral negotiations to reserve to the State where the beneficiary of the income resides the exclusive right to tax such income, then ipso facto there is no value in inserting in the convention which fixes

their relations that provision in paragraph 5 which defines the State of source of such income. But it is equally obvious that double taxation would not be fully avoided in such a case if the payer of the interest owned, in a third State which charged its tax at the source on the interest, a permanent establishment for the account of which the loan had been borrowed and which bore the interest payable on it. The case would then be just the same as is contemplated in paragraphs 26 to 28 above.

Paragraph 6

30.   The purpose of this paragraph is to restrict the operation of the provisions concerning the taxation of interest in cases where, by reason of a special relationship between the payer and the beneficial owner or between both of them and some other person, the amount of the interest paid exceeds the amount which would have been agreed upon by the payer and the beneficial owner had they stipulated at arm's length. It provides that in such a case the provisions of the Article apply only to that last-mentioned amount and that the excess part of the interest shall remain taxable according to the laws of the two Contracting States, due regard being had to the other provisions of the Convention.

31.   It is clear from the text that for this clause to apply the interest held excessive must be due to a special relationship between the payer and the beneficial owner or between either of them and some other person. There may be cited as examples cases where interest is paid to an individual or legal person who directly or indirectly controls the payer, or who is directly or indirectly controlled by him or is subordinate to a group having common interest with him. These examples, moreover, are similar or analogous to the cases contemplated by Article 9.

32.   On the other hand, the concept of special relationship also covers relationship by blood or marriage and, in general, any community of interests as distinct from the legal relationship giving rise to the payment of the interest.

33.   With regard to the taxation treatment to be applied to the excess part of the interest, the exact nature of such excess will need to be ascertained according to the circumtances of each case, in order to determine the category of income in which it should be classified for the purposes of applying the provisions of the tax laws of the States concerned and the provisions of the Convention. If two Contracting States should have difficulty in determining the other provisions of the Convention applicable, as cases require, to the excess part of the interest, there would be nothing to prevent them from introducing additional clarifications in the last sentence of paragraph 6, as long as they do not alter its general purport.

34.   Should the principles and rules of their respective laws oblige the two Contracting States to apply different Articles of the Convention for the purpose of taxing the excess, it will be necessary to resort to the mutual agreement procedure provided by the Convention in order to resolve the difficulty.

OBSERVATIONS ON THE COMMENTARY

35.   The *United Kingdom* does not adhere to paragraph 18 above. Under United Kingdom law, certain interest payments are treated as distributions, and are therefore dealt with under Article 10.

36.   The *United States* observes that the Article does not limit the taxation by internal law of interest not attributable to a United States permanent establishment in cases where 50 per cent or more of a non-resident payer's gross income is effectively connected with a trade or business in the United States. The United States is willing, in appropriate situations, to limit such taxation by making appropriate modifications in the text of the Article.

RESERVATIONS ON THE ARTICLE

Paragraph 2

37.   *Belgium, Portugal* and *Spain* reserve their position on the rate provided in paragraph 2.

38.   *Canada* reserves its position on paragraph 2 and wishes to retain a 15 per cent rate of tax at source in its bilateral conventions.

39.   *Turkey* cannot accept a rate of tax which is lower than 20 per cent.

Paragraph 4

40.   *Italy* reserves the right to subject interest to the taxes imposed by its law whenever the recipient thereof has a permanent establishment in Italy, even if the indebtedness in respect of which the interest is paid is not effectively connected with such permanent establishment.

COMMENTARY ON ARTICLE 12
CONCERNING THE TAXATION OF ROYALTIES

I. PRELIMINARY REMARKS

1.   In principle, royalties in respect of licences to use patents and similar property and similar payments are income to the recipient from a letting. The letting may be granted in connection with an industrial or commercial enterprise (e.g. the use of literary copyright granted by a publisher) or an independent profession (e.g. use of a patent granted by the inventor) or quite independently of any activity of the grantor (e.g. use of a patent granted by the inventor's heirs).

2.   Certain countries do not allow royalties paid to be deducted for the purposes of the payer's tax unless the recipient also resides in the same State or is taxable in that State. Otherwise they forbid the deduction. The question whether the deduction should also be allowed in cases where the royalties are paid by a resident of a Contracting State to a resident of the other State, is dealt with in paragraph 5 of Article 24.

II. COMMENTARY ON THE PROVISIONS OF THE ARTICLE

Paragraph 1

3.   Paragraph 1 lays down the principle of exclusive taxation of royalties in the State of the beneficial owner's residence. The only exception to this principle is that made in the cases dealt with in paragraph 3.

4.   Under paragraph 1, the exemption from tax in the State of source is not available when an intermediary, such as an agent or nominee, is interposed between the beneficiary and the payer, unless the beneficial owner is a resident of the other Contracting State. States which wish to make this more explicit are free to do so during bilateral negotiations. The term "paid" has a very wide meaning, since the concept of payment means the fulfilment of the obligation to put funds at the disposal of the creditor in the manner required by contract or by custom.

5.   The Article deals only with royalties arising in a Contracting State and paid to a resident of the other Contracting State. It does not, therefore, apply to royalties arising in a third State as well as to royalties arising in a Contracting State which are attributable to a permanent establishment which an enterprise of that State has in the other Contracting State (for these cases cf. paragraphs 4 to 6 of the Commentary on Article 21).

6.   The paragraph does not specify whether or not the exemption in the State of source should be conditional upon the royalties being subject to tax in the State of residence. This question can be settled by bilateral negotiations.

7.   Attention is drawn generally to the following case: the beneficial owner of royalties arising in a Contracting State is a company resident in the other Con-

tracting State; all or part of its capital is held by shareholders resident outside that other State; its practice is not to distribute its profits in the form of dividends; and it enjoys preferential taxation treatment (private investment company, base company). The question may arise whether in the case of such a company it is justifiable to allow in the State of source of the royalties the tax exemption which is provided in paragraph 1. It may be appropriate, when bilateral negotiations are being conducted, to agree upon special exceptions to the taxing rule laid down in this Article, in order to define the treatment applicable to such companies.

Paragraph 2

8. Paragraph 2 contains a definition of the term "royalties". These relate, in general, to rights or property constituting the different forms of literary and artistic property, the elements of industrial and commercial property specified in the text and information concerning industrial, commercial or scientific experience. The definition applies to payments for the use of, or the entitlement to use, rights of the kind mentioned, whether or not they have been, or are required to be, registered in a public register. The definition covers both payments made under a licence and compensation which a person would be obliged to pay for fraudulently copying of infringing the right. As a guide, certain explanations are given below in order to define the scope of Article 12 in relation to that of other Articles of the Convention, as regards, in particular, equipment renting and the provision of information.

9. A clear distinction must be made between royalties paid for the use of equipment, which fall under Article 12, and payments constituting consideration for the sale of equipment, which may, depending on the case, fall under Articles 7, 13, 14 or 21. Some contracts combine the hire element and the sale element, so that it sometimes proves difficult to determine their true legal import. In the case of credit sale agreements and hire-purchase agreements, it seems clear that the sale element is the paramount use, because the parties have from the outset agreed that the ownership of the property in question shall be transferred from one to the other, although they have made this dependent upon the payment of the last instalment. Consequently, the instalments paid by the purchaser/hirer do not, in principle, constitute royalties. In the case, however, of lend-lease, and of leasing in particular, the sole, or at least the principal, purpose of the contract is normally that of hire, even if the hirer has the right thereunder to opt during its term to purchase the equipment in question outright. Article 12 therefore applies in the normal case to the rentals paid by the hirer, including all rentals paid by him up to the date he exercises any right to purchase.

10. Rents in respect of cinematograph films are also treated as royalties, whether such films are exhibited in cinemas or on the television. It may, however, be agreed through bilateral negotiations that rents in respect of cinematograph films shall be treated as industrial and commercial profits and, in consequence, subjected to the provisions of Articles 7 and 9.

11. The rules set out above in regard to rents in respect of cinematograph films could also be applied in regard to rentals derived by a shipping enterprise from the hire of its containers for the conveyance of goods on land after leaving the ship. It is considered, however, that where the hire of the containers is a supplementary or incidental activity of a transport company, the income should be treated as profits falling under Article 8.

12.   In classifying as royalties payments received as consideration for information concerning industrial, commercial or scientific experience, paragraph 2 alludes to the concept of "know-how". Various specialist bodies and authors have formulated definitions of know-how which do not differ intrinsically. One such definition, given by the "Association des Bureaux pour la Protection de la Propriété Industrielle" (ANBPPI), states that "know-how is all the undivulged technical information, whether capable of being patented or not, that is necessary for the industrial reproduction of a product or process, directly and under the same conditions; inasmuch as it is derived from experience, know-how represents what a manufacturer cannot know from mere examination of the product and mere knowledge of the progress of technique." In the know-how contract, one of the parties agrees to impart to the other, so that he can use them for his own account, his special knowledge and experience which remain unrevealed to the public. It is recognised that the grantor is not required to play any part himself in the application of the formulae granted to the licensee and that he does not guarantee the result thereof. This type of contract thus differs from contracts for the provision of services, in which one of the parties undertakes to use the customary skills of his calling to execute work himself for the other party. Thus, payments obtained as consideration for after-sales service, for services rendered by a seller to the purchaser under a guarantee, for pure technical assistance, or for an opinion given by an engineer, an advocate or an accountant, do not constitute royalties within the meaning of paragraph 2. Such payments generally fall under Article 7 or Article 14. In business practice, contracts are encountered which cover both know-how and the provision of technical assistance. One example, amongst others, of contracts of this kind is that of franchising, where the franchisor imparts his knowledge and experience to the franchisee and, in addition, provides him with varied technical assistance, which, in certain cases, is backed up with financial assistance and the supply of goods. The appropriate course to take with a mixed contract is, in principle, to break down, on the basis of the information contained in the contract or by means of a reasonable apportionment, the whole amount of the stipulated consideration according to the various parts of what is being provided under the contract, and then to apply to each part of it so determined the taxation treatment proper thereto. If, however, one part of what is being provided constitutes by far the principal purpose of the contract and the other parts stipulated therein are only of an ancillary and largely unimportant character, then it seems possible to apply to the whole amount of the consideration the treatment applicable to the principal part.

13.   The suggestions made above regarding mixed contracts could also be applied in regard to certain performances by artists and, in particular, in regard to an orchestral concert given by a conductor or a recital given by a musician. The fee for the musical performance, together with that paid for any simultaneous radio broadcasting thereof, seems to fall to be treated under Article 17. Where, whether under the same contract or under a separate one, the musical performance is recorded and the artist has stipulated that he be paid royalties on the sale or public playing of the records, then so much of the payment received by him as consists of such royalties falls to be treated under Article 12.

14.   It is further pointed out that variable or fixed payments for the working of mineral deposits, sources or other natural resources are governed by Article 6 and do not, therefore, fall within the present Article. If two Contracting States should have difficulty from the legal standpoint in applying this distinction in regard to consideration for the use of, or the right to use, equipment, they could

add to the text of paragraph 2, after the words "industrial, commercial or scientific equipment", the words "not constituting immovable property referred to in Article 6".

Paragraph 3

15.   Certain States consider that dividends, interest and royalties arising from sources in their territory and payable to individuals or legal persons who are residents of other States fall outside the scope of the arrangement made to prevent them from being taxed both in the State of source and in the State of the beneficiary's residence when the beneficiary has a permanent establishment in the former State.   Paragraph 3 is not based on such a conception which is sometimes referred to as "the force of attraction of the permanent establishment".   It does not stipulate that royalties arising to a resident of a Contracting State from a source situated in the other State must, by a kind of legal presumption, or fiction even, be related to a permanent establishment which that resident may have in the latter State, so that the said State would not be obliged to limit its taxation in such a case.   The paragraph merely provides that in the State of source the royalties are taxable as part of the profits of the permanent establishment there owned by the beneficiary which is a resident of the other State, if they are paid in respect of rights or property forming part of the assets of the permanent establishment or otherwise effectively connected with that establishment.   In that case, paragraph 3 relieves the State of source of the royalties from any limitations under the Article.   The foregoing explanations accord with those in the Commentary on Article 7.

16.   The rules set out above also apply where the beneficiary of the royalties has in the other Contracting State, for the purpose of performing any of the kinds of independent personal services mentioned in Article 14, a fixed base with which the right or property in respect of which the royalties are paid is effectively connected.

Paragraph 4

17.   The purpose of this paragraph is to restrict the operation of the provisions concerning the taxation of royalties in cases where, by reason of a special relationship between the payer and the beneficial owner or between both of them and some other person, the amount of the royalties paid exceeds the amount which would have been agreed upon by the payer and the beneficial owner had they stipulated at arm's length.   It provides that in such a case the provisions of the Article apply only to that last-mentioned amount and that the excess part of the royalty shall remain taxable according to the laws of the two Contracting States, due regard being had to the other provision of the Convention.

18.   It is clear from the text that for this clause to apply the payment held excessive must be due to a special relationship between the payer and the beneficial owner or between both of them and some other person.   There may be cited as examples cases where royalties are paid to an individual or legal person who directly or indirectly controls the payer, or who is directly or indirectly controlled by him or is subordinate to a group having common interest with him.   These examples, moreover, are similar or analogous to the cases contemplated by Article 9.

19.   On the other hand, the concept of special relationship also covers relationship by blood or marriage and, in general, any community of interests as distinct from the legal relationship giving rise to the payment of the royalty.

20.   With regard to the taxation treatment to be applied to the excess part of the royalty, the exact nature of such excess will need to be ascertained according to the circumstances of each case, in order to determine the category of income in which it should be classified for the purpose of applying the provisions of the tax laws of the States concerned and the provisions of the Convention. If two Contracting States should have difficulty in determining the other provisions of the Convention applicable, as cases required, to the excess part of the royalties, there would be nothing to prevent them from introducing additional clarifications in the last sentence of paragraph 4, as long as they do not alter its general purport.

21.   Should the principles and rules of their respective laws oblige the two Contracting States to apply different Articles of the Convention for the purpose of taxing the excess, it will be necessary to resort to the mutual agreement procedure provided by the Convention in order to resolve the difficulty.

OBSERVATION ON THE COMMENTARY

22.   The observation made by *Portugal, Spain* and *Turkey* on the Commentary on Article 8 (cf. paragraph 28 of the Commentary thereon) applies also to paragraph 11 of the present Commentary for the leasing of containers.

RESERVATIONS ON THE ARTICLE

Paragraph 1

23.   *Australia* reserves the right to tax royalties that, under Australian law, have a source in Australia.

24.   *Austria, Greece* and *Luxemburg* are unable to accept a provision which would preclude them, in bilateral conventions for the avoidance of double taxation, from stipulating a clause conferring on them the right to tax royalties at a rate of up to 10 per cent.

25.   *Canada* reserves its position on paragraph 1 and wishes to retain a 10 per cent rate of tax at source in its bilateral conventions. However, Canada would be prepared to provide an exemption from tax for copyright royalties in respect of any literary, dramatic, musical or artistic work, but not including royalties in respect of motion picture films, and films or video tapes for use in connection with television.

26.   *Finland* reserves the right to tax royalties at source. However, Finland would be prepared to provide an exemption from tax for copyright royalties in respect of any literary, artistic or scientific work.

27.   *France* reserves the right to retain some tax on royalties of French origin when flows of royalties between France and the other Contracting State are unbalanced to France's disadvantage.

28.   *Japan, New Zealand, Portugal* and *Spain* reserve the right to tax royalties at source.

29.   *Turkey* cannot accept a rate of tax which is lower than 20 per cent.

Paragraph 3

30.   *Italy* reserves the right to subject royalties and profits from the alienation of rights or property giving rise to royalties to the taxes imposed by its law whenever the recipient thereof has a permanent establishment in Italy, even if the rights or property in respect of which the royalties are paid is not effectively connected with such permanent establishment.

31.   *Belgium* reserves the right, in order to fill what it considers as a gap in the Article, to propose a provision defining the source of royalties by analogy with the provision in paragraph 5 of Article 11, which deals with the same problem in the case of interest.

COMMENTARY ON ARTICLE 13
CONCERNING THE TAXATION OF CAPITAL GAINS

I. PRELIMINARY REMARKS

1.   A comparison of the tax laws of the OECD Member countries shows that the taxation of capital gains varies considerably from country to country:

- in some countries capital gains are not deemed to be taxable income;
- in other countries capital gains accrued to an enterprise are taxed, but capital gains made by an individual outside the course of his trade or business are not taxed;
- even where capital gains made by an individual outside the course of his trade or business are taxed, such taxation often applies only in specified cases, e.g. profits from the sale of immovable property or speculative gains (where an asset was bought to be resold).

2.   Moreover, the taxes on capital gains vary from country to country. In some OECD Member countries capital gains are taxed as ordinary income and therefore added to the income from other sources. This applies especially to the capital gains made by the alienation of assets of an enterprise. In a number of OECD Member countries, however, capital gains are subjected to special taxes, such as taxes on profits from the alienation of immovable property, or general capital gains taxes, or taxes on capital appreciation (increment taxes). Such taxes are levied on each capital gain or on the sum of the capital gains accrued during a year, mostly at special rates, which do not take into account the other income (or losses) of the taxpayer. It does not seem necessary to describe all those taxes.

3.   The Article does not deal with the above-mentioned questions. It is left to the domestic law of each Contracting State to decide whether capital gains should be taxed and, if they are taxable, how they are to be taxed. The Article can in no way be construed as giving a State the right to tax capital gains if such right is not provided for in its domestic law. The Article does not specify to what kind of tax it applies. It is understood that the Article must apply to all kinds of taxes levied by a Contracting State on capital gains. The wording of Article 2 is large enough to achieve this aim and to include also special taxes on capital gains.

II. COMMENTARY ON THE PROVISIONS OF THE ARTICLE

GENERAL REMARKS

4.   It is normal to give the right to tax capital gains on a property of a given kind to the State which under the Convention is entitled to tax both the property and the income derived therefrom. The right to tax a gain from the alienation

of a business asset must be given to the same State without regard to the question whether such gain is a capital gain or a business profit. Accordingly, no distinction between capital gains and commercial profits is made nor is it necessary to have special provisions as to whether the Article on capital gains or Article 7 on the taxation of business profits should apply. It is however left to the domestic law of the taxing State to decide whether a tax on capital gains or on ordinary income must be levied. The Convention does not prejudge this question.

5.   The Article does not give a detailed definition of capital gains. This is not necessary for the reasons mentioned above. The words "alienation of property" are used to cover in particular capital gains resulting from the sale or exchange of property and also from a partial alienation, the expropriation, the transfer to a company in exchange for stock, the sale of a right, the gift and even the passing of property on death.

6.   Most States taxing capital gains do so when an alienation of capital assets takes place. Some of them, however, tax only so-called realised capital gains. Under certain circumstances, though there is an alienation no realised capital gain is recognised for tax purposes (e.g. when the alienation proceeds are used for acquiring new assets). Whether or not there is a realisation has to be determined according to the applicable domestic tax law. No particular problems arise when the State which has the right to tax does not exercise it at the time the alienation takes place.

7.   As a rule, appreciation in value not associated with the alienation of a capital asset is not taxed, since, as long as the owner still holds the asset in question, the capital gain exists only on paper. There are, however, tax laws under which capital appreciation and revaluation of business assets are taxed even if there is no alienation.

8.   Special circumstances may lead to the taxation of the capital appreciation of an asset that has not been alienated. This may be the case if the value of a capital asset has increased in such a manner that the owner proceeds to the revaluation of this asset in his books. Such revaluation of assets in the books may also occur in the case of a depreciation of the national currency. A number of States levy special taxes on such book profits, amounts put into reserve, an increase in the paid-up capital and other revaluations resulting from the adjustment of the book-value to the intrinsic value of a capital asset. These taxes on capital appreciation (increment taxes) are covered by the Convention according to Article 2.

9.   Where capital appreciation and revaluation of business assets are taxed, the same principle should, as a rule, apply as in the case of the alienation of such assets. It has not been found necessary to mention such cases expressly in the Article or to lay down special rules. The provisions of the Article as well as those of Articles 6, 7 and 21, seem to be sufficient. As a rule, the right to tax is conferred by the above-mentioned provisions on the State of which the alienator is a resident, except that in the cases of immovable property or of movable property forming part of the business property of a permanent establishment or pertaining to a fixed base, the prior right to tax belongs to the State where such property is situated. Special attention must be drawn, however, to the cases dealt with in paragraphs 13 to 17 below.

10.   In some States the transfer of an asset from a permanent establishment situated in the territory of such State to a permanent establishment or the head

office of the same enterprise situated in another State is assimilated to an alienation of property. The Article does not prevent these States from taxing profits or gains deemed to arise in connection with such a transfer, provided, however, that such taxation is in accordance with Article 7.

11.   The Article does not distinguish as to the origin of the capital gain. Therefore all capital gains, those accruing over a long term, parallel to a steady improvement in economic conditions, as well as those accruing in a very short period (speculative gains) are covered. Also capital gains which are due to depreciation of the national currency are covered. It is, of course, left to each State to decide whether or not such gains should be taxed.

12.   The Article does not specify how to compute a capital gain, this being left to the domestic law applicable. As a rule, capital gains are calculated by deducting the cost from the selling price. To arrive at cost all expenses incidental to the purchase and all expenditure for improvements are added to the purchase price. In some cases the cost after deduction of the depreciation allowances already given is taken into account. Some tax laws prescribe another base instead of cost, e.g. the value previously reported by the alienator of the asset for capital tax purposes.

13.   Special problems may arise when the basis for the taxation of capital gains is not uniform in the two Contracting States. The capital gain from the alienation of an asset computed in one State according to the rules mentioned in paragraph 12 above, may not necessarily coincide with the capital gain computed in the other State under the accounting rules used there. This may occur when one State has the right to tax capital gains because it is the State of situs while the other State has the right to tax because the enterprise is a resident of that other State.

14.   The following example may illustrate this problem; an enterprise of State A bought immovable property situated in State B. The enterprise may have entered depreciation allowances in the books kept in State A. If such immovable property is sold at a price which is above cost, a capital gain may be realised and, in addition, the depreciation allowances granted earlier may be recovered. State B in which the immovable property is situated and where no books are kept does not have to take into account, when taxing the income from the immovable property, the depreciation allowances booked in State A. Neither can State B substitute the value of the immovable property shown in the books kept in State A for the cost at the time of the alienation. State B cannot, therefore, tax the depreciation allowances realised in addition to the capital gain as mentioned in paragraph 12 above.

15.   On the other hand, State A of which the alienator is a resident, cannot be obliged in all cases to exempt such book profits fully from its taxes under paragraph 1 of the Article and Article 23 A (there will be hardly any problems for States applying the tax credit method). To the extent that such book profits are due to the realisation of the depreciation allowances previously claimed in State A and which had reduced the income or profits taxable in such State A, that State cannot be prevented from taxing such book profits. The situation corresponds to that dealt with in paragraph 44 of the Commentary on Article 23 A.

16.   Further problems may arise in connection with profits due to changes of the rate of exchange between the currencies of State A and State B. After the devaluation of the currency of State A, enterprises of such State A may, or may

have to, increase the book value of the assets situated outside the territory of State A. Apart from any devaluation of the currency of a State, the usual fluctuations of the rate of exchange may give rise to so-called currency gains or losses. Take for example an enterprise of State A having bought and sold immovable property situated in State B. If the cost and the selling price, both expressed in the currency of State B, are equal, there will be no capital gain in State B. When the value of the currency of State B has risen between the purchase and the sale of the asset in relation to the currency of State A, in the currency of that State a profit will accrue to such enterprise. If the value of the currency of State B has fallen in the meantime, the alienator will sustain a loss which will not be recognised in State B. Such currency gains or losses may also arise in connection with claims and debts contracted in a foreign currency. If the balance-sheet of a permanent establishment situated in State B of an enterprise of State A shows claims and debts expressed in the currency of State B, the books of the permanent establishment do not show any gain or loss when repayments are made. Changes of the rate of exchange may be reflected, however, in the accounts of the head office. If the value of the currency of State B has risen (fallen) between the time the claim has originated and its repayment, the enterprise, as a whole, will realise a gain (sustain a loss). This is true also with respect to debts if between the time they have originated and their repayment, the currency of State B has fallen (risen) in value.

17.   The provisions of the Article do not settle all questions regarding the taxation of such currency gains. Such gains are in most cases not connected with an alienation of the asset; they may often not even be determined in the State on which the right to tax capital gains is conferred by the Article. Accordingly, the question, as a rule, is not, whether the State in which a permanent establishment is situated has a right to tax, but whether the State of which the taxpayer is a resident must, if applying the exemption method, refrain from taxing such currency gains which, in many cases, cannot be shown but in the books kept in the head office. The answer to that latter question depends not only on the Article but also on Article 7 and on Article 23 A. If in a given case differing opinions of two States should result in an actual double taxation, the case should be settled under the mutual agreement procedure provided for by Article 25.

18.   Moreover the question arises which Article should apply when there is paid for property sold an annuity during the lifetime of the alienator and not a fixed price. Are such annuity payments, as far as they exceed costs, to be dealt with as a gain from the alienation of the property or as "income not dealt with" according to Article 21? Both opinions may be supported by arguments of equivalent weight, and it seems difficult to give one rule on the matter. In addition such problems are rare in practice, so it therefore seems unnecessary to establish a rule for insertion in the Convention. It may be left to Contracting States, who may be involved in such a question, to adopt a solution in the mutual agreement procedure provided for by Article 25.

19.   The Article is not intended to apply to prizes in a lottery or to premiums and prizes attaching to bonds or debentures.

20.   The Article deals first with the gains which may be taxed in the State where the alienated property is situated. For all other capital gains, paragraph 4 gives the right to tax to the State of which the alienator is a resident.

21.   As capital gains are not taxed by all States, it may be considered reasonable to avoid only actual double taxation of capital gains. Therefore, Contracting

States are free to supplement their bilateral convention in such a way that a State has to forego its right to tax conferred on it by the domestic laws only if the other State on which the right to tax is conferred by the Convention makes use thereof. In such a case, paragraph 4 of the Article should be supplemented accordingly. Besides, a modification of Article 23 A as suggested in paragraph 35 of the Commentary on Article 23 A is needed.

Paragraph 1

22.   Paragraph 1 states that gains from the alienation of immovable property may be taxed in the State in which it is situated. This rule corresponds to the provisions of Article 6 and of paragraph 1 of Article 22. It applies also to immovable property forming part of the assets of an enterprise or used for performing independent personal services. For the definition of immovable property paragraph 1 refers to Article 6. Paragraph 1 of Article 13 deals only with gains which a resident of a Contracting State derives from the alienation of immovable property situated in the other Contracting State. It does not, therefore, apply to gains derived from the alienation of immovable property situated in the Contracting State of which the alienator is a resident in the meaning of Article 4 or situated in a third State; the provisions of paragraph 1 of Article 21 shall apply to such gains.

23.   Certain tax laws assimilate the alienation of all or part of the shares in a company, the exclusive or main aim of which is to hold immovable property, to the alienation of such immovable property. In itself paragraph 1 does not allow that practice: a special provision in the bilateral convention can alone provide for such an assimilation. Contracting States are of course free either to include in their bilateral conventions such special provision, or to confirm expressly that the alienation of shares cannot be assimilated to the alienation of the immovable property.

Paragraph 2

24.   Paragraph 2 deals with movable property forming part of the business property of a permanent establishment of an enterprise or pertaining to a fixed base used for performing independent personal services. The term "movable property" means all property other than immovable property which is dealt with in paragraph 1. It includes also incorporeal property, such as goodwill, licences, etc. Gains from the alienation of such assets may be taxed in the State in which the permanent establishment or fixed base is situated, which corresponds to the rules for business profits and for income from independent personal services (Articles 7 and 14).

25.   The paragraph makes clear that its rules apply when movable property of a permanent establishment or fixed base is alienated as well as when the permanent establishment as such (alone or with the whole enterprise) or the fixed base as such is alienated. If the whole enterprise is alienated, then the rule applies to such gains which are deemed to result from the alienation of movable property forming part of the business property of the permanent establishment. The rules of Article 7 should then apply mutatis mutandis without express reference thereto. For the transfer of an asset from a permanent establishment in one State to a permanent establishment (or the head office) in another State, cf. paragraph 10 above.

26.   On the other hand, paragraph 2 may not always be applicable to capital gains from the alienation of a participation in an enterprise. The provision applies only to property which was owned by the alienator, either wholly or jointly with another person.   Under the laws of some countries, capital assets of a partnership are considered to be owned by the partners. Under some other laws, however, partnerships and other associations are treated as body corporate for tax purposes, distinct from their partners (members), which means that participations in such entities are dealt with in the same way as shares in a company. Capital gains from the alienation of such participations like capital gains from the alienation of shares, are therefore taxable only in the State of residence of the alienator. Contracting States may agree bilaterally on special rules governing the taxation of capital gains from the alienation of a participation in a partnership.

27.   Certain States consider that all capital gains arising from sources in their territory should be subject to their taxes according to their domestic laws, if the alienator has a permanent establishment within their territory. Paragraph 2 is not based on such a conception which is sometimes referred to as "the force of attraction of the permanent establishment". The paragraph merely provides that gains from the alienation of movable property forming part of the business property of a permanent establishment or of movable property pertaining to a fixed base used for performing independent personal services may be taxed in the State where the permanent establishment or the fixed base is situated. The gains from the alienation of all other movable property are taxable only in the State of residence of the alienator as provided in paragraph 4. The foregoing explanations accord with those in the Commentary on Article 7.

Paragraph 3

28.   An exception from the rule of paragraph 2 is provided for ships and aircraft operated in international traffic and for boats engaged in inland waterways transport and movable property pertaining to the operation of such ships, aircraft and boats. Gains from the alienation of such assets are taxable only in the State in which the place of effective management of the enterprise operating such ships, aircraft and boats is situated. This rule corresponds to the provisions of Article 8 and of paragraph 3 of Article 22. It is understood that paragraph 3 of Article 8 is applicable if the place of effective management of such enterprise is aboard a ship or a boat. Contracting States which would prefer to confer the exclusive taxing right on the State of residence or to use a combination of the residence criterion and the place of effective management criterion are free, in bilateral conventions, to substitute to paragraph 3 a provision corresponding to those proposed in paragraphs 2 and 3 of the Commentary on Article 8.

Paragraph 4

29.   As regards gains from the alienation of any property other than that referred to in paragraphs 1, 2 and 3, paragraph 4 provides that they are taxable only in the State of which the alienator is a resident. This corresponds to the rules laid down in Article 22.

30.   The Article does not contain special rules for gains from the alienation of shares in a company or of securities, bonds, debentures and the like. Such gains are, therefore, taxable only in the State of which the alienator is a resident.

31.   If shares are sold by a shareholder to the issuing company in connection with the liquidation of such company or the reduction of its paid-up capital, the difference between the selling price and the par value of the shares may be treated in the State of which the company is a resident as a distribution of accumulated profits and not as a capital gain.   The Article does not prevent the State of residence of the company from taxing such distributions at the rates provided for in Article 10: such taxation is permitted because such difference is covered by the definition of the term "dividends" contained in paragraph 3 of Article 10 and interpreted in paragraph 27 of the Commentary relating thereto.   The same interpretation may apply if bonds or debentures are redeemed by the debtor at a price which is higher than the parvalue or the value at which the bonds or debentures have been issued; in such a case, the difference may represent interest and, therefore, be subjected to a limited tax in the State of source of the interest in accordance with Article 11 (cf. also paragraphs 18 and 19 of the Commentary on Article 11).

SPECIAL DEROGATION

32.   In view of its particular situation in relation to shipping, *Greece* will retain its freedom of action with regard to the provisions in the Convention relating to profits from the operation of ships in international traffic, to remuneration of crews of such ships, to capital represented by ships in international traffic and by movable property pertaining to the operation of such ships, and to capital gains from the alienation of such ships and assets.

RESERVATIONS ON THE ARTICLE

33.   *Australia* reserves the right to propose changes to reflect the facts that Australia does not levy a capital gains tax and that the terms "movable property" and "immovable property" are terms not used in Australian law.

34.   *Canada* reserves its position on paragraph 4 of the Article, in order to reserve the right to tax gains from the alienation of property, other than those mentioned in the first three paragraphs.

35.   *Finland* reserves the right to tax gains from the alienation of shares or other corporate rights in Finnish companies, where the ownership of such shares or other corporate rights entitles to the enjoyment of immovable property situated in Finland and owned by the company.

36.   *France* can accept the provisions of paragraph 4, but wishes to retain the possibility of applying the provisions in its laws relative to the taxation of gains from the alienation of shares or rights which are part of a substantial participation in a company which is a resident of France, or of shares or rights of companies the assets of which consist mainly of immovable property situated in France.

37.   *Italy* reserves the right to subject capital gains from Italian sources to the taxes imposed by its law whenever the alienator has a permanent establishment in Italy, even if the property or assets alienated did not form part of the business property employed in such permanent establishment.

38.   *New Zealand* reserves its position on paragraphs 3 and 4.

39.   *Portugal* reserves the right to tax gains from the increase in capital of companies with a head office or place of effective management in Portugal, when the increase results from the capitalisation of reserves or the issue of shares.

40.   *Turkey* reserves the right, in accordance with its legislation, to tax capital gains from the alienation, within its territory, of movable capital and any property other than those mentioned in paragraph 2 if the delay between their acquisition and their alienation is less than two years.

COMMENTARY ON ARTICLE 14
CONCERNING THE TAXATION OF INDEPENDENT
PERSONAL SERVICES

1. The Article is concerned with what are commonly known as professional services and with other activities of an independent character. This excludes industrial and commercial activities and also professional services performed in employment, e.g. a physician serving as a medical officer in a factory. It should, however, be observed that the Article does not concern independent activities of entertainers and athletes, these being covered by Article 17.

2. The meaning of the term "professional services" is illustrated by some examples of typical liberal professions. The enumeration has an explanatory character only and is not exhaustive. Difficulties of interpretation which might arise in special cases may be solved by mutual agreement between the competent authorities of the Contracting States concerned.

3. The provisions of the Article are similar to those for business profits and rest in fact on the same principles as those of Article 7. The provisions of Article 7 and the Commentary thereon could therefore be used as guidance for interpreting and applying Article 14. Thus the principles laid down in Article 7 for instance as regards allocation of profits between head office and permanent establishment could be applied also in apportioning income between the State of residence of a person performing independent personal services and the State where such services are performed from a fixed base. Equally, expenses incurred for the purposes of a fixed base, including executive and general expenses, should be allowed as deductions in determining the income attributable to a fixed base in the same way as such expenses incurred for the purposes of a permanent establishment (cf. paragraph 3 of Article 7). Also in other respects Article 7 and the Commentary thereon could be of assistance for the interpretation of Article 14.

4. Even if Articles 7 and 14 are based on the same principles, it was thought that the concept of permanent establishment should be reserved for commercial and industrial activities. The term "fixed base" has therefore been used. It has not been thought appropriate to try to define it, but it would cover, for instance, a physician's consulting room or the office of an architect or a lawyer. A person performing independent personal services would probably not as a rule have premises of this kind in any other State than of his residence. But if there is in another State a centre of activity of a fixed or a permanent character, then that State should be entitled to tax the person's activities.

RESERVATIONS ON THE ARTICLE

5. *New Zealand* and *Turkey* reserve the right to tax persons performing professional services or other activities of an independent character if they are present

in these countries for a period or periods exceeding in the aggregate 183 days in the fiscal (for New Zealand) or calendar (for Turkey) year, even if they do not have a fixed base available to them for the purpose of performing such services or activities.

6.   *Portugal* and *Spain* reserve their position on paragraph 1.

7.   The *United States* reserves the right to tax services performed by individuals who are present in the United States for more than 183 days during the taxable year.   The United States also believes that this Article should be limited to individuals and to income from the performance of personal services.

COMMENTARY ON ARTICLE 15
CONCERNING THE TAXATION OF DEPENDENT
PERSONAL SERVICES

1.   Paragraph 1 establishes the general rule as to the taxation of income from employment (other than pensions), namely, that such income is taxable in the State where the employment is actually exercised.   One consequence of this would be that a resident of a Contracting State who derived remuneration, in respect of an employment, from sources in the other State could not be taxed in that other State in respect of that remuneration merely because the results of this work were exploited in that other State.

2.   The general rule is subject to exception only in the case of pensions (Article 18) and of remuneration and pensions in respect of government service (Article 19).   Remuneration of members of boards of directors of companies is the subject of Article 16.

3.   Paragraph 2 contains, however, a general exception to the rule in paragraph 1.   This exception, which concerns employment of short duration abroad, is mainly intended to facilitate the international movement of qualified personnel, as in the case of firms which sell capital goods and are responsible for installing and assembling them abroad.   The three conditions prescribed in this paragraph must be satisfied for the remuneration to qualify for the exemption.   The exemption is limited to the 183-day period.   It is further stipulated that this time period may not be exceeded "in the fiscal year concerned".   The formulation used may create difficulties in cases where the fiscal years of the Contracting States do not coincide.   In order to avoid these difficulties such Contracting States may prefer to use another phrasing, for instance "fiscal year of that other State" or "calendar year".   The employer paying the remuneration must not be a resident of the State in which the employment is exercised.   Furthermore, should the employer have in that State a permanent establishment (or a fixed base if he performs professional services or other activities of an independent character), the exemption is given only on condition that the remuneration is not borne by a permanent establishment or a fixed base which the employer has in the other State.   It should be noted that, under the provisions of Article 17, the exemption does not apply to remuneration of artistes and athletes.

4.   Paragraph 3 applies to the remuneration of crews of ships or aircraft operated in international traffic, or of boats engaged in inland waterways transport, a rule which follows up to a certain extent the rule applied to the income from shipping, inland waterways transport and air transport—that is, to tax them in the Contracting State in which the place of effective management of the enterprise concerned is situated.   In the Commentary on Article 8, it is indicated that Contracting States may agree to confer the right to tax such income on the State of the enterprise operating the ships, boats or aircraft.   The reasons for introducing

that possibility in the case of income from shipping, inland waterways and air transport operations are valid also in respect of remuneration of the crew. Accordingly Contracting States are left free to agree on a provision which gives the right to tax such remuneration to the State of the enterprise. Such a provision, as well as that of paragraph 3 of Article 15, assumes that the domestic laws of the State on which the right to tax is conferred allows it to tax the remuneration of a person in the service of the enterprise concerned, irrespective of his residence. It is understood that paragraph 3 of Article 8 is applicable if the place of effective management of a shipping enterprise or of an inland waterways transport enterprise is aboard a ship or a boat. According to the domestic laws of some Member countries, tax is levied on remuneration received by non-resident members of the crew in respect of employment aboard ships only if the ship has the nationality of such a State. For that reason conventions concluded between these States provide that the right to tax such remuneration is given to the State of the nationality of the ship. On the other hand many States cannot make use of such a taxation right and the provision could in such cases lead to non-taxation. However, States having that taxation principle in their domestic laws may agree bilaterally to confer the right to tax remuneration in respect of employment aboard ships on the State of the nationality of the ship.

5.   It should be noted that no special rule regarding the taxation of income of frontier workers is included as it would be more suitable for the problems created by local conditions to be solved directly between the States concerned.

6.   No special provision has been made regarding remuneration derived by visiting professors or students employed with a view to their acquiring practical experience. Many conventions contain rules of some kind or other concerning such cases, the main purpose of which is to facilitate cultural relations by providing for a limited tax exemption. Sometimes, tax exemption is already provided under domestic taxation laws. The absence of specific rules should not be interpreted as constituting an obstacle to the inclusion of such rules in bilateral conventions whenever this is felt desirable.

SPECIAL DEROGATION

7.   In view of its particular situation in relation to shipping, *Greece* will retain its freedom of action with regard to the provisions in the Convention relating to profits from the operation of ships in international traffic, to remuneration of crews of such ships, to capital represented by ships in international traffic and by movable property pertaining to the operation of such ships, and to capital gains from the alienation of such ships and assets.

COMMENTARY ON ARTICLE 16
CONCERNING THE TAXATION OF DIRECTORS' FEES

1.   This Article relates to remuneration received by a resident of a Contracting State, whether an individual or a legal person, in the capacity of a member of a board of directors of a company which is a resident of the other Contracting State.   Since it might sometimes be difficult to ascertain where the services are performed, the provision treats the services as performed in the State of residence of the company.

2.   A member of the board of directors of a company often also has other functions with the company, e.g. as ordinary employee, adviser, consultant, etc. It is clear that the Article does not apply to remuneration paid to such a person on account of such other functions.

3.   In some countries organs of companies exist which are similar in function to the board of directors.   Contracting States are free to include in bilateral conventions such organs of companies under a provision corresponding to Article 16.

RESERVATIONS ON THE ARTICLE

4.   *Portugal* reserves the right to tax under Article 15 any remuneration of a member of the board of directors or of any other body of a company, for the carrying out of a permanent activity.

5.   The *United States* reserves its position with regard to this Article.   The United States believe that directors' fees should be subject to tax under Article 14.

COMMENTARY ON ARTICLE 17
CONCERNING THE TAXATION OF ARTISTES AND ATHLETES

1.   Paragraph 1 provides that entertainers and athletes who are residents of a Contracting State may be taxed in the other Contracting State in which their personal activities as such are performed, whether these are of an independent or of a dependent nature. This provision is an exception to the rules in Article 14 and to that in paragraph 2 of Article 15, respectively.

2.   This provision makes it possible to avoid the practical difficulties which often arise in taxing entertainers and athletes performing abroad. Moreover, too strict provisions might in certain cases impede cultural exchanges. In order to overcome this disadvantage, the States concerned may, by common agreement, limit the application of paragraph 1 to independent activities by adding its provisions to those of Article 14. In such a case, entertainers and athletes performing for a salary or wages would automatically come within Article 15 and thus be entitled to the exemptions provided for in paragraph 2 of that Article.

3.   The provisions of the Article do not apply when the entertainer or athlete is employed by a Government and derives the income from that Government. Such income is to be treated under the provisions of Article 19. Certain conventions contain provisions excluding entertainers and athletes employed in organisations which are subsidised out of public funds from the application of Article 17. The provisions of the Article shall not prevent Contracting States from agreeing bilaterally on particular provisions concerning such entertainers and athletes.

4.   The purpose of paragraph 2 is to counteract certain tax avoidance devices in cases where remuneration for the performance of an entertainer or athlete is not paid to the entertainer or athlete himself but to another person, e.g. a so-called artiste-company, in such a way that the income is taxed in the State where the activity is performed neither as personal service income to the entertainer or athlete nor as profits of the enterprise in the absence of a permanent establishment. Paragraph 2 permits the State in which the performance is given to impose a tax on the profits diverted from the income of the entertainer or athlete to the enterprise where for instance the entertainer or athlete has control over or rights to the income thus diverted or has obtained or will obtain some benefit directly or indirectly from that income. It may be, however, that the domestic laws of some States do not enable them to apply such a provision. Such States are free to agree to alternative solutions or to leave paragraph 2 out of their bilateral convention.

5.   Where in the cases dealt with in paragraph 2 the exemption method for relieving double taxation is used by the State of residence of the person receiving the income, that State would be precluded from taxing such income even if the State where the activities were performed could not make use of its right to tax.

It is therefore understood that the credit method should be used in such cases. The same result could be achieved by stipulating a subsidiary right to tax for the State of residence of the person receiving the income, if the State where the activities are performed cannot make use of the right conferred on it by paragraph 2. Contracting States are free to choose any of these methods in order to ensure that the income does not escape taxation.

OBSERVATION ON THE COMMENTARY

6.   *Canada* and the *United States* are of the opinion that paragraph 2 of the Article applies only to cases mentioned in paragraph 4 above and these countries will propose an amendment to that effect when negotiating conventions with other Member countries.

RESERVATIONS ON THE ARTICLE

7.   *Greece* and *Portugal* reserve the right to apply the provisions of Article 17, not 19, to income of Government artistes and athletes.

8.   *Japan* reserves the right to apply the provisions of this Article to income derived in connection with trade or business by entertainers or athletes who are employed by the Government.

9.   The *United States* reserves the right to limit paragraph 1 to situations where the entertainer or athlete is present in the other State for a specified period or earns a specified amount.

COMMENTARY ON ARTICLE 18
CONCERNING THE TAXATION OF PENSIONS

1.   According to this Article, pensions paid in respect of private employment are taxable only in the State of residence of the recipient.   The provision also covers widows' and orphans' pensions and other similar payments such as annuities paid in respect of past employment.   It also applies to pensions in respect of services rendered to a State or a political subdivision or local authority thereof which are not covered by the provisions of paragraph 2 of Article 19.

2.   Some States consider pensions paid out under a public pension scheme which is part of their social security system similar to Government pensions. Such States argue on that basis that the State of source, i.e. the State from which the pension is paid, should have a right to tax such pensions.   Many conventions concluded by these States contain provisions to that effect, sometimes including also other payments made under the social security legislation of the State of source.   Such payments are for instance sickness benefits, unemployment benefits and benefits on account of industrial injury.   Contracting States having that view may agree bilaterally on an additional paragraph to the Article giving the State of source a right to tax payments made under its social security legislation.   A paragraph of that kind could be drafted along the following lines:

> "Notwithstanding the provisions of paragraph 1, pensions and other payments made under the social security legislation of a Contracting State may be taxed in that State."

Where the State of which the recipient of such payments is a resident applies the exemption method the payments will be taxable only in the State of source while States using the credit method may tax the payments and give credit for the tax levied in the State of source.   Some States using the credit method as the general method in their conventions may, however, consider that the State of source should have an exclusive right to tax such payments.   Such States should then substitute the words "shall be taxable only" for the words "may be taxed" in the above draft provision.

3.   The treatment under the taxation laws of the OECD Member countries of amounts paid to an employee on the cessation of his employment is highly diversified.   Some States regard such a payment as a pension, private or Government as the case may be, paid as a lump sum.   In such a case it would be natural to consider the income as falling under Article 18 or 19.   In the tax laws of other States such a payment is looked upon as the final remuneration for the work performed.   Then it should of course be treated under Article 15 or 19, as the case may be.   Others again consider such a payment as a bonus which is not taxable under their income tax laws but perhaps subjected to a gift tax or a similar tax.   It has not been possible to reach a common solution on the tax treatment of payments of this kind under the Model Convention.   If the question of taxing

such payments should arise between Contracting States, the matter therefore has to be solved by recourse to the provisions of Article 25.

RESERVATIONS ON THE ARTICLE

4.   *Australia* reserves its position on this Article. When negotiating with other Member countries, the Australian authorities will propose that all pensions be taxable only in the country of residence of the recipient.

5.   *Canada* reserves its position on this Article. When negotiating conventions, the Canadian authorities will propose that the country in which the pensions arise be given a limited right to tax. Canada would also wish to apply this rule to pensions referred to in Article 19 in order to achieve uniformity of treatment.

6.   *Sweden,* when negotiating conventions with other Member countries, would wish to retain the right to tax pensions paid to non-residents of Sweden, where such pensions are paid in respect of past services rendered mainly within Sweden.

COMMENTARY ON ARTICLE 19
CONCERNING THE TAXATION OF REMUNERATION
IN RESPECT OF GOVERNMENT SERVICE

1.   This Article applies to remuneration in respect of government service. Similar provisions in old bilateral conventions were framed in order to conform with the rules of international courtesy and mutual respect between sovereign States. They were therefore rather limited in scope. However, the importance and scope of Article 19 has increased on account of the fact that, consequent on the growth of the public sector in many countries, governmental activities abroad have been considerably extended. According to the original version of paragraph 1 of Article 19 in the 1963 Draft Convention the paying State had a right to tax payments made for services rendered to that State or political subdivision or local authority thereof. The expression "may be taxed" was used and this did not connote an exclusive right of taxation.

2.   On revision of the Article, paragraph 1 was split into two paragraphs, paragraph 1 concerning remuneration other than a pension and paragraph 2 concerning pensions, respectively. Unlike the original provision, sub-paragraph *a*) of paragraphs 1 and 2 are both based on the principle that the paying State shall have an exclusive right to tax the payments. Countries using the credit method as the general method for relieving double taxation in their conventions are thus, as an exception to that method, obliged to exempt from tax such payments to their residents as are dealt with under paragraphs 1 and 2. If both Contracting States apply the exemption method for relieving double taxation, they can continue to use the expression "may be taxed" instead of "shall be taxable only". In relation to such countries the effect will of course be the same irrespective of which of these expressions they use. It is understood that the expression "shall be taxable only" shall not prevent a Contracting State from taking into account the income exempted under sub-paragraph *a*) of paragraphs 1 and 2 in determining the rate of tax to be imposed on income derived by its residents from other sources. The principle of giving the exclusive taxing right to the paying State is contained in so many of the existing conventions between OECD Member countries that it can be said to be already internationally accepted. It is also in conformity with the conception of international courtesy which is at the basis of the Article and with the provisions of the Vienna Conventions on Diplomatic and Consular Relations. It should, however, be observed that the Article is not intended to restrict the operation of any rules originating from international law in the case of diplomatic missions and consular posts (cf. Article 27) but deals with cases not covered by such rules.

3.   The provisions of the Article apply to payments made not only by a State but also by its political subdivisions and local authorities (constituent states, regions, provinces, "départements", cantons, districts, "arrondissements", "Kreise", municipalities, or groups of municipalities, etc.).

138

4.   An exception from the principle of giving exclusive taxing power to the paying State is contained in sub-paragraph *b*) of paragraph 1.   It is to be seen against the background that, according to the Vienna Conventions mentioned above, the receiving State is allowed to tax remuneration paid to certain categories of personnel of foreign diplomatic missions and consular posts, who are permanent residents or nationals of that State.   Given that pensions paid to retired government officials ought to be treated for tax purposes in the same way as salaries or wages paid to such employees during their active time, an exception like the one in sub-paragraph *b*) of paragraph 1 is incorporated also in sub-paragraph *b*) of paragraph 2 regarding pensions.   Since the condition laid down in sub-paragraph *b*) (*ii*) of paragraph 1 cannot be valid in relation to a pensioner, the only pre-requisite for the receiving State's power to tax the pension is that the pensioner must be one of its own residents and nationals.   It should be noted that the expression "out of funds created by" in sub-paragraph *a*) of paragraph 2 covers the situation where the pension is not paid directly by the State, a political subdivision or a local authority but out of separate funds created by them.

5.   According to Article 19 of the 1963 Draft Convention, the services rendered to the State, political subdivision or local authority had to be rendered "in the discharge of functions of a governmental nature".   In the course of the revision of the Article, it was decided to delete that expression.   Some OECD Member countries, however, thought that the exclusion would lead to a widening of the scope of the Article.   Contracting States who are of that view and who feel that such a widening is not desirable may continue to use, and preferably specify, the expression "in the discharge of functions of a governmental nature" in their bilateral conventions.

6.   Paragraphs 1 and 2 do not apply if the services are performed in connection with business carried on by the State, or one of its political subdivisions or local authorities, paying the remuneration.   In such cases the ordinary rules apply: Article 15 for wages and salaries, Article 16 for directors' fees and other similar payments and Article 18 for pensions.   Article 17 is not mentioned because paragraphs 1 and 2 of Article 19 are to apply to remuneration paid to artistes employed by the State, a political subdivision or a local authority thereof, irrespective of whether such artistes could be said to be rendering services in connection with business carried on by the State, the political subdivision or the local authority.   Contracting States, wishing for specific reasons to dispense with paragraph 3 in their bilateral conventions, are free to do so thus bringing in under paragraphs 1 and 2 also services rendered in connection with business.   In view of the specific functions carried out by certain public bodies, e.g. State Railways, the Post Office, State-owned theatres etc., Contracting States wanting to keep paragraph 3 may agree in bilateral negotiations to include under the provisions of paragraphs 1 and 2 remuneration paid by such bodies, even if they could be said to be performing business activities.

RESERVATIONS ON THE ARTICLE

7.   *Japan* and the *United States* believe that a reference to Article 17 should be added to paragraph 3, so that government-employed artistes may be governed by Article 17 if their services are rendered in connection with a business.

8.   The *United States* reserves the right to modify the text to indicate that its application is not limited by Article 1.

COMMENTARY ON ARTICLE 20
CONCERNING THE TAXATION OF STUDENTS

1.   The rule established in this Article concerns certain payments received by students or business apprentices for the purpose of their maintenance, education or training. All such payments received from sources outside the State in which the student or business apprentice concerned is staying shall be exempted from tax in that State.

2.   In the course of revision of the 1963 Draft Convention it was decided to insert the word "immediately" in order to make clear that the Article does not cover a person who has once been a resident of a Contracting State but has subsequently moved his residence to a third State before visiting the other Contracting State.

RESERVATION ON THE ARTICLE

3.   *Australia* reserves the right to have the operation of this Article limited to students.

COMMENTARY ON ARTICLE 21
CONCERNING THE TAXATION OF OTHER INCOME

1.   This Article provides a general rule relating to income not dealt with in the foregoing Articles of the Convention.   The income concerned is not only income of a class not expressly dealt with but also income from sources not expressly mentioned.   The scope of the Article is not confined to income arising in a Contracting State; it extends also to income from third States.

Paragraph 1

2.   Under this paragraph the exclusive right to tax is given to the State of residence.   In cases of conflict between two residences, Article 4 will also allocate the taxation right in respect of third State income.

3.   The rule set out in the paragraph applies irrespective of whether the right to tax is in fact exercised by the State of residence, and thus when the income arises in the other Contracting State, that State cannot impose tax even if the income is not taxed in the first-mentioned State.   Likewise, when income arises in a third State and the recipient of this income is considered as a resident by both Contracting States under their domestic law, the application of Article 4 will result in the recipient being treated as a resident of one Contracting State only and being liable to comprehensive taxation ("full tax liability") in that State only. In this case, the other Contracting State may not impose tax on the income arising from the third State, even if the recipient is not taxed by the State of which he is considered a resident under Article 4.   In order to avoid non-taxation, Contracting States may agree to limit the scope of the Article to income which is taxed in the Contracting State of which the recipient is a resident and may modify the provisions of the paragraph accordingly.   In fact, this problem is merely a special aspect of the general problem dealt with in paragraphs 34 and 35 of the Commentary on Article 23 A.

Paragraph 2

4.   This paragraph provides for an exception from the provisions of paragraph 1 where the income is associated with the activity of a permanent establishment or fixed base which a resident of a Contracting State has in the other Contracting State.   The paragraph includes income from third States.   In such a case, a right to tax is given to the Contracting State in which the permanent establishment or the fixed base is situated.   Paragraph 2 does not apply to immovable property for which, according to paragraph 4 of Article 6, the State of situs has a primary right to tax (cf. paragraphs 3 and 4 of the Commentary on Article 6).   Therefore, immovable property situated in a Contracting State and forming part of the business property of a permanent establishment of an enterprise of that State situated in the other Contracting State shall be taxable only in the

first-mentioned State in which the property is situated and of which the recipient of the income is a resident. This is in consistency with the rules laid down in Articles 13 and 22 in respect of immovable property since paragraph 2 of those Articles applies only to movable property of a permanent establishment.

5.   The paragraph also covers the case where the beneficiary and the payer of the income are both residents of the same Contracting State, and the income is attributed to a permanent establishment or a fixed base, which the beneficiary of the income has in the other Contracting State. In such a case a right to tax is given to the Contracting State in which the permanent establishment or the fixed base is situated. Where double taxation occurs, the State of residence should give relief under the provisions of Article 23 A or 23 B. However a problem may arise as regards the taxation of dividends and interest in the State of residence as the State of source: the combination of Articles 7 and 23 A prevents that State from levying tax on that income, whereas if it were paid to a resident of the other State, the first State, being the State of source of the dividends or interest, could tax such dividends or interest at the rates provided for in paragraph 2 of Articles 10 and 11. Contracting States which find this position unacceptable may include in their conventions a provision according to which the State of residence would be entitled, as State of source of the dividends or interest, to levy a tax on such income at the rates provided for in paragraph 2 of Articles 10 and 11. The State where the permanent establishment is situated would give a credit for such tax on the lines of the provisions of paragraph 2 of Article 23 A or of paragraph 1 of Article 23 B; of course, this credit should not be given in cases where the State in which the permanent establishment is situated does not tax the dividends or interest attributed to the permanent establishment, in accordance with its domestic laws.

6.   Some States which apply the exemption method (Article 23 A) may have reason to suspect that the treatment accorded in paragraph 2 may provide an inducement to an enterprise of a Contracting State to attach assets such as shares, bonds or patents, to a permanent establishment situated in the other Contracting State in order to obtain more favourable tax treatment there. To counteract such arrangements which they consider would represent abuse, some States might take the view that the transaction is artificial and, for this reason, would regard the assets as not effectively connected with the permanent establishment. Some other States may strengthen their position by adding in paragraph 2 a condition providing that the paragraph shall not apply to cases where the arrangements were primarily made for the purpose of taking advantage of this provision.

Reservations on the Article

7.   *Australia, Canada, New Zealand, Portugal and Spain* reserve their positions on this Article and would wish to maintain the right to tax income arising from sources in their own country.

8.   *Sweden*, when negotiating conventions with other Member countries, would wish to retain the right to tax certain annuities and similar payments to non-residents of Sweden, where such payments are made on account of a pension insurance issued in Sweden.

9.   In negotiating conventions with other Member States, the *United Kingdom* also wishes to maintain the right to tax income paid by residents of the United Kingdom to non-residents of the United Kingdom in the form of income from a trust.

COMMENTARY ON ARTICLE 22
CONCERNING THE TAXATION OF CAPITAL

1.   This Article deals only with taxes on capital, to the exclusion of taxes on estates and inheritances and on gifts and of transfer duties.   Taxes on capital to which the Article applies are those referred to in Article 2.

2.   Taxes on capital generally constitute complementary taxation of income from capital.   Consequently, taxes on a given element of capital can be levied, in principle, only by the State which is entitled to tax the income from this element of capital.   However, it is not possible to refer purely and simply to the rules relating to the taxation of such class of income, for not all items of income are subject to taxation exclusively in one State.

3.   The Article, therefore, enumerates first property which may be taxed in the State in which they are situated.   To this category belong immovable property, referred to in Article 6 which a resident of a Contracting State owns and which is situated in the other Contracting State (paragraph 1), and movable property forming part of the business property of a permanent establishment which an enterprise of a Contracting State has in the other Contracting State, or pertaining to a fixed base which a resident of a Contracting State has in the other Contracting State for the performance of independent personal services (paragraph 2).

4.   Ships and aircraft operated in international traffic and boats engaged in inland waterways transport and movable property pertaining to the operation of such ships, boats or aircraft shall be taxable only in the State in which the place of effective management of the enterprise is situated (paragraph 3). This rule corresponds to the provisions of Article 8 and of paragraph 3 of Article 13.   It is understood that paragraph 3 of Article 8 is applicable if the place of effective management of a shipping enterprise or of an inland waterways transport enterprise is aboard a ship or boat.   Contracting States which would prefer to confer the exclusive taxing right on the State of residence or to use a combination of the residence criterion and the place of effective management criterion are free in bilateral conventions to substitute for paragraph 3 a provision corresponding to those proposed in paragraphs 2 and 3 of the Commentary on Article 8.   Immovable property pertaining to the operation of ships, boats or aircraft may be taxed in the State in which they are situated, in accordance with the rule laid down in paragraph 1.

5.   As regards elements of capital other than those listed in paragraphs 1 to 3, the Article provides that they are taxable only in the Contracting State of which the person to whom they belong is a resident (paragraph 4).

6.   If, when the provisions of paragraph 4 are applied to elements of movable property under usufruct, double taxation subsists because of the disparity between domestic laws, the States concerned may resort to the mutual agreement procedure or settle the question by means of bilateral negotiations.

7.   The Article does not provide any rule about the deductions of debts.   The laws of OECD Member countries are too different to allow a common solution for such a deduction.   The problem of the deduction of debts which could arise when the taxpayer and the creditor are not residents of the same State is dealt with in paragraph 5 of Article 24.

SPECIAL DEROGATION

8.   In view of its particular situation in relation to shipping, *Greece* will retain its freedom of action with regard to the provisions in the Convention relating to profits from the operation of ships in international traffic, to remuneration of crews of such ships, to capital represented by ships in international traffic and by movable property pertaining to the operation of such ships, and to capital gains from the alienation of such ships and assets.

RESERVATIONS ON THE ARTICLE

9.   *Finland* reserves the right to tax shares or other corporate rights in Finnish companies, where the ownership of such shares or other corporate rights entitles to the enjoyment of immovable property situated in Finland and owned by the company.

10.   *New Zealand* and *Portugal* reserve their positions on this Article if and when they impose taxes on capital.

11.   The *United Kingdom* reserves its position on this Article pending the introduction of a wealth tax.

COMMENTARY ON ARTICLES 23 A AND 23 B
CONCERNING THE METHODS FOR ELIMINATION
OF DOUBLE TAXATION

I. PRELIMINARY REMARKS

A. THE SCOPE OF THE ARTICLES

1.   These Articles deal with the so-called juridical double taxation where the same income or capital is taxable in the hands of the same person by more than one State.

2.   This case has to be distinguished especially from the so-called economic double taxation, i.e. where two different persons are taxable in respect of the same income or capital. If two States wish to solve problems of economic double taxation, they must do so in bilateral negotiations.

3.   International juridical double taxation may arise in three cases:

   a)   where each Contracting State subjects the same person to tax on his worldwide income or capital (concurrent full liability to tax, cf. paragraph 4 below);

   b)   where a person is a resident of a Contracting State (R)[1] and derives income from, or owns capital in, the other Contracting State (S or E) and both States impose tax on that income or capital (cf. paragraph 5 below);

   c)   where each Contracting State subjects the same person, not being a resident of either Contracting State to tax on income derived from, or capital owned in, a Contracting State; this may result, for instance, in the case where a non-resident person has a permanent establishment or fixed base in one Contracting State (E) through which he derives income from, or owns capital in, the other Contracting State (S) (concurrent limited tax liability, cf. paragraph 11 below).

4.   The conflict in case *a)* is reduced to that of case *b)* by virtue of Article 4. This is because that Article defines the term "resident of a Contracting State" by reference to the liability to tax of a person under domestic law by reason of his domicile, residence, place of management or any other criterion of a similar nature (paragraph 1 of Article 4) and by listing special criteria for the case of double residence to determine which of the two States is the State of residence (R) within the meaning of the Convention (paragraphs 2 and 3 of Article 4).

---

1. Throughout the Commentary on Articles 23 A and 23 B, the letter "R" stands for the State of residence within the meaning of the Convention, "S" for the State of source or situs, and "E" for the State where a permanent establishment of a fixed base is situated.

5.   The conflict in case *b*) may be solved by allocation of the right to tax between the Contracting States.   Such allocation may be made by renunciation of the right to tax either by the State of source or situs (S) or of the situation of the permanent establishment or the fixed base (E), or by the State of residence (R), or by a sharing of the right to tax between the two States.   The provisions of the Chapters III and IV of the Convention, combined with the provisions of Article 23 A or 23 B, govern such allocation.

6.   For some items of income or capital, an exclusive right to tax is given to one of the Contracting States, and the relevant Article states that the income or capital in question "shall be taxable only" in a Contracting State[1].   The words "shall be taxable only" in a Contracting State preclude the other Contracting State from taxing, thus double taxation is avoided.   The State to which the exclusive right to tax is given is normally the State of which the taxpayer is a resident within the meaning of Article 4, that is State R, but in four Articles[2] the exclusive right may be given to the other Contracting State (S) of which the taxpayer is not a resident within the meaning of Article 4.

7.   For other items of income or capital, the attribution of the right to tax is not exclusive, and the relevant Article then states that the income or capital in question "may be taxed" in the Contracting State (S or E) of which the taxpayer is not a resident within the meaning of Article 4.   In such case the State of residence (R) must give relief so to avoid the double taxation.   Paragraphs 1 and 2 of Article 23 A and paragraph 1 of Article 23 B are designed to give the necessary relief.

8.   Articles 23 A and 23 B apply to the situation in which a resident of State R derives income from, or owns capital in, the other Contracting State E or S (not being the State of residence within the meaning of the Convention) and that such income or capital, in accordance with the Convention, may be taxed in such other State E or S.   The Articles, therefore, apply only to the State of residence and do not prescribe how the other Contracting State E or S has to proceed.

9.   Where a resident of the Contracting State R derives income from the same State R through a permanent establishment or a fixed base which he has in the other Contracting State E, State E may tax such income (except income from immovable property situated in State R) if it is attributable to the said permanent establishment or fixed base (paragraph 2 of Article 21).   In this instance too, State R must give relief under Article 23 A or Article 23 B for income attributable to the permanent establishment or fixed base situated in State E, notwithstanding the fact that the income in question originally arises in State R (cf. paragraph 5 of the Commentary on Article 21).   However, where the Contracting States agree to give to State R which applies the exemption method a limited right to tax as the State of source of dividends or interest within the limits fixed in paragraph 2 of the Articles 10 or 11 (cf. paragraph 5 of the Commentary on Article 21), then the two States should also agree upon a credit to be given by State E for the tax levied by State R, on the lines of paragraph 2 of Article 23 A or of paragraph 1 of Article 23 B.

---

1. Cf. first sentence of paragraph 1 of Article 7, paragraphs 1 and 2 of Article 8, paragraph 1 of Article 12, paragraphs 2, 3 and 4 of Article 13, first sentence of paragraph 1 of Article 14, first sentence of paragraph 1 and paragraph 2 of Article 15, Article 18, paragraphs 1 and 2 of Article 19, paragraph 1 of Article 21 and paragraphs 3 and 4 of Article 22.
2. Cf. paragraphs 1 and 2 of Article 8, paragraph 3 of Article 13, sub-paragraph *a*) of paragraphs 1 and 2 of Article 19 and paragraph 3 of Article 22.

10.   Where a resident of State R derives income from a third State through a permanent establishment or a fixed base which he has in State E, such State E may tax such income (except income from immovable property situated in the third State) if it is attributable to such permanent establishment or fixed base (paragraph 2 of Article 21). State R must give relief under Article 23 A or Article 23 B in respect of income attributable to the permanent establishment or fixed base in State E. There is no provision in the Convention for relief to be given by Contracting State E for taxes levied in the third State where the income arises; however, under paragraph 4 of Article 24 any relief provided for in the domestic laws of State E (double taxation conventions excluded) for residents of State E is also to be granted to a permanent establishment in State E of an enterprise of State R (cf. paragraphs 51 to 55 of the Commentary on Article 24). Cases in which more than two States are involved (triangular cases) raise many problems in regard to which not only the convention between the States R and E but also conventions between States R and/or E with State S may come into play. It could be argued that a provision in a convention between State R and State E obliging State E to give credit or exemption for income derived from a third State leads to a more favourable treatment of the permanent establishment than is granted by State E to its own residents, and that the effect of the combined application of domestic laws and of one or more conventions may even result in double or multiple relief. It is, therefore, left to Contracting States to settle the question bilaterally either generally in a convention to be concluded between them or by way of a mutual agreement procedure (Article 25).

11.   The conflict in case *c*) of paragraph 3 above is outside the scope of the Convention as, under Article 1, it applies only to persons who are residents of one or both of the States. It can, however, be settled by applying the mutual agreement procedure (cf. also paragraph 10 above).

B.   DESCRIPTION OF METHODS FOR ELIMINATION OF DOUBLE TAXATION

12.   In the existing conventions, two leading principles are followed for the elimination of double taxation by the State of which the taxpayer is a resident. For purposes of simplicity, only income tax is referred to in what follows; but the principles apply equally to capital tax.

1. *The principle of exemption*

13.   Under the principle of exemption, the State of residence R does not tax the income which according to the Convention may be taxed in State E or S (nor, of course, also income which shall be taxable only in State E or S; cf. paragraph 6 above).

14.   The principle of exemption may be applied by two main methods:
- *a)*   the income which may be taxed in State E or S is not taken into account at all by State R for the purposes of its tax; State R is not entitled to take the income so exempted into consideration when determining the tax to be imposed on the rest of the income; this method is called "full exemption";
- *b)*   the income which may be taxed in State E or S is not taxed by State R, but State R retains the right to take that income into consideration when determining the tax to be imposed on the rest of the income; this method is called "exemption with progression".

147

2. *The principle of credit*

15.   Under the principle of credit, the State of residence R calculates its tax on the basis of the taxpayer's total income including the income from the other State E or S which, according to the Convention, may be taxed in that other State (but not including income which shall be taxable only in State S; cf. paragraph 6 above). It then allows a deduction from its own tax for the tax paid in the other State.

16.   The principle of credit may be applied by two main methods:

a)   State R allows the deduction of the total amount of tax paid in the other State on income which may be taxed in that State; this method is called "full credit";

b)   The deduction given by State R for the tax paid in the other State is restricted to that part of its own tax which is appropriate to the income which may be taxed in the other State; this method is called "ordinary credit".

17.   Fundamentally, the difference between the methods is that the exemption methods look at income, while the credit methods look at tax.

C.   OPERATION AND EFFECTS OF THE METHODS

18.   An example in figures will facilitate the explanation of the effects of the various methods.   Suppose the total income to be 100,000, of which 80,000 is derived from one State (State of residence R) and 20,000 from the other State (State of source S).   Assume that in State R the rate of tax on an income of 100,000 is 35 per cent and on an income of 80,000 is 30 per cent.   Assume further that in State S the rate of tax is either 20 per cent—case (*i*)—or 40 per cent—case (*ii*), so that the tax payable therein on 20,000 is 4,000 in case (*i*) or 8,000 in case (*ii*), respectively.

19.   If the taxpayer's total income of 100,000 arises in State R, his tax would be 35,000.   If he had an income of the same amount, but derived in the manner set out above, and if no relief is provided for in the domestic laws of State R and no conventions exists between State R and State S, then the total amount of tax would be, in case (*i*): 35,000 plus 4,000 = 39,000, and in case (*ii*): 35,000 plus 8,000 = 43,000.

1. *Exemption methods*

20.   Under the exemption methods, State R limits its taxation to that part of the total income which, in accordance with the various Articles of the Convention, it has a right to tax, i.e. 80,000.

a) *Full exemption:*

State R imposes tax on 80,000 at the rate of tax applicable to 80,000, i.e. at 30 per cent.

	Case (*i*)	Case (*ii*)
Tax in State R, 30% of 80,000	24,000	24,000
plus tax in State S	4,000	8,000
Total taxes	28,000	32,000
Relief has been given by State R in the amount of	11,000	11,000

b) *Exemption with progression:*

State R imposes tax on 80,000 at the rate of tax applicable to total income wherever it arises (100,000), i.e. at 35 per cent.

	Case (*i*)	Case (*ii*)
Tax in State R, 35% of 80,000	28,000	28,000
plus tax in State S	4,000	8,000
Total Taxes	32,000	36,000
Relief has been given by State R in the amount of	7,000	7,000

21.   In both cases, the level of tax in States S does not affect the amount of tax given up by State R.   If the tax on the income from State S is lower in State S than the relief to be given by State R—cases *a* (*i*), *a* (*ii*), and *b* (*i*)—then the taxpayer will fare better than if his total income were derived solely from State R. In the converse case—case *b* (*ii*)—the taxpayer will be worse off.

22.   The example shows also that the relief given where State R applies the full exemption method may be higher than the tax levied in State S, even if the rates of tax in State S are higher than those in State R.   This is due to the fact that under the full exemption method, not only the tax of State R on the income from State S is surrendered (35 per cent of 20,000 = 7,000; as under the exemption with progression), but that also the tax on remaining income (80,000) is reduced by an amount corresponding to the differences in rates at the two income levels in State R (35 less 30 = 5 per cent applied to 80,000 = 4,000).

2. *Credit methods*

23.   Under the credit methods, State R retains its right to tax the total income of the taxpayer, but against the tax so imposed, it allows a deduction.

a) *Full credit*

State R computes tax on total income of 100,000 at the rate of 35 per cent and allows the deduction of the tax due in State S on the income from S.

	Case (*i*)	Case (*ii*)
Tax in State R, 35% of 100,000	35,000	35,000
less tax in State S	— 4,000	— 8,000
Tax due	31,000	27,000
Total taxes	35,000	35,000
Relief has been given by State R in the amount of	4,000	8,000

b) *Ordinary credit*

State R computes tax on total income of 100,000 at the rate of 35 per cent and allows the deduction of the tax due in State S on the income from S, but in no case it allows more than the portion of tax in State R attributable to the income from S (maximum deduction).   The maximum deduction would be 35 per cent of 20,000 = 7,000.

	Case (*i*)	Case (*ii*)
Tax in State R, 35% of 100,000	35,000	35,000
less tax in State S	— 4,000	
less maximum deduction		— 7,000
Tax due	31,000	28,000
Total taxes	35,000	36,000
Relief has been given by State R in the amount of	4,000	7,000

Table I. TOTAL AMOUNT OF TAX IN THE DIFFERENT CASES ILLUSTRATED
ABOVE

A. All income arising in State R	Total tax = 35,000	
B. Income arising in two States, viz. 80,000 in State R and 20,000 in State S	Total tax if tax in State S is	
	4,000 (case *i*)	8,000 (case *ii*)
No convention (19)[1]	39,000	43,000
Full exemption (20*a*)	28,000	32,000
Exemption with progression (20*b*)	32,000	36,000
Full credit (23*a*)	35,000	35,000
Ordinary credit (23*b*)	35,000	36,000

1. Numbers in brackets refer to paragraphs in this Commentary.

Table II. AMOUNT OF TAX GIVEN UP BY THE STATE OF RESIDENCE

	If tax in State S is	
	4,000 (case *i*)	8,000 (case *ii*)
No convention	0	0
Full exemption (20*a*)[1]	11,000	11,000
Exemption with progression (20*b*)	7,000	7,000
Full credit (23*a*)	4,000	8,000
Ordinary credit (23*b*)	4,000	7,000

1. Numbers in brackets refer to paragraphs in this Commentary.

24.   A characteristic of the credit methods compared with the exemption methods is that State R is never obliged to allow a deduction of more than the tax due in State S.

25.   Where the tax due in State S is lower than the tax of State R appropriate to the income from State S (maximum deduction), the taxpayer will always have to pay the same amount of taxes as he would have had to pay if he were taxed only in State R, i.e. as if his total income were derived solely from State R.

26.   The same result is achieved, where the tax due in State S is the higher, while State R applies the full credit, at least as long at the total tax due to State R is as high or higher than the amount of the tax due in State S.

27.   Where the tax due in State S is higher and where the credit is limited (ordinary credit), the taxpayer will not get a deduction for the whole of the tax paid in State S. In such event the result would be less favourable to the taxpayer than if his whole income arose in State R, and in these circumstances the ordinary credit method would have the same effect as the method of exemption with progression.

D. THE METHODS PROPOSED IN THE ARTICLES

28.   In the conventions concluded between OECD Member countries both leading principles have been followed. Some States have a preference for the first one, some for the other. Theoretically a single principle could be held to be more desirable, but, on account of the preferences referred to, each State has been left free to make its own choice.

29.   On the other hand, it has been found important to limit the number of methods based on each leading principle to be employed. In view of this limitation, the Articles have been drafted so that Member countries are left free to choose between two methods:

— the exemption method with progression (Article 23 A), and
— the ordinary credit method (Article 23 B).

30.   If two Contracting States both adopt the same method, it will be sufficient to insert the relevant Article in the convention. On the other hand, if the two Contracting States adopt different methods, both Articles may be amalgamated in one, and the name of the State must be inserted in each appropriate part of the Article, according to the method adopted by that State.

31.   Contracting States may use a combination of the two methods. Such combination is indeed necessary for a Contracting State R which generally adopts the exemption method in the case of income which under Articles 10 and 11 may be subjected to a limited tax in the other Contracting State S. For such case, Article 23 A provides in paragraph 2 a credit for the limited tax levied in the other Contracting State S. Moreover, States which in general adopt the exemption method may wish to exclude specific items of income from exemption and to apply to such items the credit method. In such case, paragraph 2 of Article 23 A could be amended to include these items of income.

32.   The two Articles are drafted in a general way and do not give detailed rules on how the exemption or credit is to be computed, this being left to the domestic laws and practice applicable. Contracting States which find it necessary to settle any problem in the convention itself are left free to do so in bilateral negotiations.

II.   COMMENTARY ON THE PROVISIONS OF ARTICLE 23A
(EXEMPTION METHOD)

Paragraph 1

A.   THE OBLIGATION OF THE STATE OF RESIDENCE TO GIVE EXEMPTION

33.   In the Article it is laid down that the State of residence R shall exempt from tax income and capital, which in accordance with the Convention "may be taxed" in the other State E or S.

34.   The State of residence must accordingly give exemption whether or not the right to tax is in effect exercised by the other State. This method is regarded as the most practical one since it relieves the State of residence from undertaking investigations of the actual taxation position in the other State.

35.   Occasionally, negotiating States may find it reasonable in certain circumstances to make an exception to the absolute obligation on the State of residence to give exemption. Such may be the case, in order to avoid non-taxation, where under the domestic laws of the State of source no tax on specific items of income or capital is provided, or tax is not effectively collected owing to special circumstances such as the set-off of losses, a mistake, or the statutory time limit having expired. To avoid non-taxation of specific items of income, Contracting States may agree to amend the relevant Article itself (cf. paragraph 4 of the Commentary on Article 15 and paragraph 5 of the Commentary on Article 17; for

the converse case where relief in the State of source is subject to actual taxation in the State of residence, cf. paragraph 20 of the Commentary on Article 10, paragraph 10 of the Commentary on Article 11, paragraph 6 of the Commentary on Article 12, paragraph 21 of the Commentary on Article 13 and paragraph 3 of the Commentary on Article 21). One might also make an exception to the general rule, in order to achieve a certain reciprocity, where one of the States adopts the exemption method and the other the credit method. Finally, another exception to the general rule may be made where a State wishes to apply to specific items of income the credit method rather than exemption (cf. paragraph 31 above).

36. As already mentioned in paragraph 31 above, the exemption method does not apply to such items of income which according to the Convention may be taxed in the State of residence but may also be subjected to a limited tax in the other Contracting State. For such items of income, paragraph 2 of Article 23A provides for the credit method (cf. paragraph 47 below).

B. ALTERNATIVE FORMULATION OF THE ARTICLE

37. An effect of the exemption method as it is drafted in the Article is that the taxable income or capital in the State of residence is reduced by the amount exempted in that State. If in a particular State the amount of income as determined for income tax purposes is used as a measure for other purposes, e.g. social benefits, the application of the exemption method in the form proposed may have the effect that such benefits may be given to persons who ought not to receive them. To avoid such consequences, the Article may be altered so that the income in question is included in the taxable income in the State of residence. The State of residence must, in such cases, give up that part of the total tax appropriate to the income concerned. This procedure would give the same result as the Article in the form proposed. States can be left free to make such modifications in the drafting of the Article. If a State wants to draft the Article as indicated above, paragraph 1 may be drafted as follows:

"Where a resident of a Contracting State derives income or owns capital which, in accordance with the provisions of this Convention, shall be taxable only or may be taxed in the other Contracting State, the first mentioned State shall, subject to the provisions of paragraph 2, allow as a deduction from the income tax or capital tax that part of the income tax or capital tax, respectively, which is applicable, as the case may be, to the income derived from or the capital owned in that other State."

If the Article is so drafted, paragraph 3 would not be necessary and could be omitted.

C. MISCELLANEOUS PROBLEMS

38. Article 23A contains the principle that the State of residence has to give exemption, but does not give detailed rules on how the exemption has to be implemented. This is consistent with the general pattern of the Convention. Articles 6 to 22 too lay down rules attributing the right to tax in respect of the various types of income or capital without dealing, as a rule, with the determination of taxable income or capital, deductions, rate of tax, etc. (cf., however, paragraph 3 of Article 7 and Article 24). Experience has shown that many problems may arise. This is especially true with respect to Article 23A. Some of them are dealt with in the following paragraphs. In the absence of a specific

provision in the Convention, the domestic laws of each Contracting State are applicable. Some conventions contain an express reference to the domestic laws but of course this would not help where the exemption method is not used in the domestic laws. In such cases, Contracting States which face this problem should establish rules for the application of Article 23A, if necessary, after having consulted with the competent authority of the other Contracting State (paragraph 3 of Article 25).

1. *Amount to be exempted*

39.   The amount of income to be exempted from tax by the State of residence is the amount which, but for the Convention, would be subjected to domestic income tax according to the domestic laws governing such tax. It may, therefore, differ from the amount of income subjected to tax by the State of source according to its domestic laws.

40.   Normally, the basis for the calculation of income tax is the total net income, i.e. gross income less allowable deductions. Therefore, it is the gross income derived from the State of source less any allowable deductions (specified or proportional) connected with such income which is to be exempted.

41.   Problems arise from the fact that most countries provide in their respective taxation laws for additional deductions from total income or specific items of income to arrive at the income subject to tax. A numerical example may illustrate the problem:

a)	Domestic income (gross less allowable expenses)	100
b)	Income from the other State (gross less allowable expenses)	100
c)	Total income	200
d)	Deductions for other expenses provided for under the laws of the State of residence which are not connected with any of the income under a or b, such as insurance premiums, contributions to welfare institutions	—20
e)	"Net" income	180
f)	Personal and family allowances	—30
g)	Income subject to tax	150

The question is, what amount should be exempted from tax, e.g.

—   100 (line *b*), leaving a taxable amount of 50;
—   90 (half of line *e*, according to the ratio between line *b* and line *c*), leaving 60 (line *f* being fully deducted from domestic income);
—   75 (half of line *g*, according to the ratio between line *b* and line *c*), leaving 75;
— or any other amount.

42.   A comparison of the laws and practices of the OECD Member countries shows that the amount to be exempted varies considerably from country to country. The solution adopted by a State will depend on the policy followed by that State and its tax structure. It may be the intention of a State that its residents always enjoy the full benefit of their personal and family allowances and other deductions. In other States these tax free amounts are apportioned. In

many States personal or family allowances form part of the progressive scale, are granted as a deduction from tax, or are even unknown, the family status being taken into account by separate tax scales.

43.   In view of the wide variety of fiscal policies and techniques in the different States regarding the determination of tax, especially deductions, allowances and similar benefits, it is preferable not to propose an express and uniform solution in the Convention, but to leave each State free to apply its own legislation and technique.   Contracting States which prefer to have special problems solved in their convention are, of course, free to do so in bilateral negotiations.   Finally, attention is drawn to the fact that the problem is also of importance for States applying the credit method (cf. paragraph 62 below).

2.   *Treatment of losses*

44.   Several States in applying Article 23A treat losses incurred in the other State in the same manner as they treat income arising in that State: as State of residence (State R), they do not allow deduction of a loss incurred from immovable property or a permanent establishment situated in the other State (E or S).   Provided that this other State allows carry over of such loss, the taxpayer will not be at any disadvantage as he is merely prevented from claiming a double deduction of the same loss namely in State E (or S) and in State R. Other States may, as State of residence R, allow a loss incurred in State E (or S) as a deduction from the income they assess.   In such a case State R should be free to restrict the exemption under paragraph 1 of Article 23A for profits or income which are made subsequently in the other State E (or S) by deducting from such subsequent profits or income the amount of earlier losses which the taxpayer can carry over in State E (or S).   As the solution depends primarily on the domestic laws of the Contracting States and as the laws of the OECD Member countries differ from each other substantially, no solution can be proposed in the Article itself, it being left to the Contracting States, if they find it necessary, to clarify the above-mentioned question and other problems connected with losses (cf. paragraph 62 below for the credit method) bilaterally, either in the Article itself or by way of a mutual agreement procedure (paragraph 3 of Article 25).

3.   *Taxation of the rest of income*

45.   Apart from the application of progressive tax rates which is now dealt with in paragraph 3 of the Article (cf. paragraphs 55 and 56 below), some problems may arise from specific provisions of the tax laws.   Thus, e.g. some tax laws provide that taxation starts only if a minimum amount of taxable income is reached or exceeded (tax exempt threshold).   Total income before application of the Convention may clearly exceed such tax free threshold; but by virtue of the exemption resulting from the application of the Convention which leads to a deduction of the tax exempt income from total taxable income, the remaining taxable income may be reduced to an amount below this threshold.   For the reasons mentioned in paragraph 43 above, no uniform solution can be proposed. It may be noted, however, that the problem will not arise, if the alternative formulation of paragraph 1 of Article 23A (as set out in paragraph 37 above) is adopted.

46.   Certain States have introduced special systems for taxing corporate income (cf. paragraphs 36 to 65 of the Commentary on Article 10).   In States applying

a split rate corporation tax (paragraph 39 of the said Commentary), the problem may arise whether the income to be exempted has to be deducted from undistributed income (to which the normal rate of tax applies) or from distributed income (to which the reduced rate applies) or whether the income to be exempted has to be attributed partly to distributed and partly to undistributed income. Where, under the laws of a State applying the split rate corporation tax, a supplementary tax is levied in the hands of a parent company on dividends which it received from a domestic subsidiary company but which it does not redistribute (on the grounds that such supplementary tax is a compensation for the benefit of a lower tax rate granted to the subsidiary on the distributions), the problem arises, whether such supplementary tax may be charged where the subsidiary pays its dividends out of income exempt from tax by virtue of the Convention. Finally a similar problem may arise in connection with taxes ("précompte", Advance Corporation Tax) which are levied on distributed profits of a corporation in order to cover the tax credit attributable to the shareholders (cf. paragraph 43 of the Commentary on Article 10). The question is whether such special taxes connected with the distribution of profits, could be levied insofar as distributions are made out of profits exempt from tax. It is left to Contracting States to settle these questions by bilateral negotiations.

Paragraph 2

47.   In Articles 10 and 11 the right to tax dividends and interest is divided between the State of residence and the State of source. In these cases, the State of residence is left free not to tax if it wants to do so (cf. e.g. paragraphs 70 to 76 below) and to apply the exemption method also to the above-mentioned items of income. However, where the State of residence prefers to make use of its right to tax such items of income, it cannot apply the exemption method to eliminate the double taxation since it would thus give up fully its right to tax the income concerned. For the State of residence, the application of the credit method would normally seem to give a satisfactory solution. Moreover, as already indicated in paragraph 31 above, States which in general apply the exemption method may wish to apply to specific items of income the credit method rather than exemption. Consequently, the paragraph is drafted in accordance with the ordinary credit method. The Commentary on Article 23B hereafter applies mutatis mutandis to paragraph 2 of Article 23A.

48.   In the cases referred to in the previous paragraph, certain maximum percentages are laid down for tax reserved to the State of source. In such cases, the rate of tax in the State of residence will very often be higher than the rate in the State of source. The limitation of the deduction which is laid down in the second sentence of paragraph 2 and which is in accordance with the ordinary credit method is therefore of consequence only in a limited number of cases. If, in such cases, the Contracting States prefer to waive the limitation and to apply the full credit method, they can do so by deleting the second sentence of paragraph 2 (cf. also paragraph 63 below).

DIVIDENDS FROM SUBSTANTIAL HOLDINGS BY A COMPANY

49.   The combined effect of paragraphs 1 and 2 of Article 10 and Article 23 (Article 23A and 23B as appropriate) is that the State of residence of the shareholder is allowed to tax dividends arising in the other State, but that it must credit against its own tax on such dividends the tax which has been collected by

the State where the dividends arise at a rate fixed under paragraph 2 of Article 10. This regime equally applies when the recipient of the dividends is a parent company receiving dividends from a subsidiary; in this case, the tax withheld in the State of the subsidiary—and credited in the State of the parent company— is limited to 5 per cent of the gross amount of the dividends by the application of sub-paragraph *a*) of paragraph 2 of Article 10.

50.   These provisions effectively avoid the juridical double taxation of dividends but they do not prevent recurrent corporate taxation on the profits distributed to the parent company: first at the level of the subsidiary and again at the level of the parent company.   Such recurrent taxation creates a very important obstacle to the development of international investment.   Many States have recognised this and have inserted in their domestic laws provisions designed to avoid this obstacle.   Moreover, provisions to this end are frequently inserted in double taxation conventions.

51.   The Committee on Fiscal Affairs has considered whether it would be appropriate to modify Article 23 of the Convention in order to settle this question. Although many States favoured the insertion of such a provision in the Model Convention this met with many difficulties, resulting from the diverse opinions of States and the variety of possible solutions.   Some States, fearing tax evasion, preferred to maintain their freedom of action and to settle the question only in their domestic laws.

52.   In the end, it appeared preferable to leave States free to choose their own solution to the problem.   For States preferring to solve the problem in their conventions, the solutions would most frequently follow one of the principles below:

a)   *Exemption with progression*

The State of which the parent company is a resident exempts the dividends it receives from its subsidiary in the other State, but it may nevertheless take these dividends into account in computing the tax due by the parent company on the remaining income (such a provision will frequently be favoured by States applying the exemption method specified in Article 23A).

b)   *Credit for underlying taxes*

As regards dividends received from the subsidiary, the State of which the parent company is a resident gives credit as provided for in paragraph 2 of Article 23A or in paragraph 1 of Article 23B, as appropriate, not only for the tax on dividends as such, but also for the tax paid by the subsidiary on the profits distributed (such a provision will frequently be favoured by States applying as a general rule the credit method specified in Article 23B).

c)   *Assimilation to a holding in a domestic subsidiary*

The dividends that the parent company derives from a foreign subsidiary are treated, in the State of the parent company, in the same way for tax purposes as dividends received from a subsidiary which is a resident of that State.

53.   When the State of the parent company levies taxes on capital, a similar solution should also be applied to such taxes.

54.   Moreover, States are free to fix the limits and methods of application of these provisions (definition and minimum duration of holding of the shares, proportion of the dividends deemed to be taken up by administrative or financial expenses) or to make the relief granted under the special regime subject to the condition that the subsidiary is carrying out a genuine economic activity in the State of which it is a resident, or that it derives the major part of its income from that State or that it is subject to a substantial taxation on profits therein.

Paragraph 3

55.   The 1963 Draft Convention reserved expressly the application of the progressive scale of tax rates by the State of residence (last sentence of paragraph 1 of Article 23A) and most conventions concluded between OECD Member countries, which adopt the exemption method follow this principle. According to paragraph 3 of Article 23A, as amended, the State of residence retains the right to take the amount of exempted income or capital into consideration when determining the tax to be imposed on the rest of the income or capital. The rule applies even where the exempted income (or items of capital) and the taxable income (or items of capital) accrue to those persons (e.g. husband and wife) whose incomes (or items of capital) are taxed jointly according to the domestic laws. This principle of progression applies to income or capital exempted by virtue of paragraph 1 of Article 23A as well as to income or capital which under any other provision of the Convention "shall be taxable only" in the other Contracting State (cf. paragraph 6 above). This is the reason why the principle of progression is transferred from paragraph 1 of Article 23A to a new paragraph 3 of the said Article, and reference is made to exemption "in accordance with any provision of the Convention".

56.   Paragraph 3 of Article 23A relates only to the State of residence. The form of the Article does not prejudice the application by the State of source of the provisions of its domestic laws concerning the progression.

III.   COMMENTARY ON THE PROVISIONS OF ARTICLE 23B (CREDIT METHOD)

Paragraph 1

A.   METHODS

57.   Article 23B based on the credit principle, follows the ordinary credit method: the State of residence (R) allows, as a deduction from its own tax on the income or capital of its resident, an amount equal to the tax paid in the other State E (or S) on the income derived from, or capital owned in, that other State E (or S), but the deduction is restricted to the appropriate proportion of its own tax.

58.   The ordinary credit method is intended to apply also for a State which follows the exemption method but has to give credit, under paragraph 2 of Article 23A, for the tax levied at limited rates in the other State on dividends and interest (cf. paragraph 47 above). The possibility of some modification as mentioned in paragraphs 47 and 48 above (full credit) could, of course, also be of relevance in the case of dividends and interest paid to a resident of a State which adopted the ordinary credit method (cf. also paragraph 63 below).

59.   It is to be noted that Article 23B applies in a State R only to items of income or capital which, in accordance with the Convention, "may be taxed" in the other State E (or S).   Items of income or capital which according to Article 8, to paragraph 3 of Article 13, to sub-paragraph *a*) of paragraphs 1 and 2 of Article 19 and to paragraph 3 of Article 22, "shall be taxable only" in the other State, are from the outset exempt from tax in State R (cf. paragraph 6 above), and the Commentary on Article 23A applies to such exempted income and capital.   As regards progression, reference is made to paragraph 2 of the Article (and paragraph 77 below).

60.   Article 23B sets out the main rules of the credit method, but does not give detailed rules on the computation and operation of the credit.   This is consistent with the general pattern of the Convention.   Experience has shown that many problems may arise.   Some of them are dealt with in the following paragraphs.   In many States, detailed rules on credit for foreign tax already exist in their domestic laws.   A number of conventions, therefore, contain a reference to the domestic laws of the Contracting States and further provide that such domestic rules shall not affect the principle laid down in Article 23B.   Where the credit method is not used in the domestic laws of a Contracting State, this State should establish rules for the application of Article 23B, if necessary after consultation with the competent authority of the other Contracting State (paragraph 3 of Article 25).

61.   The amount of foreign tax for which a credit has to be allowed is the tax effectively paid in accordance with the Convention in the other Contracting State.   Problems may arise, e.g. where such tax is not calculated on the income of the year for which it is levied but on the income of a preceding year or on the average income of two of more preceding years.   Other problems may arise in connection with different methods of determining the income or in connection with changes in the currency rates (devaluation or revaluation).   However, such problems could hardly be solved by an express provision in the Convention.

62.   According to the provisions of the second sentence of paragraph 1 of Article 23B, the deduction which the State of residence (R) is to allow is restricted to that part of the income tax which is appropriate to the income derived from the State S, or E (so-called "maximum deduction").   Such maximum deduction may be computed either by apportioning the total tax on total income according to the ratio between the income for which credit is to be given and the total income, or by applying the tax rate for total income to the income for which credit is to be given.   In fact, in cases where the tax in State E (or S) equals or exceeds the appropriate tax of State R, the credit method will have the same effect as the exemption method with progression.   Also under the credit method, similar problems as regards the amount of income, tax rate, etc. may arise as are mentioned in the Commentary on Article 23A (cf. especially paragraphs 39 to 41 and 44 above).   For the same reasons mentioned in paragraphs 42 and 43 above, it is preferable also for the credit method, not to propose an express and uniform solution in the Convention, but to leave each State free to apply its own legislation and technique.   This is also true for some further problems which are dealt with below.

63.   The maximum deduction is normally computed as the tax on net income, i.e. on the income from State E (or S) less allowable deductions (specified or proportional) connected with such income (cf. paragraph 40 above).   For such reason, the maximum deduction in many cases may be lower than the tax

effectively paid in State E (or S). This may especially be true in the case where, for instance, a resident of State R deriving interest from State S has borrowed funds from a third person to finance the interest-producing loan. As the interest due on such borrowed money may be offset against the interest derived from State S, the amount of net income subject to tax in State R may be very small, or there may even be no net income at all. This problem could be solved by using the full credit method in State R as mentioned in paragraph 48 above. Another solution would be to exempt such income from tax in State S, as it is proposed in the Commentary in respect of interest on credit sales and on loans granted by banks (cf. paragraph 15 of the Commentary on Article 11).

64.   If a resident of State R derives income of different kinds from State S, and the latter State, according to its tax laws imposes tax only on one of these items, the maximum deduction which State R is to allow will normally be that part of its tax which is appropriate only to that item of income which is taxed in State S. However, other solutions are possible, especially in view of the following broader problem: the fact that credit has to be given, e.g. for several items of income on which tax at different rates is levied in State S, or for income from several States, with of without conventions, raises the question whether the maximum deduction or the credit has to be calculated separately for each item of income, or for each country, or for all foreign income qualifying for credit under domestic laws and under conventions. Under an "overall credit" system, all foreign income is aggregated, and the total of foreign taxes is credited against the domestic tax appropriate to the total foreign income.

65.   Further problems may arise in case of losses. A resident of State R, deriving income from State E (or S), may have a loss in State R, or in State E (or S) or in a third State. For purposes of the tax credit, in general, a loss in a given State will be set off against other income from the same State. Whether a loss suffered outside State R (e.g. in a permanent establishment) may be deducted from other income, whether derived from State R or not depends on the domestic laws of State R. Here similar problems may arise, as mentioned in the Commentary on Article 23A (paragraph 44 above). When the total income is derived from abroad, and no income but a loss not exceeding the income from abroad arises in State R, then the total tax charged in State R will be appropriate to the income from State S, and the maximum deduction which State R is to allow will consequently be the tax charged in State R. Other solutions are possible.

66.   The aforementioned problems depend very much on domestic laws and practice, and the solution must, therefore, be left to each State. In this context, it may be noted that some States are very liberal in applying the credit method. Some States are also considering or have already adopted the possibility of carrying over unused tax credits. Contracting States are, of course, free in bilateral negotiations to amend the Article to deal with any of the aforementioned problems.

67.   As regards dividends from a substantial holding by a company, reference is made to paragraphs 49 to 54 above.

B.   REMARKS CONCERNING CAPITAL TAX

68.   As paragraph 1 is drafted, credit is to be allowed for income tax only against income tax and for capital tax only against capital tax. Consequently,

credit for or against capital tax will be given only if there is a capital tax in both Contracting States.

69.   In bilateral negotiations, two Contracting States may agree that a tax called a capital tax is of a nature closely related to income tax and may, therefore, wish to allow credit for it against income tax and vice versa.   There are cases where because one State does not impose a capital tax or because both States impose capital taxes only on domestic assets, no double taxation of capital will arise. In such cases it is, of course, understood that the reference to capital taxation may be deleted.   Furthermore, States may find it desirable, regardless of the nature of the taxes under the convention, to allow credit for the total amount of tax in the State of source or situs against the total amount of tax in the State of residence.   Where, however, a convention includes both real capital taxes and capital taxes which are in their nature income taxes, the States may wish to allow credit against income tax only for the latter capital taxes.   In such cases, States are free to alter the proposed Article so as to achieve the desired effect.

C.   THE RELATION IN SPECIAL CASES BETWEEN THE TAXATION IN THE STATE OF SOURCE AND THE ORDINARY CREDIT METHOD

70.   In certain cases a State, especially a developing country, may for particular reasons give concessions to taxpayers, e.g. tax incentive reliefs to encourage industrial output.   In a similar way, a State may exempt from tax certain kinds of income, e.g. pensions to war wounded soldiers.

71.   When such a State concludes a convention with a State which applies the exemption method, no restriction of the relief given to the taxpayers arises, because that other State must give exemption regardless of the amount of tax, if any, imposed in the State of source (see paragraph 34 above).   But when the other State applies the credit method, the concession may be nullified to the extent that such other State will allow a deduction only of the tax paid in the State of source.   By reason of the concessions, that other State secures what may be called an uncovenanted gain for its own Exchequer.

72.   Should the two States agree that the benefit of the concessions given to the taxpayers in the State of source are not to be nullified, a derogation from paragraph 2 of Article 23A, or from Article 23B will be necessary.

73.   Various formulae can be used to this effect as for example:
  a)   the State of residence will allow as a deduction the amount of tax which the State of source could have imposed in accordance with its general legislation or such amount as limited by the Convention (e.g. limitations of rates provided for dividends and interest in Articles 10 and 11) even if the State of source, as a developing country, has waived all or part of that tax under special provisions for the promotion of its economic development;
  b)   as a counterpart for the tax sacrifice which the developing country makes by reducing in a general way its tax at the source, the State of residence agrees to allow a deduction against its own tax of an amount (in part fictitious) fixed at a higher rate;
  c)   the State of residence exempts the income which has benefited from tax incentives in the developing country.

Contracting States are free to devise other formulae in the course of bilateral negotiations.

74.   If a Contracting State agrees to stimulate especially investments in the other State being a developing country, the above provisions will generally be accompanied by guarantees for the investors, that is to say, the convention will limit the rate of tax which can be imposed in the State of source on dividends, interest and royalties.

75.   Moreover, time restrictions or time limits can be provided for the application of the advantages referred to in formula *a*), and possibly *c*), above: the extended credit (or the exemption) may be granted only in respect of incentives applied temporarily in developing countries, or only for investments made or contracts concluded in the future (for instance, from the date of entry into force of the convention) or for a determined period of time.

76.   Thus, there exists a considerable number of solutions to this problem. In fact, the concrete effects of the provisions concerned can also vary as a result of other factors such as the amount to be included in the taxable income in the State of residence (formulae *a*) and *b*) above); it may be the net income derived (after deduction of the tax effectively paid in the State of source), or the net income grossed-up by an amount equal to the tax effectively paid in the State of source, or to the tax which could have been levied in accordance with the convention (rates provided for in Articles 10 and 11) or to the tax which the State of residence agrees to allow as a deduction.

Paragraph 2

77.   This paragraph has been added to enable the State of residence to retain the right to take the amount of income or capital exempted in that State into consideration when determining the tax to be imposed on the rest of the income or capital. The right so retained extends to income or capital which "shall be taxable only" in the other State. The principle of progression is thus safeguarded for the State of residence, not only in relation to income or capital which "may be taxed" in the other State, but also for income or capital which "shall be taxable only" in that other State. The Commentary on paragraph 3 of Article 23A in relation to the State of source also applies to paragraph 2 of Article 23B.

COMMENTARY ON ARTICLE 24
CONCERNING NON-DISCRIMINATION

Paragraph 1

1.   This paragraph establishes the principle that for purposes of taxation discrimination on the grounds of nationality is forbidden, and that, subject to reciprocity, the nationals of a Contracting State may not be less favourably treated in the other Contracting State than nationals of the latter State in the same circumstances.

2.   It is noteworthy that the principle of non-discrimination, under various descriptions and with a more or less wide scope, was applied in international fiscal relations well before the appearance, at the end of the 19th Century, of the classic type of double taxation conventions. Thus, in a great many agreements of different kinds (consular or establishment conventions, treaties of friendship or commerce, etc.) concluded by States, especially in the 19th Century, in order to extend and strengthen the diplomatic protection of their nationals wherever resident, there are clauses under which each of the two Contracting States undertakes to accord nationals of the other State equality of treatment with its own nationals. The fact that such clauses subsequently found their way into double taxation conventions has in no way affected their original justification and scope. The text of paragraph 1 provides that the application of this paragraph is not restricted by Article 1 to nationals solely who are residents of a Contracting State, but on the contrary, extends to all nationals of each Contracting State, whether or not they be residents of one of them. In other words, all nationals of a Contracting State are entitled to invoke the benefit of this provision as against the other Contracting State. This holds good, in particular, for nationals of the Contracting States who are not residents of either of them but of a third State.

3.   The expression "in the same circumstances" refers to taxpayers (individuals, legal persons, partnerships and associations) placed, from the point of view of the application of the ordinary taxation laws and regulations, in substantially similar circumstances both in law and in fact.

4.   Consequently if a Contracting State, in giving relief from taxation on account of family responsibilities, distinguishes between its own nationals according to whether they reside in its territory or not, that State cannot be obliged to give nationals of the other State who do not reside in its territory the same treatment as it gives its resident nationals but it undertakes to extend to them the same treatment as is available to its non-resident nationals.

5.   Likewise, the provisions of paragraph 1 are not to be construed as obliging a State which accords special taxation privileges to its own public bodies or services as such, to extend the same privileges to the public bodies and services of the other State.

6.   Neither are they to be construed as obliging a State which accords special taxation privileges to private institutions not for profit whose activities are performed for purposes of public benefit, which are specific to that State, to extend the same privileges to similar institutions whose activities are not for its benefit.

7.   To take the first of these two cases, if a State accords immunity from taxation to its own public bodies and services, this is justified because such bodies and services are integral parts of the State and at no time can their circumstances be comparable to those of the public bodies and services of the other State.   Nevertheless, this reservation is not intended to apply to State corporations carrying on gainful undertakings.   To the extent that these can be regarded as being on the same footing as private industrial and commercial undertakings, the provisions of paragraph 1 will apply to them.

8.   As for the second case, if a State accords taxation privileges to certain private institutions not for profit, this is clearly justified by the very nature of these institutions' activities and by the benefit which that State and its nationals will derive from those activities.

9.   Furthermore, paragraph 1 has been deliberately framed in a negative form. By providing that the nationals of a Contracting State may not be subjected in the other Contracting State to any taxation or any requirement connected therewith which is other or more burdensome than the taxation and connected requirements to which nationals of the other Contracting State in the same circumstances are or may be subjected, this paragraph has the same mandatory force as if it enjoined the Contracting States to accord the same treatment to their respective nationals.   But since the principal object of this clause is to forbid discrimination in one State against the nationals of the other, there is nothing to prevent the first State from granting to persons of foreign nationality, for special reasons of its own, or in order to comply with a special stipulation in a double taxation convention, such as, notably, the requirement that profits of permanent establishments are to be taxed on the basis of separate accounts, certain concessions or facilities which are not available to its own nationals.   As it is worded, paragraph 1 would not prohibit this.

10.   Subject to the foregoing observation, the words "...shall not be subjected... to any taxation or any requirement connected therewith which is other or more burdensome..." mean that when a tax is imposed on nationals and foreigners in the same circumstances, it must be in the same form as regards both the basis of charge and the method of assessment, its rate must be the same and, finally, the formalities connected with the taxation (returns, payment, prescribed times, etc.) must not be more onerous for foreigners than for nationals.

Paragraph 2

11.   Paragraph 2 merely stipulates that the term "nationals" applies to all individuals possessing the nationality of a Contracting State.   It has not been judged necessary here to introduce into the text of the Article any considerations on the signification of the concept of nationality, any more than it seemed indispensable to make any special comment here on the meaning and application of the word.   Obviously, in determining in relation to individuals, what is meant by "the nationals of a Contracting State", reference must be made to the sense in which the term is usually employed and each State's particular rules on the acquisition or loss of nationality.

12.   But paragraph 2 is more specific as to legal persons, partnerships and associations.   By declaring that all legal persons, partnerships and associations deriving their status as such from the laws in force in a Contracting State are considered to be nationals for the purposes of paragraph 1, the provision disposes of a difficulty which often arises in determining the nationality of companies. In defining the nationality of companies, certain States have regard less to the law which governs the company than to the origin of the capital with which the company was formed or the nationality of the individuals or legal persons controlling it.

13.   Moreover, in view of the legal relationship created between the company and the State under whose law it is constituted, which from certain points of view is closely akin to the relationship of nationality in the case of individuals, it seems justifiable not to deal with legal persons, partnerships and associations in a special provision, but to assimilate them with individuals under the term "nationals".

Paragraph 3

14.   On 28th September, 1954, a number of States concluded in New York a Convention relating to the status of stateless persons, under Article 29 of which stateless persons must be accorded national treatment.   The signatories of the Convention include several OECD Member countries.

15.   It should, however, be recognised that the provisions of paragraph 3 will, in a bilateral convention, enable national treatment to be extended to stateless persons who, because they are in one of the situations enumerated in paragraph 2 of Article 1 of the above-mentioned Convention of 28th September, 1954, are not covered by that Convention.   This is mainly the case, on the one hand, of persons receiving at the time of signature of that Convention, protection or assistance from organs or agencies of the United Nations other than the United Nations High Commissioner for Refugees, and, on the other hand, of persons who are residents of a country and who there enjoy and are subject to the rights and obligations attaching to the possession of that country's nationality.

16.   The purpose of paragraph 3 is to limit the scope of the clause concerning equality of treatment with nationals of a Contracting State solely to stateless persons who are residents of that of the other Contracting State.

17.   By thus excluding stateless persons who are residents of neither Contracting State, such a clause prevents their being privileged in one State as compared with nationals of the other State.

18.   However, if States were to consider it desirable in their bilateral relations, to extend the application of paragraph 3 to all stateless persons, whether residents of a Contracting State or not, so that in all cases they enjoy the most favourable treatment accorded to nationals of the State concerned, in order to do this they would need only to adopt the following text which contains no condition as to residence in a Contracting State:

> "Notwithstanding the provisions of Article 1, stateless persons shall not be subjected in a Contracting State to any taxation or any requirement connected therewith which is other or more burdensome than the taxation and connected requirements to which nationals of that State in the same circumstances are or may be subjected."

19.   It is possible that in the future certain States will take exception to the provisions of paragraph 3 as being too liberal insofar as they entitle stateless persons who are residents of one State to claim equality of treatment not only in the other State but also in their State of residence and thus benefit in particular in the latter from the provisions of double taxation conventions concluded by it with third States. If such States wished to avoid this latter consequence, they would have to modify paragraph 3 as follows:

> "Stateless persons who are residents of a Contracting State shall not be subjected in the other Contracting State to any taxation or any requirement connected therewith which is other or more burdensome than the taxation and connected requirements to which nationals of that other State in the same circumstances are or may be subjected."

20.   Finally, it should be understood that the definition of the term "stateless person" to be used for the purposes of such a clause can only be that laid down in paragraph 1 of Article 1 of the Convention of 28th September, 1954, which defines a stateless person as "a person who is not considered as a national by any State under the operation of its law".

Paragraph 4

21.   Strictly speaking, the type of discrimination which this paragraph is designed to end is discrimination based not on nationality but on the actual situs of an enterprise. It therefore affects without distinction, and irrespective of their nationality, all residents of a Contracting State who have a permanent establishment in the other Contracting State.

22.   It appears necessary first to make it clear that the wording of the first sentence of paragraph 4 must be interpreted in the sense that it does not constitute discrimination to tax non-resident persons differently, for practical reasons, from resident persons, as long as this does not result in more burdensome taxation for the former than for the latter. In the negative form in which the provision concerned has been framed, it is the result alone which counts, it being permissible to adapt the mode of taxation to the particular circumstances in which the taxation is levied.

23.   By the terms of the first sentence of paragraph 4, the taxation of a permanent establishment shall not be less favourably levied in the State concerned than the taxation levied on enterprises of that State carrying on the same activities. The purpose of this provision is to end all discrimination in the treatment of permanent establishments as compared with resident enterprises belonging to the same sector of activities, as regards taxes based on industrial and commercial activities, and especially taxes on business profits.

24.   However, the second sentence of paragraph 4 specifies the conditions under which the principle of equal treatment set forth in the first sentence should be applied to individuals who are residents of a Contracting State and have a permanent establishment in the other State. It is designed mainly to ensure that such persons do not obtain greater advantages than residents, through entitlement to personal allowances and reliefs for family responsibilities, both in the State of which they are residents, by the application of its domestic laws, and in the other State by virtue of the principle of equal treatment. Consequently, it leaves it open to the State in which the permanent establishment is situated whether or not to give personal allowances and reliefs to the persons

165

concerned in the proportion which the amount of the permanent establishment's profits bears to the world income taxable in the other State.

25.   As regards the first sentence, experience has shown that it was difficult to define clearly and completely the substance of the principle of equal treatment and this has led to wide differences of opinion with regard to the many implications of this principle.   The main reason for difficulty seems to reside in the actual nature of the permanent establishment, which is not a separate legal entity but only a part of an enterprise that has its head office in another State.   The situation of the permanent establishment is different from that of a domestic enterprise, which constitutes a single entity all of whose activities, with their fiscal implications, can be fully brought within the purview of the State where it has its head office.   The implications of the equal treatment clause will be examined below under several aspects of the levying of tax.

A.   ASSESSMENT OF TAX

26.   With regard to the basis of assessment of tax, the principle of equal treatment normally has the following implications:

   a)   Permanent establishments must be accorded the same right as resident enterprises to deduct the trading expenses that are, in general, authorised by the taxation law to be deducted from taxable profits in addition to the right to attribute to the permanent establishment a proportion of the overheads of the head office of the enterprise.   Such deductions should be allowed without any restrictions other than those also imposed on resident enterprises.

   b)   Permanent establishments must be accorded the same facilities with regard to depreciation and reserves.   They should be entitled to avail themselves without restriction not only of the depreciation facilities which are customarily available to enterprises (straight line depreciation, declining balance depreciation), but also of the special systems that exist in a number of countries ("wholesale" writing down, accelerated depreciation, etc.).   As regards reserves, it should be noted that these are sometimes authorised for purposes other than the offsetting—in accordance with commercial accounting principles—of depreciation on assets, expenses or losses which have not yet occurred but which circumstances make likely to occur in the near future.   Thus, in certain countries, enterprises are entitled to set aside, out of taxable profit, provisions or "reserves" for investment.   When such a right is enjoyed by all enterprises, or by all enterprises in a given sector of activity, it should normally also be enjoyed, under the same conditions, by non-resident enterprises, or by all enterprises in a given sector of activity, it should in the State concerned, insofar, that is, as the activities to which such provisions or reserves would pertain are taxable in that State.

   c)   Permanent establishments should also have the option that is available in most countries to resident enterprises of carrying forward or backward a loss brought out at the close of an accounting period within a certain period of time (e.g. 5 years).   It is hardly necessary to specify that in the case of permanent establishments it is the loss on their own business activities, as shown in the separate accounts for these activities, which will qualify for such carry-forward.

   d)   Permanent establishments should further have the same rules applied to resident enterprises, with regard to the taxation of capital gains realised on the alienation of assets, whether during or on the cessation of business.

27.   Although the general rules mentioned above rarely give rise to any difficulties with regard to the principle of non-discrimination, the same does not always hold good for the tax incentive measures which most countries, faced with such problems as decentralisation of industry, development of economically backward regions, or the promotion of new activities necessary for the expansion of the economy, have introduced in order to facilitate the solution of these problems by means of tax exemptions, reductions or other tax advantages given to enterprises for investment which is in line with official objectives.

28.   As such measures are in furtherance of objectives directly related to the economic activity proper of the State concerned, it is right that the benefit of them should be extended to permanent establishments of enterprises of another State which has a double taxation convention with the first embodying the provisions of Article 24, once they have been accorded the right to engage in industrial or commercial activity in that State, either under its legislation or under an international agreement (treaties of commerce, establishment conventions, etc.) concluded between the two States.

29.   It should, however, be noted that although non-resident enterprises are entitled to claim these tax advantages in the State concerned, they must fulfil the same conditions and requirements as resident enterprises. They may, therefore, be denied such advantages if their permanent establishments are unable or refuse to fulfil the special conditions and requirements attached to the granting of them.

30.   Finally, it goes without saying that non-resident enterprises are not entitled to tax advantages attaching to activities the exercise of which is strictly reserved, on grounds of national interest, defence, protection of the national economy, etc., to domestic enterprises, since non-resident enterprises are not allowed to engage in such activities.

B. SPECIAL TREATMENT OF DIVIDENDS RECEIVED IN RESPECT OF HOLDINGS OWNED BY PERMANENT ESTABLISHMENTS

31.   In many countries special rules exist for the taxation of dividends distributed between companies (parent company-subsidiary treatment, the "Schachtelprivileg", the rule "non bis in idem"). The question arises whether such treatment should by effect · of the provisions of paragraph 4 also be enjoyed by permanent establishments in respect of dividends on holdings forming part of their assets.

32.   On this point opinions differ. Some States consider that such special treatment should be accorded to permanent establishments. They take the view that such treatment was enacted in order to avoid double taxation on profits made by a subsidiary and distributed to a parent company. In principle profits tax should be levied once, in the hands of the subsidiary performing the profit-generating activities. The parent company should be exempted from tax on such profits when received from the subsidiary or should, under the indirect credit method, be given relief for the taxation borne by the subsidiary. In cases where shares are held as direct investment by a permanent establishment the same principle implies that such a permanent establishment receiving dividends

from the subsidiary should likewise be granted the special treatment in view of the fact that a profits tax has already been levied in the hands of the subsidiary. On the other hand, it is hardly conceivable on this line of thought to leave it to the State where the head office of the parent company is situated to give relief from double taxation brought about by a second levying of tax in the State of the permanent establishment. The State of the parent company, in which no activities giving rise to the doubly taxed profits have taken place, will normally exempt the profits in question or will levy a profits tax which is not sufficient to bear a double credit (i.e. for the profits tax on the subsidiary as well as for such tax on the permanent establishment). All this assumes that the shares held by the permanent establishment are effectively connected with its activity. Furthermore, an obvious additional condition is that the profits out of which the dividends are distributed should have borne a profits tax.

33.   Other States, on the contrary, consider that assimilating permanent establishments to their own enterprises does not entail any obligation to accord such special treatment to the former. They justify their position on various grounds. The purpose of such special treatment is to avoid economic double taxation of dividends and it should be for the recipient company's State of residence and not the permanent establishment's State to bear its cost, because it is more interested in the aim in view. Another reason put forward related to the sharing of tax revenue between States. The loss of tax revenue incurred by a State in applying such special treatment is partly offset by the taxation of the dividends when they are redistributed by the parent company which has enjoyed such treatment (withholding tax on dividends, shareholder's tax). A State which accorded such treatment to permanent establishments would not have the benefit of such a compensation. Another argument made is that when such treatment is made conditional upon redistribution of the dividends its extension to permanent establishments would not be justified, for in such a case the permanent establishment, which is only a part of a company of another State and does not distribute dividends, would be more favourably treated than a resident company. Finally, the States which feel that paragraph 4 does not entail any obligation to extend such treatment to permanent establishments argue that there is a risk that companies of one State might transfer their holdings in companies of another State to their permanent establishments in that other State for the sole purpose of availing themselves of such treatment.

34.   The fact remains that there can be very valid reasons for a holding being owned and managed by a permanent establishment rather than by the head office of the enterprise, viz.,

— reasons of necessity arising principally from a legal or regulatory obligation on banks and financial institutions and insurance companies to keep deposited in countries where they operate a certain amount of assets, particularly shares, as security for the performance of their obligations;

— or reasons of expediency, where the holdings are in companies which have business relations with the permanent establishment or whose head offices are situated in the same country as the permanent establishment;

— or simple reasons of practical convenience, in line with the present tendency towards decentralisation of management functions in large enterprises.

35.   In view of these divergent attitudes, as well as of the existence of the situations just described, it would be advisable for States, when concluding bilateral conventions, to make clear the interpretation they give to the first sentence of paragraph 4.   They can, if they so desire, explain their position, or change it as compared with their previous practice, in a protocol or any other document annexed to the convention.

36.   A solution could also be provided in such a document to meet the objection mentioned above that the extension of the treatment of holdings in a State (A) to permanent establishments of companies which are residents of another State (B) results in such companies unduly enjoying privileged treatment as compared with other companies which are residents of the same State and whose head offices own holdings in the capital of companies which are residents of State A, in that whereas the dividends on their holdings can be repatriated by the former companies without bearing withholding tax, such tax is levied on dividends distributed to the latter companies at the rate of 5 or 15 per cent as the case may be.   Tax neutrality and the equality of tax burdens as between permanent establishments and subsidiary companies, as advocated by the States concerned, could be ensured by adapting, in the bilateral convention between States A and B, the provisions of paragraphs 2 and 4 of Article 10, so as to enable withholding tax to be levied in State A on dividends paid by companies which are residents of that State to permanent establishments of companies which are residents of State B in the same way as if they are received directly i.e. by the head offices of the latter companies, viz., at the rate of:

— 5 per cent in the case of a holding of at least 25 per cent;
— 15 per cent in all other cases.

37.   Should it not be possible, because of the absence of appropriate provisions in the domestic laws of the State concerned to levy a withholding tax there on dividends paid to permanent establishments, the treatment of inter-company dividends could be extended to permanent establishments, as long as its application is limited in such manner that the tax levied by the State of source of the dividends is the same whether the dividends are received by a permanent establishment of a company which is a resident of the other State or are received directly by such a company.

C.   STRUCTURE AND RATE OF TAX

38.   In countries where enterprises, mainly companies, are charged a tax on their profits which is specific to them, the provisions of paragraph 4 raise, with regard to the rate applicable in the case of permanent establishments, especially difficult and delicate problems, which here too arise from the fact that the permanent establishment is only a part of a legal entity which is not under the jurisdiction of the State where the permanent establishment is situated.

39.   When the taxation of profits made by companies which are residents of a given State is calculated according to a progressive scale of rates, such a scale should, in principle, be applied to permanent establishments situated in that State.   If in applying the progressive scale, the permanent establishment's State takes into account the profits of the whole company to which such a permanent establishment belongs, such a rule would not appear to conflict with the equal treatment rule, since resident companies are in fact treated in the same way (cf. paragraphs 55, 56 and 77 of the Commentary on Articles 23A and 23B).   States

that tax their own companies in this way could therefore define in their bilateral conventions the treatment applicable to permanent establishments.

40.   When a system of taxation based on a progressive scale of rates includes a rule that a minimum rate is applicable to permanent establishments, it cannot be claimed a priori that such a rule is incompatible with the equal treatment principle. The profits of the whole enterprise to which the permanent establishment belongs should be taken into account in determining the rate applicable according to the progressive scale. The provisions of the first sentence of paragraph 4 are not observed only if the minimum rate is higher.

41.   However, even if the profits of the whole enterprise to which the permanent establishment belongs is taken into account when applying either a progressive scale of rates or a minimum rate, this should not conflict with the principle of the distinct and separate enterprise, according to which the profits of the permanent establishment must be determined under paragraph 2 of Article 7. The minimum amount of the tax levied in the State where the permanent establishment is situated is, therefore, the amount which would be due if it were a distinct and separate enterprise, without reference to the profits of the whole enterprise to which it belongs. The State where the permanent establishment is situated is, therefore, justified in applying the progressive scale applicable to resident enterprises solely to the profits of the permanent establishment, leaving aside the profits of the whole enterprise when the latter are less than those of the permanent establishment. This State may likewise tax the profits of the permanent establishment at a minimum rate, provided that the same rate applies also to resident enterprises, even if taking into account the profits of the whole enterprise to which it belongs would result in a lower amount of tax, or no tax at all.

42.   As regards the split-rate system of company tax, it should first be pointed out as being a fact central to the issue here that most OECD Member countries which have adopted this system do not consider themselves bound by the provisions of paragraph 4 to extend it to permanent establishments of non-resident companies. This attitude is based, in particular, on the view that the split-rate is only one element amongst others (in particular a withholding tax on distributed income) in a system of taxing company profits and dividends which must be considered as a whole and is therefore, both for legal and technical reasons, of domestic application only. The State where the permanent establishment is situated could claim the right not to tax such profits at the reduced rate as, generally, it does not tax the dividends distributed by the company to which the permanent establishment belongs. Moreover, a State which has adopted a split-rate system usually has other economic policy objectives, such as the promotion of the capital market, by encouraging resident companies to distribute dividends. The extension of the reduced rate to the profits of the permanent establishment would not serve such a purpose at all, as the company distributing the dividends is not a resident of the State concerned.

43.   This view is, however, disputed. The States in favour of extending the split-rate system to permanent establishments urge that as the essential feature of this system is a special technique of taxing profits which enterprises in a corporate form derive from their activities, and is designed to afford immediate relief from the double taxation levied on the profits distributed, it should be applied to permanent establishments in bilateral conventions against double taxation. It is generally recognised that, by the effects of their provisions, such

conventions necessarily result in some integration of the taxation systems of the Contracting States. On this account, it is perfectly conceivable that profits made in a State (A) by a permanent establishment of a company resident in another State (B) should be taxed in State A according to the split-rate system. As a practical rule, the tax could in such case be calculated at the reduced rate (applicable to distributed profits) on that proportion of an establishment's profits which corresponds to the ratio between the profit distributed by the company to which it belongs and the latter's total profit; the remaining profit could be taxed at the higher rate. Of course, the two Contracting States would have to consult together and exchange all information necessary for giving practical effect to this solution. Similar considerations apply to systems where distributions of profits made can be deducted from the taxable income of a company.

44. As regards the imputation system ("avoir fiscal" or "tax credit"), it seems doubtful, at least on a literal interpretation of the provisions of paragraph 4, whether it should be extended to non-resident companies in respect of dividends paid out of profits made by their permanent establishments. In fact, it has identical effects to those of the split-rate system but these effects are not immediate as they occur only at the time of the shareholder's personal taxation. From a purely economic and financial standpoint, however, it is conceivable that such profits should be treated as though they were profits of a distinct company in State A where the permanent establishment of a company which is a resident of State B is situated, and, to the extent that they are distributed, carry the "avoir fiscal" or "tax credit". But to take the matter further, to avoid all discrimination it is necessary that this advantage should already have been accorded to shareholders who are residents of State B of companies which are residents of State A. From the practical standpoint, the two States concerned should, of course, agree upon the conditions and procedures for allowing the "avoir fiscal" or "tax credit" to shareholders who are themselves residents of either State, of the companies concerned that are residents of State B.

45. Contracting States which are faced with the problems described above may settle them in bilateral negotiations in the light of their peculiar circumstances.

D. WITHHOLDING TAX ON DIVIDENDS, INTEREST AND ROYALTIES RECEIVED BY A PERMANENT ESTABLISHMENT

46. When permanent establishments receive dividends, interest, or royalties such income, by virtue of paragraph 4 of Articles 10 and 11 and paragraph 3 of Article 12, respectively, comes under the provisions of Article 7 and consequently—subject to the observations made in paragraph 36 above as regards dividends received on holdings of permanent establishment—falls to be included in the taxable profits of such permanent establishments (cf. paragraph 34 of the Commentary on Article 7).

47. According to the respective Commentaries on the above-mentioned provisions of Articles 10, 11 and 12 (cf. respectively paragraphs 30, 22 and 15), these provisions dispense the State of source of the dividends, interest or royalties received by the permanent establishment from applying any limitation provided for in those Articles, which means—and this is the generally accepted interpretation—that they leave completely unaffected the right of the State of source, where the permanent establishment is situated, to apply its withholding tax at the full rate.

48. While this approach does not create any problems with regard to the provisions of paragraph 4 of Article 24 in the case of countries where a with-holding tax is levied on all such income, whether the latter be paid to residents (permanent establishments, like resident enterprises, being allowed to set such withholding tax off against the tax on profits due by virtue of Article 7) or to non-residents (subject to the limitations provided for in Articles 10, 11 and 12), the position is different when withholding tax is applied exclusively to income paid to non-residents.

49. In this latter case, in fact, it seems difficult to reconcile the levy of withholding tax with the principle set out in paragraph 4 that for the purpose of taxing the income which is derived from their activity, or which is normally connected with it—as is recognised to be the case with dividends, interest and royalties referred to in paragraph 4 of Articles 10 and 11 and in paragraph 3 of Article 12—permanent establishments must be treated as resident enterprises and hence in respect of such income be subjected to tax on profits solely.

50. In any case, it is for Contracting States which have this difficulty to settle it in bilateral negotiations in the light of their peculiar circumstances.

E. CREDIT FOR FOREIGN TAX

51. In a related context, when a permanent establishment receives foreign income which is included in its taxable profits, it is right by virtue of the same principle to grant to the permanent establishment credit for foreign tax borne by such income when such credit is granted to resident enterprises under domestic laws.

52. If in a Contracting State (A) in which is situated a permanent estab-lishment of an enterprise of the other Contracting State (B) credit for tax levied in a third State (C) can be allowed only by virtue of a convention, then the more general question arises, as to the extension to permanent establishments of the benefit of conventions concluded with third States, which is examined in pa-ragraph 54 below.

53. It should, however, be pointed out that difficulties may arise as to the amount of the credit to be allowed, if permanent establishments in State A benefit from the convention which State B has concluded with State C. Such amount may be either the amount of tax effectively collected by State C or the amount of tax which State C may collect by virtue either of its convention with State A or its convention with State B. Moreover, the question arises whether such credit is not given twice, i.e. once in State A, where the permanent estab-lishment is situated and again in State B, the State of residence. It is for Contracting States to settle such problems, if necessary, in their bilateral negotiations.

F. EXTENSION TO PERMANENT ESTABLISHMENTS OF THE BENEFIT OF DOUBLE TAXATION CONVENTIONS CONCLUDED WITH THIRD STATES

54. While an enterprise of a State (A) can normally claim, in respect of the permanent establishment which it possesses in another State (B), the benefit of the provisions of the convention between those two States A and B, it never-theless cannot, should such permanent establishment derive income from a third State (C), invoke the provisions of the convention between States B and C for the

benefit of such permanent establishment since it, the enterprise, is in fact resident of neither of those two States (cf. Article 1). This is the consequence of the well-known principle of the relative effect of treaties, which means that they have effect only as between the Contracting States.

55.   Nor could such an enterprise invoke for this purpose a most-favoured-nation clause, however general its terms, included in a treaty or agreement concluded between States A and B. In fact, it has alway been accepted that such a clause did not apply in the case of double taxation conventions because these are essentially based on the principle of reciprocity. It should, however, be noted that some States have made provision in their double taxation conventions enabling the provisions of the latter to be applied, "in special cases", to permanent establishments of enterprises of a third State.

Paragraph 5

56.   This paragraph is designed to end a particular form of discrimination resulting from the fact that in certain countries the deduction of interest, royalties and other disbursements allowed without restriction when the recipient is resident, is restricted or even prohibited when he is a non-resident. The same situation may also be found in the sphere of capital taxation, as regards debts contracted to a non-resident. It is however open to Contracting States to modify this provision in bilateral conventions to avoid its use for tax avoidance purposes.

Paragraph 6

57.   This paragraph forbids a Contracting State to give less favourable treatment to an enterprise, the capital of which is owned or controlled, wholly or partly, directly or indirectly, by one or more residents of the other Contracting State. This provision, and the discrimination which it puts an end to, relates to the taxation only of enterprises and not of the persons owning or controlling their capital. Its object therefore is to ensure equal treatment for taxpayers residing in the same State, and not to subject foreign capital, in the hands of the partners or shareholders, to identical treatment to that applied to domestic capital.

Paragraph 7

58.   This paragraph states that the scope of the Article is not restricted by the provisions of Article 2. The Article therefore applies to taxes of every kind and description levied by, or on behalf of, the State, its political sub-divisions or local authorities.

OBSERVATIONS ON THE COMMENTARY

59.   The interpretation given in paragraphs 40 and 41 above is not endorsed by *Germany,* the tax laws of which require the application of a minimum rate with respect to non-residents. Under German tax laws, the profits of a permanent establishment of an enterprise operated in Germany by a non-resident individual are charged income tax at a minimum rate of 25 per cent. On the other hand, the German tax laws restrict the application of higher rates by strictly limiting the basis for determining the rate applicable to profits derived from German sources—thus excluding any profits derived by those parts of the enterprise which are situated abroad. Moreover, since the minimum rate of 25 per cent is close to

the lower end of the progressive tax scale which ranges from 22 per cent to 56 per cent, Germany is of the opinion that the application of the minimum rate of 25 per cent does not violate the provisions of paragraph 4.

60.   The *United States* observes that its non-resident citizens are not in the same circumstances as other non-residents, since the United States taxes its non-resident citizens on their worldwide income.

RESERVATIONS ON THE ARTICLE

61.   *Autralia, Canada* and *New Zealand* reserve their positions on this Article.

Paragraph 1

62.   *France* accepts the provisions of paragraph 1 but wishes to reserve the possibility of granting only to French nationals the exemption, provided for in its domestic laws, of gains from the alienation of immovable property which constitutes, whether in whole or in part, the residence in France of French nationals who are domiciled abroad.

63.   The *United Kingdom* reserves its position on the second sentence of paragraph 1.

Paragraph 4

64.   *Belgium* reserves the right to apply the provisions of its internal law for the purpose of taxing the profits of Belgian permanent establishments of companies and associations resident in countries with which it undertakes negotiations, whenever such an attitude is warranted by the general treatment accorded in such countries to permanent establishments of companies and associations resident in Belgium (paragraph 4).

65.   *Japan* reserves the right not to extend to the permanent establishments of non-residents the benefit of tax incentive measures introduced for national policy objectives.

Paragraph 5

66.   France accepts the provisions of paragraph 5 but wishes to reserve the possibility of applying the provisions in its domestic laws relative to the limitation to the deduction of interest paid by a French company to a foreign parent company.

COMMENTARY ON ARTICLE 25
CONCERNING THE MUTUAL AGREEMENT PROCEDURE

I. PRELIMINARY REMARKS

1.   This Article institutes a mutual agreement procedure for resolving difficulties arising out of the application of the Convention in the broadest sense of the term.

2.   It provides first, in paragraphs 1 and 2, that the competent authorities shall endeavour by mutual agreement to resolve the situation of taxpayers subjected to taxation not in accordance with the provisions of the Convention.

3.   It also, in paragraph 3, invites and authorises the competent authorities of the two States to resolve by mutual agreement problems relating to the interpretation or application of the Convention and, furthermore, to consult together for the elimination of double taxation in cases not provided for in the Convention.

4.   Finally, as regards the practical operation of the mutual agreement procedure, the Article, in paragraph 4, merely authorises the competent authorities to communicate with each other directly, without going through diplomatic channels, and, if it seems advisable to them, to have an oral exchange of opinions through a Joint Commission appointed especially for the purpose.

5.   Since the Article merely lays down general rules concerning the mutual agreement procedure, the comments now following are intended to clarify the purpose of such rules, and also to amplify them, if necessary, by referring, in particular, to the rules followed at international level in the conduct of mutual agreement procedures or at the internal level in the conduct of the procedures which exist in most OECD Member countries for dealing with disputed claims regarding taxes.

II. COMMENTARY ON THE PROVISIONS OF THE ARTICLE

Paragraphs 1 and 2

6.   The rules laid down in paragraphs 1 and 2 provide for the elimination in a particular case of taxation which does not accord with the Convention. As is known, in such cases it is normally open to taxpayers to litigate in the tax court, either immediately or upon the dismissal of their objections by the taxation authorities. When taxation not in accordance with the Convention arises from an incorrect application of the Convention in both States, taxpayers are then obliged to litigate in each State, with all the disadvantages and uncertainties that such a situation entails. So paragraph 1 makes available to taxpayers affected, without depriving them of the ordinary legal

remedies available, a procedure which is called the mutual agreement procedure because it is aimed, in its second stage, at resolving the dispute on an amicable basis, i.e. by agreement between competent authorities, the first stage being conducted exclusively in the State of residence (except where the procedure for the application of paragraph 1 of Article 24 is set in motion by the taxpayer in the State of which he is a national) from the presentation of the objection up to the decision taken regarding it by the competent authority on the matter.

7.   In any case, the mutual agreement procedure is clearly a special procedure outside the domestic law. It follows that it can be set in motion solely in cases coming within paragraph 1, i.e. cases where tax has been charged, or is going to be charged, in disregard of the provisions of the Convention. So where a charge of tax has been made contrary both to the Convention and the domestic law, this case is amenable to the mutual agreement procedure to the extent only that the Convention is affected. unless a connecting link exists between the rules of the Convention and the rules of the domestic law which have been misapplied.

8.   In practice, the procedure applies to cases—by far the most numerous— where the measure in question leads to double taxation which it is the specific purpose of the Convention to avoid. Among the most common cases, mention must be made of the following:

— the questions relating to attribution to a permanent establishment of a proportion of the executive and general administrative expenses incurred by the enterprise, under paragraph 3 of Article 7;
— the taxation in the State of the payer—in case of a special relationship between the payer and the beneficial owner—of the excess part of interest and royalties, under the provisions of Article 9, paragraph 6 of Article 11 or paragraph 4 of Article 12;
— cases where lack of information as to the taxpayer's actual situation has led to misapplication of the Convention, especially in regard to the determination of residence (paragraph 2 of Article 4), the existence of a permanent establishment (Article 5), or the temporary nature of the services performed by an employee (paragraph 2 of Article 15).

9.   As regards adjustments to be made correlatively with the reinstatement of profits in the trading results of associated enterprises under the provisions of paragraphs 1 and 2 of Article 9, there is ground for considering that they may properly be dealt with through the mutual agreement procedure when determining their amount gives rise to difficulty.

10.   The mutual agreement procedure is also applicable in the absence of any double taxation contrary to the Convention, once the taxation in dispute is in direct contravention of a rule in the Convention. Such is the case when one State taxes a particular class of income in respect of which the Convention gives an exclusive right to tax to the other State even though the latter is unable to exercise it owing to a gap in its domestic laws. Another category of cases concerns persons who, being nationals of one Contracting State but residents of the other State, are subjected in that other State to taxation treatment which is discriminatory under the provisions of paragraph 1 of Article 24.

11.   It should be noted that the mutual agreement procedure, unlike the disputed claims procedure under domestic law, can be set in motion by a taxpayer without waiting until the taxation considered by him to be "not in accordance with the Convention" has been charged against or notified to him. To be able to

set the procedure in motion, he must, and it is sufficient if he does, establish that the "actions for one or both of the Contracting States" will result in such taxation, and that this taxation appears as a risk which is not merely possible but probable. Such actions mean all acts or decisions, whether of a legislative or a regulatory nature, and whether of general or individual application, having as their direct and necessary consequence the charging of tax against the complainant contrary to the provisions of the Convention.

12.   To be admissible objections presented under paragraph 1 must first meet a twofold requirement expressly formulated in that paragraph: in principle, they must be presented to the competent authority of the taxpayer's State of residence (except where the procedure for the application of paragraph 1 of Article 24 is set in motion by the taxpayer in the State of which he is a national), and they must be so presented within three years of the first notification of the action which gives rise to taxation which is not in accordance with the Convention. The Convention does not lay down any special rule as to the form of the objections. The competent authorities may prescribe special procedures which they feel to be appropriate. If no special procedure has been specified, the objections may be presented in the same way as objections regarding taxes are presented to the tax authorities of the State concerned.

13.   The requirement laid on the taxpayer to present his case to the competent authority of the State of which he is a resident (except where the procedure for the application of paragraph 1 of Article 24 is set in motion by the taxpayer in the State of which he is a national) is of general application, regardless of whether the taxation objected to has been charged in that or the other State and regardless of whether it has given rise to double taxation or not. If the taxpayer should have transferred his residence to the other Contracting State subsequently to the measure or taxation objected to, he must nevertheless still present his objection to the competent authority of the State of which he was a resident during the year in respect of which such taxation has been or is going to be charged.

14.   However, in the case already alluded to where a person who is a national of one State but a resident of the other complains of having been subjected in that other State to an action or taxation which is discriminatory under paragraph 1 of Article 24, it appears more appropriate for obvious reasons to allow him, by way of exception to the general rule set forth above, to present his objection to the competent authority of the Contracting State of which he is a national. Finally, it is to the same competent authority that an objection has to be presented by a person who, while not being a resident of a Contracting State, is a national of a Contracting State, and whose case comes under paragraph 1 of Article 24.

15.   On the other hand, Contracting States may, if they consider it preferable, give taxpayers the option of presenting their cases to the competent authority of either State. In such a case, paragraph 1 would have to be modified as follows:

> "1. Where a person considers that the actions of one or both of the Contracting States result or will result for him in taxation not in accordance with the provisions of this Convention, he may, irrespective of the remedies provided by the domestic law of those States, present his case to the competent authority of either Contracting State. The case must be presented within three years from the first notification of the action resulting in taxation not in accordance with the provisions of the Convention."

16.   The time limit of three years set by the second sentence of paragraph 1 for presenting objections is intended to protect administrations against late objections.   This time limit must be regarded as a minimum, so that Contracting States are left free to agree in their bilateral conventions upon a longer period in the interests of taxpayers, e.g. on the analogy in particular of the time limits laid down by their respective domestic regulations in regard to tax conventions. Contracting States may omit the second sentence of paragraph 1 if they concur that their respective domestic regulations apply automatically to such objections and are more favourable in their effects to the taxpayers affected, either because they allow a longer time for presenting objections or because they do not set any time limits for such purpose.

17.   The provision fixing the starting point of the three-year time limit as the date of the "first notification of the action resulting in taxation not in accordance with the provisions of the Convention" should be interpreted in the way most favourable to the taxpayer.   Thus, even if such taxation should be directly charged in pursuance of an administrative decision or action of general application, the time limit begins to run only from the date of the notification of the individual action giving rise to such taxation, that is to say, under the most favourable interpretation, from the act of taxation itself, as evidenced by a notice of assessment or an official demand or other instrument for the collection or levy of tax.   If the tax is levied by deduction at the source, the time limit begins to run from the moment when the income is paid; however, if the taxpayer proves that only at a later date did he know that the deduction had been made, the time limit will begin from that date.   Furthermore, where it is the combination of decisions or actions taken in both Contracting States resulting in taxation not in accordance with the Convention, it begins to run only from the first notification of the most recent decision or action.

18.   As regards the procedure itself, it is necessary to consider briefly the two distinct stages into which it is divided (cf. paragraph 6 above).

19.   In the first stage, which opens with the presentation of the taxpayer's objections, the procedure takes place exclusively at the level of dealings between him and the competent authorities of his State of residence (except where the procedure for the application of paragraph 1 of Article 24 is set in motion by the taxpayer in the State of which he is a national).   The provisions of paragraph 1 give the taxpayer concerned the right to apply to the competent authority of the State of which he is a resident, whether or not he has exhausted all the remedies available to him under the domestic law of each of the two States.   On the other hand, that competent authority is under an obligation to consider whether the objection is justified and, if it appears to be justified, take action on it in one of the two forms provided for in paragraph 2.

20.   If the competent authority duly approached recognises that the complaint is justified and considers that the taxation complained of is due wholly or in part to a measure taken in the taxpayer's State of residence, it must give the complainant satisfaction as speedily as possible by making such adjustments or allowing such reliefs as appear to be justified.   In this situation, the issue can be resolved without resort to the mutual agreement procedure.   On the other hand, it may be found useful to exchange views and information with the competent authority of the other Contracting State, in order, for example, to confirm a given interpretation of the Convention.

21.   If, however, it appears to that competent authority that the taxation complained of is due wholly or in part to a measure taken in the other State, it will be incumbent on it, indeed it will be its duty—as clearly appears by the terms of paragraph 2—to set in motion the mutual agreement procedure proper.

22.   A taxpayer is entitled to present his case under paragraph 1 to the competent authority of the State of which he is a resident whether or not he may also have made a claim or commenced litigation under the domestic law of that State.   If litigation is pending, the competent authority of the State of residence should not wait for the final adjudication, but should say whether it considers the case to be eligible for the mutual agreement procedure.   If it so decides, it has to determine whether it is itself able to arrive at a satisfactory solution or whether the case has to be submitted to the competent authority of the other Contracting State.

23.   If a claim has been finally adjudicated by a court in the State of residence, a taxpayer may wish even so to present or pursue a claim under the mutual agreement procedure.   In some States, the competent authority may be able to arrive at a satisfactory solution which departs from the court decision.   In other States, the competent authority is bound by the court decision.   It may nevertheless present the case to the competent authority of the other Contracting State and ask the latter to take measures for avoiding double taxation.

24.   In its second stage—which opens with the approach to the competent authority of the other State by the competent authority to which the taxpayer has applied—the procedure is henceforward at the level of dealings between States, as if, so to speak, the State to which the complaint was presented had given it its backing.   But while this procedure is indisputably a procedure between States, it may, on the other hand, be asked:

—   whether, as the title of the Article and the terms employed in the first sentence of paragraph 2 suggest, it is no more than a simple procedure of mutual agreement, or constitutes the implementation of a "pactum de contrahendo" laying on the parties a mere duty to negotiate but in no way laying on them a duty to reach agreement;

—   or whether on the contrary, it is to be regarded (on the assumption of course that it takes place within the framework of a Joint Commission) as a procedure of a jurisdictional nature laying on the parties a duty to resolve the dispute.

25.   Paragraph 2 no doubt entails a duty to negotiate; but as far as reaching mutual agreement through the procedure is concerned, the competent authorities are under a duty merely to use their best endeavours and not to achieve a result. However, Contracting States could agree on a more far-reaching commitment whereby the mutual agreement procedure, and above all the discussions in the Joint Commission, would produce a solution to the dispute.   Such a rule could be established either by an amendment to paragraph 2 or by an interpretation specified in a protocol or an exchange of letters annexed to the convention.

26.   In seeking a mutual agreement, the competent authorities must first, of course, determine their position in the light of the rules of their respective taxation laws and of the provisions of the Convention, which are as binding on them as much as they are on the taxpayer.   Should the strict application of such rules or provisions preclude any agreement, it may reasonably be held that the

competent authorities, as in the case of international arbitration, can, subsidiarily, have regard to considerations of equity in order to give the taxpayer satisfaction.

27.   The purpose of the last sentence of paragraph 2 is to enable countries with time limits relating to adjustments of assessments and tax refunds in their domestic law to give effect to an agreement despite such time limits.   This provision does not prevent, however, such States as are not, on constitutional or other legal grounds, able to overrule the time limits in the domestic law from inserting in the mutual agreement itself such time limits as are adapted to their internal statute of limitation.   In certain extreme cases, a Contracting State may prefer not to enter into a mutual agreement, the implementation of which would require that the internal statute of limitation had to be disregarded.   Apart from time limits there may exist other obstacles such as "final court decisions" to giving effect to an agreement.   Contracting States are free to agree on firm provisions for the removal of such obstacles.

28.   Finally, the case may arise where a mutual agreement is concluded in relation to a taxpayer who has brought a suit for the same purpose in the competent court of either Contracting State and such suit is still pending.   In such a case, there would be no grounds for rejecting a request by a taxpayer that he be allowed to defer acceptance of the solution agreed upon as a result of the mutual agreement procedure until the court had delivered its judgment in the suit still pending.   On the other hand, it is necessary to take into account the concern of the competent authority to avoid any divergence or contradiction between the decision of the court and the mutual agreement, with the difficulties or risks of abuse that they could entail.   In short, therefore, it seems normal that the implementation of a mutual agreement should be made subject:

— to the acceptance of such mutual agreement by the taxpayer, and
— to the taxpayer's withdrawal of his suit at law concerning the points settled in the mutual agreement.

Paragraph 3

29.   The first sentence of this paragraph invites and authorises the competent authorities to resolve, if possible, difficulties of interpretation or application by means of mutual agreement.   These are essentially difficulties of a general nature which concern, or which may concern, a category of taxpayers, even if they have arisen in connection with an individual case normally coming under the procedure defined in paragraphs 1 and 2.

30.   This provision makes it possible to resolve difficulties arising from the application of the Convention.   Such difficulties are not only those of a practical nature, which might arise in connection with the setting up and operation of procedures for the relief from tax deducted from dividends, interest and royalties in the Contracting State in which they arise, but also those which could impair or impede the normal operation of the clauses of the convention as they were conceived by the negotiators, the solution of which does not depend on a prior agreement as to the interpretation of the convention.

31.   Under this provision the competent authorities can, in particular:

— where a term has been incompletely or ambiguously defined in the Convention, complete or clarify its definition in order to obviate any difficulty;

— where the laws of a State have been changed without impairing the balance or affecting the substance of the Convention, settle any difficulties that may emerge from the new system of taxation arising out of such changes.

32.   Paragraph 3 confers on the "competent authorities of the Contracting States", i.e. generally the Ministers of Finance or their authorised representatives normally responsible for the administration of the Convention, authority to resolve by mutual agreement any difficulties arising as to the interpretation of the Convention. However, it is important not to lose sight of the fact that, depending on the domestic law of Contracting States, other authorities (Ministry of Foreign Affairs, courts) have the right to interpret international treaties and agreements as well as the "competent authority" designated in the Convention, and that this is sometimes the exclusive right of such other authorities.

33.   Mutual agreements resolving general difficulties of interpretation or application are binding on administrations as long as the competent authorities do not agree to modify or rescind the mutual agreement.

34.   The second sentence of paragraph 3 enables the competent authorities to deal also with such cases of double taxation as do not come within the scope of the provisions of the Convention. Of special interest in this connection is the case of a resident of a third State having permanent establishments in both Contracting States. It is of course desirable that the mutual agreement procedure should result in the effective elimination of the double taxation which can occur in such a situation. An exception must, however, be made for the case of Contracting States whose domestic law prevents the convention from being complemented on points which are not explicitly or at least implicitly dealt with; in such a case, the convention could be complemented only by a protocol subject, like the convention itself, to ratification or approval.

Paragraph 4

35.   This paragraph determines how the competent authorities may consult together for the resolution by mutual agreement, either of an individual case coming under the procedure defined in paragraphs 1 and 2 or of general problems relating in particular to the interpretation or application of the Convention, and which are referred to in paragraph 3.

36.   It provides first that the competent authorities may communicate with each other directly. It would therefore not be necessary to go through diplomatic channels.

37.   Such exchange of opinions will normally take place by letter. However, if the competent authorities deem it useful, in order to reach an agreement more easily, they may also—as provided in the second sentence of paragraph 4—exchange views orally. They may, moreover, agree that such exchanges should take place in a commission consisting of representatives of the said authorities.

38.   As to this Joint Commission, paragraph 4 leaves it to the competent authorities of the Contracting States to determine the number of members and the rules of procedure of this body.

39.   However, while the Contracting States may avoid any formalism in this field, it is nevertheless their duty to give taxpayers whose cases are brought

before the Joint Commission under paragraph 2 certain essential guarantees, namely:

— the right to make representations in writing or orally, either in person or through a representative;
— the right to be assisted by counsel.

40.   However, disclosure to the taxpayer or his representatives of the papers in the case does not seem to be warranted, in view of the special nature of the procedure.

41.   Without infringing upon the freedom of choice enjoyed in principle by the competent authorities in designating their representatives on the Joint Commission, it would be desirable for them to agree to entrust the chairmanship of each Delegation—which might include one or more representatives of the service responsible for the procedure—to a high official or judge chosen primarily on account of his special experience; it is reasonable to believe, in fact, that the participation of such persons would be likely to facilitate reaching an agreement.

III.   Final Observations

42.   On the whole, the mutual agreement procedure has proved satisfactory. The most recent treaty practice shows that Article 25 represents the maximum that Contracting States are prepared to accept. It must, however, be admitted that this provision is not yet entirely satisfactory from the taxpayer's viewpoint. This is because the competent authorities are required only to seek a solution and are not obliged to find one (cf. paragraph 25 above). The conclusion of a mutual agreement depends to a large extent on the powers of compromise which the domestic law allows the competent authorithies. Thus, if a convention is interpreted or applied differently in two Contracting States, and if the competent authorities are unable to agree on a joint solution within the framework of a mutual agreement procedure, double taxation is still possible although contrary to the sense and purpose of a convention aimed at avoiding double taxation.

43.   It is difficult to avoid this situation without going outside the framework of the mutual agreement procedure. The first approch to a solution might consist of seeking an advisory opinion: the two Contracting States would agree to ask the opinion of an impartial third party, although the final decision would still rest with the States.

44.   The provisions embodied in this Convention, as well as the Commentary related thereto, are the result of close international joint work within the Committee on Fiscal Affairs. A possibility near at hand would be to call upon the Committee on Fiscal Affairs to give an opinion on the correct understanding of the provisions where special difficulties of interpretation arise as to particular points. Such a practice, which would be in line with the mandate and aims of the Committee on Fiscal Affairs, might well make a valuable contribution to arriving at a desirable uniformity in the application of the provisions.

45.   It might also be feasible to ask the opinion of certain persons acting as independent arbitrators. In the case of OECD Member countries, the Committee on Fiscal Affairs could, for example, periodically draw up a list of persons from among whom the competent authorities of the two States concerned could choose the third party to be asked to give an advisory opinion.

RESERVATIONS ON THE ARTICLE

46.   *Canada* and *Portugal* reserve their positions on the last sentence of paragraph 1 as they could not accept such a long time-limit.

47.   *Canada, Greece, Ireland, Italy, Portugal, Spain* and *the United Kingdom* reserve their positions on the second sentence of paragraph 2. These countries consider that the implementation of reliefs and refunds following a mutual agreement ought to remain linked to time-limits prescribed by their domestic laws.

48.   *Turkey* reserves its position on the second sentence of paragraph 2. Turkey's tax law provides that refunds of tax, like the assessment itself, must be made within a specific period. According to these provisions, if the administration finds an application for repayment acceptable, it must notify the fact to the taxpayer so that he can present his claim within a period of one year of such notification. If the taxpayer exceeds this time limit, his right to claim repayment lapses. The same procedure applies to the enforcement of judgements of courts under which repayments are required to be made. That is why Turkey is obliged to fix a time limit for the implementation of agreed mutual agreement procedures as is done for all repayments. For this reason Turkey wishes to reserve the right to mention in the text of bilateral conventions a definite time limit as regards their implementation.

COMMENTARY ON ARTICLE 26
CONCERNING THE EXCHANGE OF INFORMATION

I. PRELIMINARY REMARKS

1.   There are good grounds for including in a convention for the avoidance of double taxation provisions concerning co-operation between the tax administrations of the two Contracting States.   In the first place it appears to be desirable to give administrative assistance for the purpose of ascertaining facts in relation to which the rules of the convention are to be applied.   Moreover, in view of the increasing internationalisation of economic relations, the Contracting States have a growing interest in the reciprocal supply of information on the basis of which domestic taxation laws have to be administered, even if there is no question of the application of any particular article of the convention.

2.   Therefore the present Article embodies the rules under which information may be exchanged to the widest possible extent, with a view to laying the proper basis for the implementation of the domestic laws of the Contracting States concerning taxes covered by the Convention and for the application of specific provisions of the Convention.   The text of the Article makes it clear that the exchange of information is not restricted by Article 1, so that the information may include particulars about non-residents.

3.   The matter of administrative assistance for the purpose of tax collection is not dealt with in the Article.   This matter often forms the subject of a separate agreement, whether bilateral or multilateral, between the Contracting States; alternatively, the provisions on assistance in the field of tax collection may be introduced in the double taxation convention, whenever Contracting States find it preferable.

4.   Experience in recent years has shown that the text of the Article in the 1963 Draft Convention left room for differing interpretations.   Therefore it was felt desirable to clarify its meaning by a change in the wording of the Article and its Commentary without altering its effects. Apart from a single point of substance (cf. paragraph 13 below) the main purpose of the changes made has been to remove grounds for divergent interpretations.

II. COMMENTARY ON THE PROVISIONS OF THE ARTICLE

Paragraph 1

5.   The main rule concerning the exchange of information is contained in the first sentence of the paragraph.   The competent authorities of the Contracting States shall exchange such information as is necessary to secure the correct application of the provisions of the Convention or of the domestic laws of the Contracting States concerning taxes covered by the Convention even if, in the

latter case, a particular Article of the Convention need not be applied. In order to keep the exchange of information within the framework of the Convention, a limitation to the exchange of information is set so that information should be given only insofar as the national tax in question is covered by the Convention and the taxation under the domestic taxation laws concerned is not contrary to the Convention. An illustration may be cited in this connection: a request for the imposition of a sales tax need not be complied with by the requested State as it is not covered by the Convention.

6.   The following examples may clarify the principle dealt with in paragraph 5 above. In all such cases information can be exchanged under paragraph 1.

7.   Application of the Convention

a)   When applying Article 12, State A where the beneficiary is resident asks State B where the payer is resident, for information concerning the amount of royalty transmitted.

b)   Conversely, in order to grant the exemption provided for in Article 12, State B asks State A whether the recipient of the amounts paid is in fact a resident of the last-mentioned State and the beneficial owner of the royalties.

c)   Similarly, information may be needed with a view to the proper allocation of taxable profits between associated companies in different States or the adjustment of the profits shown in the accounts of a permanent establishment in one State and in the accounts of the head office in the other State (Articles 9, 7, 23A and 23B).

8.   Implementation of the domestic laws

a)   A company in State A supplies goods to an independent company in State B. State A wishes to know from State B what price the company in State B paid for the goods with a view to a correct application of the provisions of its domestic laws.

b)   A company in State A sells goods through a company in State C (possibly a low-tax country) to a company in State B. The companies may or may not be associated. There is no convention between State A and State C, nor between State B and State C. Under the convention between A and B, State A, with a view to ensuring the correct application of the provisions of its domestic laws to the profits made by the company situated in its territory, asks State B what price the company in State B paid for the goods.

c)   State A, for the purpose of taxing a company situated in its territory, asks State B, under the convention between A and B, for information about the prices charged by a company in State B, or a group of companies in State B with which the company in State A has no business contacts in order to enable it to check the prices charged by the company in State A by direct comparison (e.g. prices charged by a company or a group of companies in a dominant position). It should be borne in mind that the exchange of information in this case might be a difficult and delicate matter owing in particular to the provisions of sub-paragraph c) of paragraph 2 relating to business and other secrets.

9.   The rule laid down in paragraph 1 allows information to be exchanged in three different ways:

a)   on request, with a special case in mind, it being understood that the regular sources of information available under the internal taxation procedure should be relied upon in the first place before request for information is made to the other State;

b)   automatically, for example when information about one or various categories of income having their source in one Contracting State and received in the other Contracting State is transmitted systematically to the other State;

c)   spontaneously, for example in the case of a State having acquired, through certain investigations, information which it supposes to be of interest to the other State.

10.   The manner in which the exchange of information agreed to in the Convention will finally be effected can be decided upon by the competent authorities of the Contracting States.

11.   Reciprocal assistance between tax administrations is feasible only if each administration is assured that the other administration will treat with proper confidence the information which it will receive in the course of their co-operation. At the same time maintenance of such secrecy in the receiving Contracting State is a matter of domestic laws. It is therefore provided in paragraph 1 that information communicated under the provisions of the Convention shall be treated as secret in the receiving State in the same manner as information obtained under the domestic laws of that State. Sanctions for the violation of such secrecy in that State will be governed by the administrative and penal laws of that State.

12.   The information obtained may be disclosed only to persons and authorities involved in the assessment or collection of, the enforcement or prosecution in respect of, or the determination of appeals in relation to, the taxes covered by the Convention. This means that the information may also be communicated to the taxpayer, his proxy or to the witnesses. The information received by a Contracting State may be used by such persons or authorities only for the purposes mentioned in paragraph 1. If the information appears to be of value to the receiving State for other purposes than those referred to, that State may not use the information for such other purposes but it must resort to means specially designed for those purposes (e.g. in case of a non-fiscal crime, to a treaty concerning judicial assistance).

13.   As stated above, the information obtained can be communicated to the persons and authorities mentioned but it does not follow from this that it can be disclosed by them in court sessions held in public or in decisions which reveal the name of the taxpayer. The last sentence of the paragraph, however, opens up this possibility. Once information is used in public court proceedings or in court decisions and thus rendered public, it is clear that from that moment such information can be quoted from the court files or decisions for other purposes even as possible evidence. But this does not mean that the persons and authorities mentioned in paragraph 1 are allowed to provide on request additional information received. If either or both of the Contracting States object to the information being made public by courts in this way, or, once the information has been made public in this way, to the information being used for other purposes, because this is not the normal procedure under their domestic laws, they should state this expressly in their convention.

Paragraph 2

14.   This paragraph contains certain limitations to the main rule in favour of the requested State. In the first place, the paragraph contains the clarification that a Contracting State is not bound to go beyond its own internal laws and administrative practice in putting information at the disposal of the other Contracting State. However, types of administrative measures authorised for the purpose of the requested State's tax must be utilised, even though invoked solely to provide information to the other Contracting State. Likewise, internal provisions concerning tax secrecy should not be interpreted as constituting an obstacle to the exchange of information under the present Article. As mentioned above, the authorities of the requesting State are obliged to observe secrecy with regard to information received under this Article.

15.   Furthermore, the requested State does not need to go so far as to carry out administrative measures that are not permitted under the laws or practice of the requesting State or to supply items of information that are not obtainable under the laws or in the normal course of administration of the requesting State. It follows that a Contracting State cannot take advantage of the information system of the other Contracting State if it is wider than its own system.

16.   Information is deemed to be obtainable in the normal course of administration if it is in the possession of the tax authorities or can be obtained by them in the normal procedure of tax determination, which may include special investigations or special examination of the business accounts kept by the taxpayer or other persons, provided that the tax authorities would make similar investigations or examination for their own purposes. This means that the requested State has to collect the information the other State needs in the same way as if its own taxation was involved, under the proviso mentioned in paragraph 15 above.

17.   The requested State is at liberty to refuse to give information in the cases referred to in the paragraphs above. However if it does give the requested information, it remains within the framework of the agreement on the exchange of information which is laid down in the Convention; consequently it cannot be objected that this State has failed to observe the obligation to secrecy.

18.   If the structure of the information systems of two Contracting States is very different, the conditions under sub-paragraphs *a*) and *b*) of paragraph 2 will lead to the result that the Contracting States exchange very little information or perhaps none at all. In such a case, the Contracting States may find it appropriate to broaden the scope of the exchange of information.

19.   In addition to the limitations referred to above, sub-paragraph *c*) of paragraph 2 contains a reservation concerning the disclosure of certain secret information. Secrets mentioned in this sub-paragraph should not be taken in too wide a sense. Before invoking this provision, a Contracting State should carefully weigh if the interests of the taxpayer really justify its application. Otherwise it is clear that too wide an interpretation would in many cases render ineffective the exchange of information provided for in the Convention. The observations made in paragraph 17 above apply here as well. The requested State in protecting the interests of its taxpayers is given a certain discretion to refuse the requested information, but if it does supply the information deliberately the taxpayer cannot allege an infraction of the rules of secrecy. It is open to the Contracting States to add further dispensations from the obligation to supply

information to the items listed in sub-paragraph *c*), for example, information protected by provisions on banker's discretion. It has been felt necessary also to prescribe a limitation with regard to information which concerns the vital interests of the State itself. To this end, it is stipulated that Contracting States do not have to supply information the disclosure of which would be contrary to public policy (ordre public).

OBSERVATIONS ON THE COMMENTARY

20. *Japan* wishes to indicate that with respect to paragraph 11 above, it would be difficult for Japan, in view of its strict domestic laws and administrative practice as to the procedure to make public the information obtained under the domestic laws, to provide information requested unless a requesting State has comparable domestic laws and administrative practice as to this procedure.

21. With respect to paragraphs 14 to 16 above, *Japan* can only supply information obtained through special investigation or special examination as long as such investigation or examination is concerned with taxation in Japan.

RESERVATIONS ON THE ARTICLE

22. *Portugal* reserves the right to apply Article 26 of the 1963 version of the Draft Convention.

23. Under the *Swiss* concept a double taxation convention aims at avoiding international double taxation; the information necessary for the correct application and for the prevention of an abuse of such a convention can be exchanged already within the existing framework of its provisions on the mutual agreement procedure, the reduction of taxes withheld at the source, etc. Switzerland considers a particular provision on the exchange of information as unnecessary since even such an express clause could not, according to the purpose of the convention, provide for more than for an exchange of information necessary for the correct application and prevention of an abuse of the convention. Accordingly Switzerland has an express reservation on the Article on the exchange of information.

24. The *United States* believes that this Article should apply to all taxes imposed by a Contracting State, not just taxes covered by the Convention.

COMMENTARY ON ARTICLE 27
CONCERNING DIPLOMATIC AGENTS AND CONSULAR OFFICERS

1.   The aim of the provision is to secure that diplomatic agents or consular officers shall, under the provisions of a double taxation convention, receive no less favourable treatment than that to which they are entitled under international law or under special international agreements.

2.   The simultaneous application of the provisions of a double taxation convention and of diplomatic and consular privileges conferred by virtue of the general rules of international law, or under a special international agreement may under certain circumstances, have the result of discharging, in both Contracting States, tax that would otherwise have been due.   As an illustration, it may be mentioned that e.g. a diplomatic agent who is accredited by State A to State B and derives royalties, or dividends from sources in State A will not, owing to international law, be subject to tax in State B in respect of this income and may also, depending upon the provisions of the bilateral convention between the two States, be entitled as a resident of State B to an exemption from, or a reduction of, the tax imposed on the income in State A.   In order to avoid tax reliefs that are not intended, the Contracting States are free to adopt bilaterally an additional provision which may be drafted on the following lines:

> "Insofar as, due to fiscal privileges granted to diplomatic agents or consular officers under the general rules of international law or under the provisions of special international agreements, income or capital are not subject to tax in the receiving State, the right to tax shall be reserved to the sending State."

3.   In many OECD Member countries, the domestic laws contain provisions to the effect that diplomatic agents and consular officers while abroad shall for tax purposes be deemed to be residents of the sending State.   In the bilateral relations between Member countries in which provisions of this kind are operative internally, a further step may be taken by including in the convention specific rules that establish, for purposes of the convention, the sending State as the State of residence of the members of the diplomatic missions and consular posts of the Contracting States.   The special provision suggested here could be drafted as follows:

> "Notwithstanding the provisions of Article 4 an individual who is a member of a diplomatic mission, consular post or permanent mission of a Contracting State which is situated in the other Contracting State or in a third State shall be deemed for the purposes of the Convention to be a resident of the sending State if:
> a)   in accordance with international law he is not liable to tax in the receiving State in respect of income from sources outside that State or on capital situated outside that State, and
> b)   he is liable in the sending State to the same obligations in relation to tax on his total income or on capital as are residents of that State."

4.   By virtue of paragraph 1 of Article 4 the diplomatic agents and consular officers of a third State accredited to a Contracting State, are not deemed to be residents of the receiving State if they are only subject to a limited taxation in that State (cf. paragraph 8 of the Commentary on Article 4).   This consideration also holds true of the international organisations established in a Contracting State and their officials as they usually benefit from certain fiscal privileges either under the convention or treaty establishing the organisation or under a treaty between the organisation and the State in which it is established.   Contracting States wishing to settle expressly this question, or to prevent undesirable tax reliefs, may add the following provision to this Article:

> "The Convention shall not apply to international organisations, to organs or officials thereof and to persons who are members of a diplomatic mission, consular post or permanent mission of a third State, being present in a Contracting State and not treated in either Contracting State as residents in respect of taxes on income or on capital."

This means that international organisations, organs or officials who are liable in a Contracting State in respect only of income from sources therein should not have the benefit of the Convention.

5.   Although honorary consular officers cannot derive from the provisions of the Article any privileges to which they are not entitled under the general rules of international law (there commonly exists only tax exemption for payments received as consideration for expenses honorary consuls have on behalf of the sending State), the Contracting States are free to exclude, by bilateral agreement, expressly honorary consular officers from the application of the Article.

OBSERVATIONS ON THE COMMENTARY

6.   *Belgium, France,* the *Netherlands* and *Switzerland* are of the opinion that persons, who are not liable to comprehensive taxation (full liability to tax) or who do not bear on the taxable part of their income a tax which corresponds in percentage terms to the tax to which they would have been liable on their total income if it had not been partly exempt, should not be deemed to be residents.

COMMENTARY ON ARTICLE 28
CONCERNING THE TERRITORIAL EXTENSION
OF THE CONVENTION

1.   Certain double taxation conventions state to what territories they apply. Some of them also provide that their provisions may be extended to other territories and define when and how this may be done.   A clause of this kind is of particular value to States which have territories overseas or are responsible for the international relations of other States or territories, especially as it recognises that the extension may be effected by an exchange of diplomatic notes.   It is also of value when the provisions of the Convention are to be extended to a part of the territory of a Contracting State which was, by special provision, excluded from the application of the Convention.   The Article, which provides that the extension may also be effected in any other manner in accordance with the constitutional procedure of the States, is drafted in a form acceptable from the constitutional point of view of all OECD Member countries affected by the provision in question.   The only prior condition for the extension of a convention to any States or territories is that they must impose taxes substantially similar in character to those to which the convention applies.

2.   The Article provides that the Convention may be extended either in its entirety or with any necessary modifications, that the extension takes effect from such date and subject to such conditions as may be agreed between the Contracting States and, finally, that the termination of the Convention automatically terminates its application to any States or territories to which it has been extended, unless otherwise agreed by the Contracting States.

COMMENTARY ON ARTICLES 29 AND 30
CONCERNING THE ENTRY INTO FORCE AND THE TERMINATION
OF THE CONVENTION

1. The present provisions on the procedure for entry into force, ratification and termination are drafted for bilateral conventions and correspond to the rules usually contained in international treaties.

2. Some Contracting States may need an additional provision in the first paragraph of Article 29 indicating the authorities which have to give their consent to the ratification. Other Contracting States may agree that the Article should indicate that the entry into force takes place after an exchange of notes confirming that each State has completed the procedures required for such entry into force.

3. It is open to Contracting States to agree that the Convention shall enter into force when a specified period has elapsed after the exchange of the instruments of ratification or after the confirmation that each State has completed the procedures required for such entry into force.

4. No provisions have been drafted as to the date on which the Convention shall have effect or cease to have effect, since such provisions would largely depend on the domestic laws of the Contracting States concerned. Some of the States assess tax on the income received during the current year, others on the income received during the previous year, others again have a fiscal year which differs from the calendar year. Furthermore, some conventions provide, as regards taxes levied by deduction at the source, a date for the application or termination which differs from the date applying to taxes levied by assessment.

5. As it is of advantage that the Convention should remain in force at least for a certain period, the Article on termination provides that notice of termination can only be given after a certain year—to be fixed by bilateral agreement. It is open to the Contracting States to decide upon the earliest year during which such notice can be given or even to agree not to fix any such year, if they so desire.

RECOMMENDATION OF THE COUNCIL
concerning the avoidance of double taxation

(Adopted by the Council on 11th April, 1977)

THE COUNCIL,

Having regard to Article 5 (b) of the Convention on the Organisation for Economic Co-operation and Development of 14th December, 1960;

Having regard to the Recommendation of the Council of 30th July, 1963, concerning the Avoidance of Double Taxation;

Having regard to the Report of the Committee on Fiscal Affairs of 7th March, 1977 on the Revision of the OECD 1963 Draft Convention for the Avoidance of Double Taxation with respect to Taxes on Income and on Capital;

Considering the need to remove the obstacles that double taxation presents to the free movement of goods, services, capital and manpower between the Member countries of the OECD by the conclusion of conventions between them for that purpose;

Considering also the need to harmonize existing bilateral conventions on the basis of uniform principles, definitions, rules and methods, to agree on a common interpretation and to extend the existing network of such conventions to all Member countries;

Considering that efforts made in this direction by Member countries have produced substantial results since 1963 and that the new Model Convention will make it possible to confirm and extend the existing international co-operation on tax matters;

I.   RECOMMENDS the Governments of Member countries:

1.   to pursue their efforts to conclude bilateral conventions for the avoidance of double taxation with respect to taxes on income and on capital with those Member countries with which they have not yet entered into such conventions and to revise those of the existing conventions between them which may no longer be in keeping with present-day needs;

2.   when concluding new bilateral conventions or revising existing bilateral conventions between them, to conform to the Model Convention set out in the Annex hereto (hereinafter referred to as the "Model Convention"), as interpreted by the Commentaries thereto and having regard to the reservations and derogations to the Model Convention which are contained in the Report referred to above.

II.   RECOMMENDS that the Governments of Member countries which consider it appropriate examine the feasibility of concluding among themselves multilateral conventions based upon the Model Convention.

III.   REQUESTS the Governments of Member countries to notify the Organisation of the text of any new or revised double taxation convention concluded with each other and, where appropriate, the reasons why the provisions of the Model Convention have not been adopted in such conventions.

IV.   INSTRUCTS the Committee on Fiscal Affairs:

1.   to examine the notifications so supplied and to report to the Council as appropriate;

2.   to proceed to periodic reviews of situations where double taxation may occur, in the light of experience gained by Member countries, and to make appropriate proposals for its removal.

V.   DECIDES to repeal the Recommendation of the Council of 30th July, 1963 referred to above.

LIST OF DOUBLE TAXATION CONVENTIONS
ON INCOME AND ON CAPITAL
SIGNED BETWEEN OECD MEMBER COUNTRIES
FROM 1st JULY, 1963 TO 1st JANUARY, 1977

Contracting States	N (new) R (revised)		Date of signature	Date of signature of the previous convention
France-Greece	N		21. 8.63	
Austria-Finland	N		8.10.63	
Iceland-Sweden		R	23. 1.64	8. 9.37
Denmark-Ireland	N		4. 2.64	
Belgium-France		R	10. 3.64	16. 5.31
Denmark-Finland		R	7. 4.64	2.12.37
Canada-Japan	N		5. 9.64	
Germany-United Kingdom		R	26.11.64	18. 8.54
France-Japan	N		27.11.64	
Greece-Italy	N		19. 3.65	
Sweden-Switzerland		R	7. 5.65	16.10.48
Belgium-Sweden		R	2. 7.65	1. 4.53
Denmark-Italy	N		10. 3.66	
Iceland-Norway	N		30. 3.66	
Germany-Greece		R	18. 4.66	15. 6.44
Germany-Japan	N		22. 4.66	
Spain-Switzerland	N		26. 4.66	
Austria-Ireland	N		24. 5.66	
New Zealand-United Kingdom		R	13. 6.66	27. 5.47
France-Switzerland		R	9. 9.66	31.12.53
Netherlands-Norway		R	22. 9.66	29.12.50
Ireland-Switzerland	N		8.11.66	
Canada-Ireland		R	23.11.66	28.10.54
Canada-Norway	N		23.11.66	
Germany-Spain	N		5.12.66	
Canada-United Kingdom		R	12.12.66	6.12.65
Austria-Spain	N		20.12.66	
Belgium-Germany	N		11. 4.67	
Japan-Norway		R	11. 5.67	21. 2.59
Luxemburg-United Kingdom	N		24. 5.67	
Belgium-Norway	N		30. 6.67	
United States-France		R	28. 7.67	25. 7.39
Finland-Italy	N		4. 8.67	
Belgium-United Kingdom		R	29. 8.67	27. 3.53
Netherlands-United Kingdom		R	31.10.67	15.10.48
Finland-Spain	N		15.11.67	
Australia-United Kingdom		R	7.12.67	29.10.46

Contracting States	N (new) R (revised)	Date of signature	Date of signature of the previous convention
Denmark-Japan	R	3. 2.68	10. 3.59
Netherlands-Sweden	R	12. 3.68	25. 4.52
France-Ireland	N	21. 3.68	
Portugal-United Kingdom	N	27. 3.68	
Belgium-Japan	N	28. 3.68	
Luxemburg-Netherlands	N	8. 5.68	
France-United Kingdom	R	22. 5.68	14.12.50
Belgium-Greece	N	24. 5.68	
Portugal-Spain	N	29. 5.68	
Norway-United Kingdom	R	22. 1.69	2. 5.51 (Protocol 29.6.66)
Japan-United Kingdom	R	10. 2.69	4. 9.62
Ireland-Netherlands	N	11. 2.69	
Italy-Japan	N	20. 3.69	
Australia-Japan	N	20. 3.69	
Finland-Ireland	N	21. 4.69	
Austria-United Kingdom	R	30. 4.69	20. 7.56
Belgium-Portugal	N	16. 7.69	
Finland-United Kingdom	R	17. 7.69	12.12.51
Belgium-Denmark	N	16.10.69	
Ireland-Norway	N	21.10.69	
Japan-Netherlands	N	3. 3.70	
Finland-United States	R	6. 3.70	3. 3.52
Finland-Netherlands	R	13. 3.70	29. 3.54
Finland-Portugal	N	27. 4.70	
Denmark-Iceland	R	21. 5.70	24. 1.39
Norway-Portugal	N	24. 6.70	
Belgium-Ireland	N	24. 6.70	
Belgium-United States	R	9. 7.70	28.10.48 (Protoc. 9.9.52, 21.5.65, 11.12.67)
Austria-Netherlands	N	1. 9.70	
Finland-France	R	11. 9.70	25. 8.58
Belgium-Luxemburg	R	17. 9.70	9. 3.31 (exchange of letters of 1965)
Austria-Greece	N	22. 9.70	
Belgium-Spain	N	24. 9.70	
Belgium-Italy	R	19.10.70	11. 7.31
Belgium-Netherlands	R	19.10.70	20. 2.33
Austria-Turkey	N	3.11.70	
Austria-Portugal	N	29.12.70	
France-Portugal	N	14. 1.71	
Japan-Switzerland	N	19. 1.71	
Japan-United States	R	8. 3.71	16. 4.54 (Protocols 23.3.57, 7.5.60 and 14.8.62)
Germany-Iceland	N	18. 3.71	
Ireland-Italy	N	11. 6.71	
Netherlands-Spain	N	16. 6.71	
Germany-Switzerland	R	11. 8.71	15. 7.31 (Protocols 9.9.57, and 20.3.59 concerning taxes on income and on capital)
Norway-Sweden	R	1.11.71	27. 9.56 (Protocol 21.5.59)
Norway-United States	R	3.12.71	13. 6.49 (Protocol 10.6.58)
Norway-Turkey	N	16.12.71	
Austria-Belgium	N	29.12.71	

Contracting States	N (new) R (revised)		Date of signature	Date of signature of the previous convention
Finland-Norway		R	12. 1.72	29. 3.54
Ireland-Luxembourg	N		14. 1.72	
Finland-Japan	N		29. 2.72	
Finland-Iceland	N		2. 3.72	
Denmark-Portugal	N		3. 3.72	
Denmark-Spain	N		3. 7.72	
Australia-New Zealand		R	8.11.72	12. 5.60
Australia-Germany	N		24.11.72	
France-Netherlands		R	16. 3.73	du 30.12.49
Finland-Sweden		R	27. 6.73	21.12.49 (Protocols 9.9.68, 19.6.58, 25.9.52)
France-Spain		R	27. 6.73	8. 1.63
Denmark-Sweden		R	16.11.73	21. 7.58 (Protocol 13.5.59)
Denmark-Switzerland		R	23.11.73	14. 1.57
Ireland-Japan	N		18. 1.74	
Austria-Switzerland		R	30. 1.74	12.11.53
Japan-Spain	N		13. 2.74	
Portugal-Switzerland	N		26. 9.74	
Germany-Turkey	N		8.11.74	
Iceland-Luxemburg	N		29. 4.75	
Canada-France		X	2. 5.75	16. 3.51
Iceland-United States	N		18. 5.75	
Belgium-Canada	N		29. 5.75	
Spain-United Kingdom	N		21.10.75	
United Kingdom-United States		R	31.12.75	16. 4.45 (Protocols 6.6.46, 25.5.54, 19.8.57, 17.3.66)
Canada-Germany		R	22. 1.76	4. 6.56
Italy-Switzerland	N		9. 3.76	
Australia-Netherlands	N		17. 3.76	
Australia-France	N		13. 4.76	
Belgium-Finland		R	18. 5.76	11. 2.54 (supplementary convention 21.5.70)
Ireland-United Kingdom		R	2. 6.76	14. 4.26 (Protocols 25.4.28, 21.7.47, 18.5.49, 4.4.59, 23.6.60, 2.5.73 et 3.6.75)
Spain-Sweden		R	16. 6.76	25. 4.63 (Protocols 14.3.66)
Canada-Switzerland	N		20. 8.76	
Canada-Spain	N		23.11.76	
Austria-Canada	N		9.12.76	

APPENDIX III

THE 1963 DRAFT CONVENTION

Chapter I

SCOPE OF THE CONVENTION

Article 1

PERSONAL SCOPE

This Convention shall apply to persons who are residents of one or both of the Contracting States.

Article 2

TAXES COVERED

1.   This Convention shall apply to taxes on income and on capital imposed on behalf of each Contracting State or of its political subdivisions or local authorities, irrespective of the manner in which they are levied.

2.   There shall be regarded as taxes on income and on capital all taxes imposed on total income, on total capital, or on elements of income or of capital, including taxes on gains from the alienation of movable or immovable property, taxes on the total amounts of wages or salaries paid by enterprises, as well as taxes on capital appreciation.

3.   The existing taxes to which the Convention shall apply are, in particular :
    a)   In the case of (State A) : ....
    b)   In the case of (State B) : ....

4.   The Convention shall also apply to any identical or substantially similar taxes which are subsequently imposed in addition to, or in place of, the existing taxes. At the end of each year, the competent authorities of the Contracting States shall notify to each other any changes which have been made in their respective taxation laws.

DEFINITIONS

Article 3

GENERAL DEFINITIONS

1.   In this Convention, unless the context otherwise requires :
   a)   the terms "a Contracting State" and "the other Contracting State" mean (State A) or (State B), as the context requires ;
   b)   the term "person" comprises an individual, a company and any other body of persons ;
   c)   the term "company" means any body corporate or any entity which is treated as a body corporate for tax purposes ;
   d)   the terms "enterprise of a Contracting State" and "enterprise of the other Contracting State" mean respectively an enterprise carried on by a resident of a Contracting State and an enterprise carried on by a resident of the other Contracting State ;
   e)   the term "competent authority" means :
      1.   in (State A) . . . .
      2.   in (State B) . . . .

2.   As regards the application of the Convention by a Contracting State any term not otherwise defined shall, unless the context otherwise requires, have the meaning which it has under the laws of that Contracting State relating to the taxes which are the subject of the Convention.

Article 4

FISCAL DOMICILE

1.   For the purposes of this Convention, the term "resident of a Contracting State" means any person who, under the law of that State, is liable to taxation therein by reason of his domicile, residence, place of management or any other criterion of a similar nature.

2.   Where by reason of the provisions of paragraph 1 an individual is a resident of both Contracting States, then this case shall be determined in accordance with the following rules :
   a)   He shall be deemed to be a resident of the Contracting State in which he has a permanent home available to him. If he has a

permanent home available to him in both Contracting States, he shall be deemed to be a resident of the Contracting State with which his personal and economic relations are closest (centre of vital interests);

b) If the Contracting State in which he has his centre of vital interests cannot be determined, or if he has not a permanent home available to him in either Contracting State, he shall be deemed to be a resident of the Contracting State in which he has an habitual abode;

c) If he has an habitual abode in both Contracting States or in neither of them, he shall be deemed to be a resident of the Contracting State of which he is a national;

d) If he is a national of both Contracting States or of neither of them, the competent authorities of the Contracting States shall settle the question by mutual agreement.

3.   Where by reason of the provisions of paragraph 1 a person other than an individual is a resident of both Contracting States, then it shall be deemed to be a resident of the Contracting State in which its place of effective management is situated.

Article 5

PERMANENT ESTABLISHMENT

1.   For the purposes of this Convention, the term "permanent establishment" means a fixed place of business in which the business of the enterprise is wholly or partly carried on.

2.   The term "permanent establishment" shall include especially:
a) a place of management;
b) a branch;
c) an office;
d) a factory;
e) a workshop;
f) a mine, quarry or other place of extraction of natural resources;
g) a building site or construction or assembly project which exists for more than twelve months.

3.   The term "permanent establishment" shall not be deemed to include:
a) the use of facilities solely for the purpose of storage, display or delivery of goods or merchandise belonging to the enterprise;
b) the maintenance of a stock of goods or merchandise belonging to the enterprise solely for the purpose of storage, display or delivery;
c) the maintenance of a stock of goods or merchandise belonging to the enterprise solely for the purpose of processing by another enterprise;
d) the maintenance of a fixed place of business solely for the purpose of purchasing goods or merchandise, or for collecting information, for the enterprise;

e) the maintenance of a fixed place of business solely for the purpose of advertising, for the supply of information, for scientific research or for similar activities which have a preparatory or auxiliary character, for the enterprise.

4.   A person acting in a Contracting State on behalf of an enterprise of the other Contracting State — other than an agent of an independent status to whom paragraph 5 applies — shall be deemed to be a permanent establishment in the first-mentioned State if he has, and habitually exercises in that State, an authority to conclude contracts in the name of the enterprise, unless his activities are limited to the purchase of goods or merchandise for the enterprise.

5.   An enterprise of a Contracting State shall not be deemed to have a permanent establishment in the other Contracting State merely because it carries on business in that other State through a broker, general commission agent or any other agent of an independent status, where such persons are acting in the ordinary course of their business.

6.   The fact that a company which is a resident of a Contracting State controls or is controlled by a company which is a resident of the other Contracting State, or which carries on business in that other State (whether through a permanent establishment or otherwise), shall not of itself constitute either company a permanent establishment of the other.

Chapter III

TAXATION OF INCOME

Article 6

INCOME FROM IMMOVABLE PROPERTY

1.   Income from immovable property may be taxed in the Contracting State in which such property is situated.

2.   The term "immovable property" shall be defined in accordance with the law of the Contracting State in which the property in question is situated. The term shall in any case include property accessory to immovable property, livestock and equipment used in agriculture and forestry, rights to which the provisions of general law respecting landed property apply, usufruct of immovable property and rights to variable or fixed payments as consideration for the working of, or the right to work, mineral deposits, sources and other natural resources; ships, boats and aircraft shall not be regarded as immovable property.

3.   The provisions of paragraph 1 shall apply to income derived from the direct use, letting, or use in any other form of immovable property.

4.   The provisions of paragraphs 1 and 3 shall also apply to the income from immovable property of an enterprise and to income from immovable property used for the performance of professional services.

Article 7

BUSINESS PROFITS

1.   The profits of an enterprise of a Contracting State shall be taxable only in that State unless the enterprise carries on business in the other Contracting State through, a permanent establishment situated therein. If the enterprise carries on business as aforesaid, the profits of the enterprise may be taxed in the other State but only so much of them as is attributable to that permanent establishment.

2.   Where an enterprise of a Contracting State carries on business in the other Contracting State through a permanent establishment situated therein, there shall in each Contracting State be attributed to that permanent establishment the profits which it might be expected to make if it

were a distinct and separate enterprise engaged in the same or similar activities under the same or similar conditions and dealing wholly independently with the enterprise of which it is a permanent establishment.

3.   In the determination of the profits of a permanent establishment, there shall be allowed as deductions expenses which are incurred for the purposes of the permanent establishment including executive and general administrative expenses so incurred, whether in the State in which the permanent establishment is situated or elsewhere.

4.   Insofar as it has been customary in a Contracting State to determine the profits to be attributed to a permanent establishment on the basis of an apportionment of the total profits of the enterprise to its various parts, nothing in paragraph 2 shall preclude that Contracting State from determining the profits to be taxed by such an apportionment as may be customary; the method of apportionment adopted shall, however, be such that the result shall be in accordance with the principles laid down in this Article.

5.   No profits shall be attributed to a permanent establishment by reason of the mere purchase by that permanent establishment of goods or merchandise for the enterprise.

6.   For the purposes of the preceding paragraphs, the profits to be attributed to the permanent establishment shall be determined by the same method year by year unless there is good and sufficient reason to the contrary.

7.   Where profits include items of income which are dealt with separately in other Articles of this Convention, then the provisions of those Articles shall not be affected by the provisions of this Article.

Article 8

SHIPPING, INLAND WATERWAYS TRANSPORT AND AIR TRANSPORT

1.   Profits from the operation of ships or aircraft in international traffic shall be taxable only in the Contracting State in which the place of effective management of the enterprise is situated.

2.   Profits from the operation of boats engaged in inland waterways transport shall be taxable only in the Contracting State in which the place of effective management of the enterprise is situated.

3.   If the place of effective management of a shipping enterprise or of an inland waterways transport enterprise is aboard a ship or boat, then it shall be deemed to be situated in the Contracting State in which the home harbour of the ship or boat is situated, or, if there is no such home harbour, in the Contracting State of which the operator of the ship or boat is a resident.

Article 9

ASSOCIATED ENTERPRISES

Where

a) an enterprise of a Contracting State participates directly or indirectly in the management, control or capital of an enterprise of the other Contracting State, or

b) the same persons participate directly or indirectly in the management, control or capital of an enterprise of a Contracting State and an enterprise of the other Contracting State,

and in either case conditions are made or imposed between the two enterprises in their commercial or financial relations which differ from those which would be made between independent enterprises, then any profits which would, but for those conditions, have accrued to one of the enterprises, but, by reason of those conditions, have not so accrued, may be included in the profits of that enterprise and taxed accordingly.

Article 10

DIVIDENDS

1.   Dividends paid by a company which is a resident of a Contracting State to a resident of the other Contracting State may be taxed in that other State.

2.   However, such dividends may be taxed in the Contracting State of which the company paying the dividends is a resident, and according to the law of that State, but the tax so charged shall not exceed :

a) 5 per cent of the gross amount of the dividends if the recipient is a company (excluding partnership) which holds directly at least 25 per cent of the capital of the company paying the dividends ;

b) in all other cases, 15 per cent of the gross amount of the dividends.

The competent authorities of the Contracting States shall by mutual agreement settle the mode of application of this limitation.

This paragraph shall not affect the taxation of the company in respect of the profits out of which the dividends are paid.

3.   The term "dividends" as used in this Article means income from shares, "jouissance" shares or "jouissance" rights, mining shares, founders' shares or other rights, not being debt-claims, participating in profits, as well as income from other corporate rights assimilated to income from shares by the taxation law of the State of which the company making the distribution is a resident.

4.   The provisions of paragraphs 1 and 2 shall not apply if the recipient of the dividends, being a resident of a Contracting State, has in the other Contracting State, of which the company paying the dividends is a resident, a permanent establishment with which the holding by virtue of

which the dividends are paid is effectively connected. In such a case, the provisions of Article 7 shall apply.

5.   Where a company which is a resident of a Contracting State derives profits or income from the other Contracting State, that other State may not impose any tax on the dividends paid by the company to persons who are not residents of that other State, or subject the company's undistributed profits to a tax on undistributed profits, even if the dividends paid or the undistributed profits consist wholly or partly of profits or income arising in such other State.

Article 11

INTEREST

1.   Interest arising in a Contracting State and paid to a resident of the other Contracting State may be taxed in that other State.

2.   However, such interest may be taxed in the Contracting State in which it arises, and according to the law of that State, but the tax so charged shall not exceed 10 per cent of the amount of the interest. The competent authorities of the Contracting States shall by mutual agreement settle the mode of application of this limitation.

3.   The term "interest" as used in this Article means income from Government securities, bonds or debentures, whether or not secured by mortgage and whether or not carrying a right to participate in profits, and debt-claims of every kind as well as all other income assimilated to income from money lent by the taxation law of the State in which the income arises.

4.   The provisions of paragraphs 1 and 2 shall not apply if the recipient of the interest, being a resident of a Contracting State, has in the other Contracting State in which the interest arises a permanent establishment with which the debt-claim from which the interest arises is effectively connected. In such a case, the provisions of Article 7 shall apply.

5.   Interest shall be deemed to arise in a Contracting State when the payer is that State itself, a political subdivision, a local authority or a resident of that State. Where, however, the person paying the interest, whether he is a resident of a Contracting State or not, has in a Contracting State a permanent establishment in connection with which the indebtedness on which the interest is paid was incurred, and such interest is borne by such permanent establishment, then such interest shall be deemed to arise in the Contracting State in which the permanent establishment is situated.

6.   Where, owing to a special relationship between the payer and the recipient or between both of them and some other person, the amount of the interest paid, having regard to the debt claim for which it is paid, exceeds the amount which would have been agreed upon by the payer and the recipient in the absence of such relationship, the provisions of this Article shall apply only to the last-mentioned amount. In that case,

the excess part of the payments shall remain taxable according to the law of each Contracting State, due regard being had to the other provisions of this Convention.

Article 12

ROYALTIES

1.   Royalties arising in a Contracting State and paid to a resident of the other Contracting State shall be taxable only in that other State.

2.   The term "royalties" as used in this Article means payments of any kind received as a consideration for the use of, or the right to use, any copyright of literary, artistic or scientific work including cinematograph films, any patent, trade mark, design or model, plan, secret formula or process, or for the use of, or the right to use, industrial, commercial, or scientific equipment, or for information concerning industrial, commercial or scientific experience.

3.   The provisions of paragraph I shall not apply if the recipient of the royalties, being a resident of a Contracting State, has in the other Contracting State in which the royalties arise a permanent establishment with which the right or property giving rise to the royalties is effectively connected. In such a case, the provisions of Article 7 shall apply.

4.   Where, owing to a special relationship between the payer and the recipient or between both of them and some other person, the amount of the royalties paid, having regard to the use, right or information for which they are paid, exceeds the amount which would have been agreed upon by the payer and the recipient in the absence of such relationship, the provisions of this Article shall apply only to the last-mentioned amount. In that case, the excess part of the payments shall remain taxable according to the law of each Contracting State, due regard being had to the other provisions of this Convention.

Article 13

CAPITAL GAINS

1.   Gains from the alienation of immovable property, as defined in paragraph 2 of Article 6, may be taxed in the Contracting State in which such property is situated.

2.   Gains from the alienation of movable property forming part of the business property of a permanent establishment which an enterprise of a Contracting State has in the other Contracting State or of movable property pertaining to a fixed base available to a resident of a Contracting State in the other Contracting State for the purpose of performing professional services, including such gains from the alienation of such a permanent establishment (alone or together with the whole enterprise) or of such a fixed base, may be taxed in the other State. However, gains

from the alienation of movable property of the kind referred to in paragraph 3 of Article 22 shall be taxable only in the Contracting State in which such movable property is taxable according to the said Article.

3. Gains from the alienation of any property other than those mentioned in paragraphs 1 and 2, shall be taxable only in the Contracting State of which the alienator is a resident.

Article 14

INDEPENDENT PERSONAL SERVICES

1. Income derived by a resident of a Contracting State in respect of professional services or other independent activities of a similar character shall be taxable only in that State unless he has a fixed base regularly available to him in the other Contracting State for the purpose of performing his activities. If he has such a fixed base, the income may be taxed in the other Contracting State but only so much of it as is attributable to that fixed base.

2. The term "professional services" includes, especially independent scientific, literary, artistic, educational or teaching activities as well as the independent activities of physicians, lawyers, engineers, architects, dentists and accountants.

Article 15

DEPENDENT PERSONAL SERVICES

1. Subject to the provisions of Articles 16, 18 and 19, salaries, wages and other similar remuneration derived by a resident of a Contracting State in respect of an employment shall be taxable only in that State unless the employment is exercised in the other Contracting State. If the employment is so exercised, such remuneration as is derived therefrom may be taxed in that other State.

2. Notwithstanding the provisions of paragraph 1, remuneration derived by a resident of a Contracting State in respect of an employment exercised in the other Contracting State shall be taxable only in the first-mentioned State if :

   a) the recipient is present in the other State for a period or periods not exceeding in the aggregate 183 days in the fiscal year concerned, and

   b) the remuneration is paid by, or on behalf of, an employer who is not a resident of the other State, and

   c) the remuneration is not borne by a permanent establishment or a fixed base which the employer has in the other State.

3. Notwithstanding the preceding provisions of this Article, remune-

ration in respect of an employment exercised aboard a ship or aircraft in international traffic, or aboard a boat engaged in inland waterways transport, may be taxed in the Contracting State in which the place of effective management of the enterprise is situated.

Article 16

DIRECTORS' FEES

Directors' fees and similar payments derived by a resident of a Contracting State in his capacity as a member of the board of directors of a company which is a resident of the other Contracting State may be taxed in that other State.

Article 17

ARTISTES AND ATHLETES

Notwithstanding the provisions of Articles 14 and 15, income derived by public entertainers, such as theatre, motion picture, radio or television artistes, and musicians, and by athletes, from their personal activities as such may be taxed in the Contracting State in which these activities are exercised.

Article 18

PENSIONS

Subject to the provisions of paragraph I of Article 19, pensions and other similar remuneration paid to a resident of a Contracting State in consideration of past employment shall be taxable only in that State.

Article 19

GOVERNMENTAL FUNCTIONS

1.   Remuneration, including pensions, paid by, or out of funds created by, a Contracting State or a political subdivision or a local authority there-of to any individual in respect of services rendered to that State or sub-division or local authority thereof in the discharge of functions of a governmental nature may be taxed in that State.

2.   The provisions of Articles 15, 16 and 18 shall apply to remuneration or pensions in respect of services rendered in connection with any trade or business carried on by one of the Contracting States or a political sub-division or a local authority thereof.

Article 20

STUDENTS

Payments which a student or business apprentice who is or was formerly a resident of a Contracting State and who is present in the other Contracting State solely for the purpose of his education or training receives for the purpose of his maintenance, education or training shall not be taxed in that other State, provided that such payments are made to him from sources outside that other State.

Article 21

INCOME NOT EXPRESSLY MENTIONED

Items of income of a resident of a Contracting State which are not expressly mentioned in the foregoing Articles of this Convention shall be taxable only in that State.

TAXATION OF CAPITAL

Article 22

CAPITAL

1. Capital represented by immovable property, as defined in paragraph 2 of Article 6, may be taxed in the Contracting State in which such property is situated.

2. Capital represented by movable property forming part of the business property of a permanent establishment of an enterprise, or by movable property pertaining to a fixed base used for the performance of professional services, may be taxed in the Contracting State in which the permanent establishment or fixed base is situated.

3. Ships and aircraft operated in international traffic and boats engaged in inland waterways transport, and movable property pertaining to the operation of such ships, aircraft and boats, shall be taxable only in the Contracting State in which the place of effective management of the enterprise is situated.

4. All other elements of capital of a resident of a Contracting State shall be taxable only in that State.

METHODS FOR ELIMINATION OF DOUBLE TAXATION

Article 23A

EXEMPTION METHOD

1.   Where a resident of a Contracting State derives income or owns capital which, in accordance with the provisions of this Convention, may be taxed in the other Contracting State, the first-mentioned State shall, subject to the provisions of paragraph 2, exempt such income or capital from tax but may, in calculating tax on the remaining income or capital of that person, apply the rate of tax which would have been applicable if the exempted income or capital had not been so exempted.

2.   Where a resident of a Contracting State derives income which, in accordance with the provisions of Articles 10 and 11, may be taxed in the other Contracting State, the first-mentioned State shall allow as a deduction from the tax on the income of that person an amount equal to the tax paid in that other Contracting State. Such deduction shall not, however, exceed that part of the tax, as computed before the deduction is given, which is appropriate to the income derived from that other Contracting State.

Article 23B

CREDIT METHOD

1.   Where a resident of a Contracting State derives income or owns capital which, in accordance with the provisions of this Convention, may be taxed in the other Contracting State, the first-mentioned State shall allow :
   a)   as a deduction from the tax on the income of that person, an amount equal to the income tax paid in that other Contracting State ;
   b)   as a deduction from the tax on the capital of that person, an amount equal to the capital tax paid in that other Contracting State.

2.   The deduction in either case shall not, however, exceed that part of the income tax or capital tax, respectively, as computed before the deduction is given, which is appropriate, as the case may be, to the income or the capital which may be taxed in the other Contracting State.

SPECIAL PROVISIONS

Article 24

NON-DISCRIMINATION

1.   The nationals of a Contracting State shall not be subjected in the other Contracting State to any taxation or any requirement connected therewith which is other or more burdensome than the taxation and connected requirements to which nationals of that other State in the same circumstances are or may be subjected.

2.   The term "nationals" means :

   a)   all individuals possessing the nationality of a Contracting State ;
   b)   all legal persons, partnerships and associations deriving their status as such from the law in force in a Contracting State.

3.   Stateless persons shall not be subjected in a Contracting State to any taxation or any requirement connected therewith which is other or more burdensome than the taxation and connected requirements to which nationals of that State in the same circumstances are or may be subjected.

4.   The taxation on a permanent establishment which an enterprise of a Contracting State has in the other Contracting State shall not be less favourably levied in that other State than the taxation levied on enterprises of that other State carrying on the same activities.
   This provision shall not be construed as obliging a Contracting State to grant to residents of the other Contracting State any personal allowances, reliefs and reductions for taxation purposes on account of civil status or family responsibilities which it grants to its own residents.

5.   Enterprises of a Contracting State, the capital of which is wholly or partly owned or controlled, directly or indirectly, by one or more residents of the other Contracting State, shall not be subjected in the first-mentioned Contracting State to any taxation or any requirement connected therewith which is other or more burdensome than the taxation and connected requirements to which other similar enterprises of that first-mentioned State are or may be subjected.

6.   In this Article the term "taxation" means taxes of every kind and description.

Article 25

MUTUAL AGREEMENT PROCEDURE

1.　Where a resident of a Contracting State considers that the actions of one or both of the Contracting States result or will result for him in taxation not in accordance with this Convention, he may, notwithstanding the remedies provided by the national laws of those States, present his case to the competent authority of the Contracting State of which he is a resident.

2.　The competent authority shall endeavour, if the objection appears to it to be justified and if it is not itself able to arrive at an appropriate solution, to resolve the case by mutual agreement with the competent authority of the other Contracting State, with a view to the avoidance of taxation not in accordance with the Convention.

3.　The competent authorities of the Contracting States shall endeavour to resolve by mutual agreement any difficulties or doubts arising as to the interpretation or application of the Convention. They may also consult together for the elimination of double taxation in cases not provided for in the Convention.

4.　The competent authorities of the Contracting States may communicate with each other directly for the purpose of reaching an agreement in the sense of the preceding paragraphs. When it seems advisable in order to reach agreement to have an oral exchange of opinions, such exchange may take place through a Commission consisting of representatives of the competent authorities of the Contracting States.

Article 26

EXCHANGE OF INFORMATION

1.　The competent authorities of the Contracting States shall exchange such information as is necessary for the carrying out of this Convention and of the domestic laws of the Contracting States concerning taxes covered by this Convention insofar as the taxation thereunder is in accordance with this Convention. Any information so exchanged shall be treated as secret and shall not be disclosed to any persons or authorities other than those concerned with the assessment or collection of the taxes which are the subject of the Convention.

2.　In no case shall the provisions of paragraph 1 be construed so as to impose on one of the Contracting States the obligation :

    a)　to carry out administrative measures at variance with the laws or the administrative practice of that or of the other Contracting State ;

    b)　to supply particulars which are not obtainable under the laws or in the normal course of the administration of that or of the other Contracting State ;

c) to supply information which would disclose any trade, business, industrial, commercial or professional secret or trade process, or information, the disclosure of which would be contrary to public policy (ordre public).

Article 27

DIPLOMATIC AND CONSULAR OFFICIALS

Nothing in this Convention shall affect the fiscal privileges of diplomatic or consular officials under the general rules of international law or under the provisions of special agreements.

Article 28

TERRITORIAL EXTENSION

1.   This Convention may be extended, either in its entirety or with any necessary modifications, [to any part of the territory of (State A) or of (State B) which is specifically excluded from the application of the Convention or] to any State or territory for whose international relations (State A) or (State B) is responsible, which imposes taxes substantially similar in character to those to which the Convention applies. Any such extension shall take effect from such date and subject to such modifications and conditions, including conditions as to termination, as may be specified and agreed between the Contracting States in notes to be exchanged through diplomatic channels or in any other manner in accordance with their constitutional procedures.

2.   Unless otherwise agreed by both Contracting States, the denunciation of the Convention by one of them under Article 30 shall terminate, in the manner provided for in that Article, the application of the Convention [to any part of the territory of (State A) or of (State B) or] to any State or territory to which it has been extended under this Article.

Note : The words between brackets are of relevance when, by special provision, a part of the territory of a Contracting State is excluded from the application of the Convention.

FINAL PROVISIONS

Article 29

ENTRY INTO FORCE

1.   This Convention shall be ratified and the instruments of ratification shall be exchanged at .... as soon as possible.

2.   The Convention shall enter into force upon the exchange of instruments of ratification and its provisions shall have effect :

   a)   in (State A) : ....
   b)   in (State B) : ....

Article 30

TERMINATION

This Convention shall remain in force until denounced by one of the Contracting States. Either Contracting State may denounce the Convention, through diplomatic channels, by giving notice of termination at least six months before the end of any calendar year after the year ...... In such event, the Convention shall cease to have effect :

   a)   in (State A) : ....
   b)   in (State B) : ....

TERMINAL CLAUSE

Note : The terminal clause concerning the signing shall be drafted in accordance with the constitutional procedure of both Contracting States.

OECD   PUBLICATIONS
2, rue André-Pascal
75775 PARIS CEDEX 16
No. 39 067   1977.

●

PRINTED IN FRANCE